One Gospel,
Many Ears

Other Chalice Press books by Joseph R. Jeter, Jr.

Preaching Judges

Other Chalice Press books by Ronald J. Allen

Preaching and Practical Ministry

Preaching Luke-Acts

Wholly Scripture

Hearing the Sermon

Interpreting the Gospel: An Introduction to Preaching

The Vital Church: Teaching, Worship, Community, Service
(with Clark M. Williamson)

A Credible and Timely Word: Process Theology and Preaching
(with Clark M. Williamson)

Preaching in the Context of Worship
(edited by David M. Greenhaw and Ronald J. Allen)

Patterns of Preaching: A Sermon Sampler
(edited by Ronald J. Allen)

Make the Word Come Alive
(with Mary Alice Mulligan)

Believing in Preaching
(with Diane Turner-Sharazz, Dawn Ottoni Wilhelm,
and Mary Alice Mulligan)

Listening to Listeners
(with John McClure, Dale Andrews, L. Susan Bond,
Dan Moseley, and G. Lee Ramsey Jr.)

One Gospel, Many Ears

Preaching for Different Listeners in the Congregation

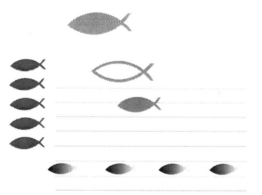

Joseph R. Jeter, Jr.,
and
Ronald J. Allen

CHALICE
PRESS

ST. LOUIS, MISSOURI

Bible quotations, unless otherwise noted, are from the *New Revised Standard Version Bible,* copyright 1989, Division of Christian Education of the National Council of the Churches of Christ in the United States of America. Used by permission. All rights reserved.

Those quotations marked RSV are from the *Revised Standard Version of the Bible,* copyright 1952, [2nd edition, 1971] by the Division of Christian Education of the National Council of the Churches of Christ in the United States of America. Used by permission. All rights reserved.

Cover art and design: Bob Currie
Interior design: Hui-Chu Wang
Art direction: Michael Domínguez

Visit Chalice Press on the World Wide Web at
www.chalicepress.com

10   9   8   7   6   5   4   06   07   08   09   10   11

Library of Congress Cataloging–in–Publication Data

Jeter, Joseph R.
  One Gospel, many ears : preaching for different listeners in the congregation / Joseph R. Jeter, Jr., & Ronald J. Allen.
      p. cm.
Includes bibliographical references.
  ISBN-10: 0-827227-16-7 (alk. paper)
  ISBN-13: 978-0-827227-16-3 (alk. paper)
  1. Preaching. 2. Sociology, Christian. 3. Multiculturalism–Religious aspects–Christianity. I. Allen, Ronald J. (Ronald James), 1949-   II. Title.
  BV4221 . J45 2002
  251–dc21
                                        2002015589

To
our colleagues in the
Academy of Homiletics,
in gratitude for the many ways
you help preachers witness to the one God.

Contents

Introduction

Sunday morning. The anthem ends. The preacher waits a moment as the choir settles into their seats, then slips from the chancel pew into the pulpit, pushes the sides and corners of the sermon manuscript into line, takes a deep breath, and looks into the faces of the congregation. G. Edwin Osborn, an influential teacher of worship in the Christian Church (Disciples of Christ) in an earlier era, painted a montage of different kinds of people who await the sermon:

- A bereft soul for whom the heavens seem shut.
- A daughter who has sacrificed her future to care for a widowed mother.
- Anxious parents who have not heard from an absent child for two months or more.
- A person under cancer's death sentence.
- A family trying to live down the scandal that sent the oldest daughter to suicide.
- An investor whose profitable ventures have inflated...pride and left that person careless with others' trust.
- A trusted employee who for months has been embezzling from the firm.
- A physician under pressure to write narcotics prescriptions for a patient to whom the physician is financially obligated.
- A high school youth torn between the license brashly advocated by the high school's social club and the standards for which this youth has stood as president of the church youth group.
- A recently promoted vice-president in a mad scramble for further advances who begins to exploit other workers, forgetting that the vice-president was once one of them.
- Social aspirants in whose heart envy and ambition have joined forces and are running wild.

1

- A lay leader in the congregation for whom religion has gradually lost its vitality and significance and has degenerated into mere formality.
- A teacher who has devoted a quarter of a century in dedicated service to the community who is becoming disillusioned because public education is made a political pawn.
- Some burning with the fires of lust; others smoldering with hatred's passion.
- A few for whom jealousy has poisoned life's cup, and others for whom the dregs of bitterness have made it the drink of death.[1]

Every time the congregation gathers for worship, many different people come from many different points in life with many different needs and perspectives. The same sermon may touch people in different ways, because they are at different places in life. Each person refracts the messages through his or her own world.

The phenomenon of diversity is even more complicated than Osborn suggested in the preceding collage of a Sunday morning congregation. In addition to being at different stations in life, people process language, thought, and feelings differently. Different people take in the world in different modes of apprehension. People express themselves and process communications in ways that are influenced by racial experience, gender, personality type, ethnicity, education, and social and economic situation. Some people hear the same words but come away with different nuances of meaning because of their built-in inclinations to receive communication in certain ways but not in others.

In this book, we explore selected aspects of such congregational diversity.[2] What does the preacher do when faced by the fact that congregations contain people who hear and process sermons in different ways?[3]

One way of describing the concern of this book is to borrow and adapt a phrase from Nancy Eiesland, who teaches at Candler School of Theology at Emory University. In her sensitive work *The Disabled God,* she writes of the importance of bringing persons with disabilities into "the speaking center" of the church (and of the wider world). Many persons with disabilities have yet to experience being at the speaking center, where they could speak about themselves as persons, talking with people with disabilities and with others within the church and the world. Generally, persons with disabilities have had to learn how to explain experiences in terms that able-bodied persons can grasp. This means translating their own experiences into someone else's way of speaking. If this translation is not accompanied by routine experiences of talking and listening to other people with disabilities, the understanding of the whole church can be limited and distorted.[4]

Eiesland's comments about disabled persons are true of other groups that make up the congregation. Each group needs to be a part of the speaking center, that is, to know that its concerns are expressed clearly and are understood by others in the community. In a similar way, each element in the congregation needs to be able to hear and understand others in the community.

A variety of activities within the life of the church can provide speaking and listening centers. In worship, the various groups within the congregation come together. The sermon has an opportunity to become the literal speaking and listening center of the church. The preacher must not only give voice to the various groups in the congregation but help them have an optimum opportunity to hear and understand the gospel and one another. That can happen as the pastor discovers the characteristics of the various listening groups in the congregation and takes them into account in the sermon.

In chapter 1, we consider the congregation as a community composed of groups (some of them quite informal) that manifest multiple and sometimes contrasting characteristics that affect ways in which listeners receive and process sermons. We then turn to six modes of diversity found within most congregations. In chapter 2, the focus is on preaching to different generations. How might the preacher take account of the listening characteristics of Builders, Silents, Boomers, Generation 13, and subsequent generations? Chapter 3 ponders preaching in the light of the differing ways in which people know and the differing ways in which they receive and process communications. Chapter 4 engages preaching and gender. We begin with matters related to heterosexual women and men, and then consider preaching and other sexual orientations. Chapter 5 deals with preaching in a multicultural community. What does the preacher need to consider when the congregation contains European Americans, African Americans, Native Americans, Hispanic Americans, Asian Americans, and others? Chapter 6 concentrates on preaching for the least, for those who are on the margins of the congregation. How might the preacher speak to—and in behalf of—the widow, those who are mentally or physically challenged, the economically poor, and the out-groups in the congregation? In chapter 7, we think about preaching in a congregation in which people hold different theological worldviews. How does a preacher make theological sense to both liberals and conservatives who sometimes sit on the same pew? These six foci are not the only variables in a listening community, but they are a place to begin systematic thinking about the enormous plurality of the listening congregation.

The two authors shared in the conception of the book and talked about the contents of the various chapters. We jointly drafted chapter 1. Joseph Jeter took the lead in chapters 4, 5 and 6, with Ronald Allen generating the first drafts on chapters 2, 3, and 7. The two writers discussed and reshaped each chapter. To be honest, we do not see eye to eye on each and every matter. But the differences are largely matters of degree and not of substance. We send this book forth in our first authorial partnership in the hope that it will enhance the preaching and hearing of the gospel in our time. We had a great time working on the book. We hope readers have a great time using it, even when they disagree with some of our ideas.

1

Varieties of Listeners in the Congregation

A few years ago, Ron spent a summer teaching in Jamaica. While vacationing at a beach, he went boating on the Caribbean. Looking into the water from the boat Ron could see fish moving. From the deck of the boat the fish looked much the same: dark blurs lacking definition in shape.

After a few minutes, he put on goggles and splashed into the water. Submerged with the fish, Ron could see their remarkable variety and distinctiveness. Long fish. Short fish. Round fish. Fish in bold stripes of color. Fish whose colors gently shaded from one color to the next. Hues of red, orange, yellow, green, and blue. Fish that appeared to glow. Indeed, the whole underwater world became luminescent. The fish ate different things ranging from plankton to other fish. From the surface, the fish looked dim and much the same. But in the underwater world itself, Ron could see their remarkable variety.

Preachers sometimes view the congregation from the surface. The listeners appear to be much the same. But when preachers penetrate below the surface of the congregation, a more complex picture comes into view. In the same way that the ocean contains many different kinds of fish, the typical congregation contains many different kinds of people who are defined by many different traits. These traits include phenomena such as gender, race, ethnicity, age, personality type, patterns of mental operation, modes of perception, and theological worldview. Different traits incline people to hear the sermon differently.

People who fish know that different kinds of bait attract different kinds of fish. In order to catch a certain kind of fish, a certain kind of bait is often used. Making an approximate parallel between fishing and arranging material in one of his theological works, the second-century theologian Clement of Alexandria offers a comment that elucidates the situation of the preacher. "We must provide a large variety of baits owing to the varieties of fish."[1] Preaching calls for variety that corresponds to the variegation in the listening community.[2]

In this chapter we first explore the notion that the congregation is a community made up of people who have different listening tendencies. We then focus on approaches that the preacher might take to help make the sermon accessible to persons who hear and process sermons in diverse ways.

The Congregation Composed of Multiple Kinds of Listeners

Some traits in the congregation are constituted by self-conscious, chosen, institutionally formal relationships. A formally constituted group often has a life as a distinct community within the larger congregation. In a sense, a congregation is a community of such groups.[3] For example, people belong to Bible school classes or prayer groups or other small (cell) groups. Koinonia groups sometimes convene around life situations (e.g., single people). Family networks within a congregation are sometimes connected by blood or marriage. In some congregations, people rally around a shared theological or political agenda. In some congregations, members appear to have deeper loyalty to their small groups than to the congregation as a whole. Members of a Sunday school class, for instance, may immediately put considerable financial muscle behind a call from the class for financial resources, whereas the same people might be much slower and less generous in response to a call from the leadership of the wider congregation.

The congregational collage also contains constellations of people who may not be related to one another by a formal church structure but who share a characteristic (or constellation of characteristics). Some of these traits present themselves fairly readily and, therefore, claim a preacher's attention. Gender, for example, is often related to tendencies in speaking and listening. In chapter 4, we examine the spectrum of women's "ways of knowing," that is, patterns by which women perceive the world, ranging from women who are almost altogether dependent on the perceptions of others to women who assertively and critically take responsibility for their own worldviews. Women are often inclined to pick up tones of feeling in sermons that do not come to the consciousness of some men. Some verbal expressions are characteristic of (though by no means unique to) women. Many women respond more positively to certain kinds of speech than to other kinds. Similarly, many men have a proclivity to pick up ideas in speech, but not catch undertones of feeling.

Age, as discussed in chapter 2, is another trait that is easily recognizable and that sometimes affects how people hear and talk. Persons at different ages often have somewhat different life issues, tastes, and modes of expression, and worldviews. Persons of different ages even hear some words differently. A preacher who brings the cross section of age-related concerns into sermons not only helps members of individual age cohorts reflect on their own situations from the perspective of the gospel but helps the congregation understand the gospel and the world from the perspective of other ages. Such preaching deepens the spirit of community in the congregation.

While congregations were once largely composed of persons of one race or ethnicity, congregations increasingly contain persons of multiple races and ethnic backgrounds. This is one aspect of the multiculturalism discussed in chapter 5. Without meaning to fall into the pit of racial and ethnic stereotyping, we observe that modes of expression and response are sometimes associated with particular racial or ethnic groups. European Americans in the long-established denominations tend to be restrained in preaching and in responding to preaching, whereas African Americans and Latinos tend to be more exuberant. However, these patterns are not true across the board. Differences exist within racial and ethnic communities. For instance, some European American Pentecostals are as exuberant as demonstrative as many African Americans and Latinos. Some African American preachers are as subdued as their European American counterparts. Some African American and Latino laity seek congregations that are quiet. The challenge to the preacher is multiplied in the multicultural setting in which European Americans, African Americans, Latinos, Asian Americans, and Native Americans sit side by side.

Multiculturalism is a phenomenon of more than race and ethnicity. Every congregation is multicultural, for people from different cultures comprise nearly every congregation. A typical congregation contains persons from a panorama of cultures, such as corporate leadership, blue-collar labor, welfare subsistence, higher education, professional life, volunteerism, various sexual orientations, and youth (with its many subcultures). People of the same race, ethnicity, and social class can operate out of very different worldviews. For instance, a corporate manager often exercises quite a different set of values in making decisions than someone from the culture of a college or seminary faculty.

In some settings, the differences of culture are more dramatic than in others. In a multicultural congregation, the preaching event brings together people who often have marked differences in oral expression and in expectations of what constitutes good and not so good communication. In a multicultural setting people may even have varying levels of familiarity with the language spoken by the preacher. Some multicultural congregations make use of a translator (or more than one translator), a phenomenon that introduces its own dynamics in a congregation.

The congregational collage also contains other traits that are less obvious and require conscientious pastoral discernment. For instance, it is well known that people differ according to personality. A warm and generous personality often responds positively to a preacher whose preaching has a personal quality and who is warm and generous in theology and demeanor, whereas the same listener may be put off by a pastor whose preaching is cast in abstractions and who is distant in personal relationships. According to our discussion of the Myers-Briggs Type Indicator in chapter 3, this aspect of congregational pluralism can be immensely complex.

People also differ in their patterns of mental operation. Some members of the community are, by nature, more deductive in the ways in which they think, while others of the community are more inductive. Some persons in the community require precise statements pointing toward definite conclusions to feel that they are in a safe space, while others are much more comfortable with ambiguity and open-ended patterns of thinking. The former may think that the latter are hiding from the hard work of reaching definite conclusions, while those who are comfortable with ambiguity think that the precisionists have vastly oversimplified the complexities of life. As someone said to one of the authors of this book, "Life just can't be boiled down to a proposition." In chapter 3 we explore such differences in connection with research into stages of faith development proposed by James Fowler.

In the preceding paragraphs, we have only begun to illustrate the elements that are part of the typical congregational sea. Sensitive pastors who listen carefully and who discern the signs of the times in the community will be able to identify many other distinctive fish below the surface of the congregational sea.

As we note below, these traits are only listener *tendencies*. Persons are not prisoners of their proclivities. Henry Mitchell, a great African American scholar of preaching, sometimes uses an expression that describes this situation. Mitchell frequently says that African American preachers are "prone" to do certain things, for example, use colorful speech. Not all African American preachers use colorful speech, but many such preachers have that tendency. They are prone to it. Similarly, we may say that persons with certain traits (e.g., age, gender, personality type, theological orientation) are prone to ways of thinking, feeling, or behaving that are associated with that trait, but they can transcend their traits.

The Preacher's Challenge: One Gospel, Many Patterns of Listening

Preachers face a challenge in these respects. On the one hand, the church draws its life and witness from the one gospel of the one living God. On the other hand, a given congregation has many different listeners who process the sermon with their own particular sets of receptors. A further complication is that each preacher has her or his tendencies of speaking and listening, cultural proclivities, and modes of apprehending the world.

By one gospel, we mean a core of meaning that is shared by most Christians across time and space, and that has implications for every situation in the cosmos. The preacher's call is to interpret the world–both its human and trans-human dimensions–from the standpoint of the gospel. The preacher also considers points at which the world might prompt the congregation to enlarge, refocus, or otherwise reformulate its understanding of the gospel.

The gospel can be formulated in many different ways. Christians sometimes debate the precise formulation and content of the gospel. But in this book, we operate with an understanding of the gospel that, we believe, can be accepted in most Christian communities. The gospel is the good news "that God is the God of a singular promise and a singular command: the promise is that God's love, confirmed in Jesus Christ, is freely, graciously, offered to each and all, and the command is the twofold requirement that we are to love God with our whole selves and to love and do justice to our neighbors as ourselves."[4]

The gospel is thus dipolar, an ellipse with two centers: the promise of the unconditional love of God for each and all, and the command of God for justice for each and all. In this context, the term *justice* takes its cue from its Hebrew roots. In the world of the Bible, justice primarily refers to right relationships in community. To do justice is to live in covenantal relationship with all neighbors.

A part of the preacher's vocation in each situation (and on each Sunday) is to determine whether to emphasize the word of promise or the word of command. In either case, appropriateness to the whole gospel is the norm for the content and style of the sermon. The heart of the preacher's creativity is to witness to the gospel in language and communication patterns that offer the listeners a good opportunity to understand the witness. When the congregation understands the witness of the sermon, they can then decide how, or whether, to respond.

The preacher effects mutual critical correlation.[5] This correlation involves three dimensions. In one dimension, the pastor correlates the gospel with values, thoughts, practices, ideas, and communication preferences of a given group. What are the similarities and positive points of contact between the gospel and the group? In another dimension, the preacher calls attention to ways in which the gospel criticizes the contemporary world and calls for repentance and new birth. What are points at which the gospel calls the congregation (and the world) to change ways of thinking, acting, and feeling to be more consistent with God's unconditional love for all and God's call for justice for all? In still another dimension, the preacher is open to reformulating the gospel in the light of current inclinations and insights. Do insights from the tradition or from the contemporary world prompt the pastor and congregation to recognize that their understanding of the gospel is inadequate and consequently should be considered afresh?

The preacher's challenge is to prepare sermons so that they have a good *opportunity* to be received and processed by the different kinds of listeners in the congregation. No amount of homiletical skill can guarantee that the congregation will grasp the message in the full dimensions intended by the preacher. Factors in the congregation over which the preacher has no control (and about which the preacher may have no knowledge) can cause the congregation to listen on one wavelength when the preacher is broadcasting on another. Nonetheless, conscientious preachers shape material so that the gospel and its implications for life are expressed in ways that are most congenial to the hearers, recognizing that under ordinary circumstances their efforts will facilitate communication.

Transcending One's Own Style

Preachers, likewise, often spend considerable effort developing their own styles of preaching. They search for ways to bring the gospel to life that are consistent with their theologies, with who they are as persons, with their own patterns of perception and expression, and with their presuppositions about how people hear sermons. For instance, in introductory preaching courses, we discover that many students are innately inclined toward inductive and intuitive patterns of movement and the use of story and image. They tend to develop a style that includes those qualities. Other students, however, have a more deductive and linear approach to preaching.

A preacher's style is typically well received by listeners who share traits that are similar to those of the preacher. Hearers whose traits differ from those of the preacher sometimes experience some uneasiness, or even frustration, with the preacher. For example, congregants who are innately inductive and intuitive often feel an innate empathy with the inductive and intuitive sermon. Listeners who tend toward the deductive and linear sometimes feel that inductive and intuitive sermons are incomplete. After hearing a sermon that many intuitives experienced as powerful, an engineer was heard to say, "But the preacher never got to the point."

On the one hand, the attempt to find one's style helps bring congruity between the preacher and the message. On the other hand, exclusive reliance on one style can leave some listeners feeling that they have not been full participants in the preaching conversation. Indeed, they can come away from such sermons feeling a little empty.

This situation is represented in Figure 1 on page 12. For the sake of illustration, we will say that a congregation represented by circle E contains sixteen listening groups (Clement's variety of fish). A pastor who preaches in only one style is represented by circle A. It is readily apparent that group 6 (whoever they might be) loves this kind of sermon. "Oh, that was preaching," they might say at the door. They may even tell their friends what a wonderful preacher they have. Groups 2, 5, 7, and 10 also like the preaching. It seems interesting and relevant. Groups 1, 3, 9 and 11 find some points of contact with the sermon, and would probably say that the preaching is satisfactory, though not exciting. But the preaching misses altogether groups 4, 8, 12, 13, 14, 15, and 16. They may continue to come to worship (perhaps out of habit, loyalty to the congregation, duty, or spousal command), but they get very little out of the sermon. The preacher may never become aware of these groups' response (or lack thereof) because they never mention anything as they slip out the side door. Circles A, B, C, and D represent different approaches that a preacher might take in order to communicate with persons whose traits are represented within those boundaries.

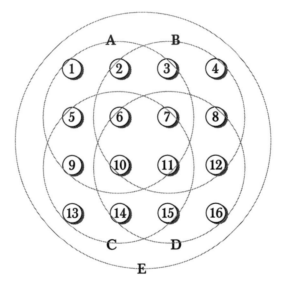

Figure 1

Some preachers actually grow a church just of people who respond to the preacher's style. The congregation not only thinks the content that the preacher thinks, but thinks it after the pattern of the preacher's own modes of thought and expression. People with other patterns of thought unconsciously (in some cases consciously) feel unwelcome.

Furthermore, not all subject matters and situations are congenial to a single approach to the sermon. In one sermon, a preacher may need to ring the fire bell of immediate warning, while another sermon may need to apply a healing salve, while still another sermon may need to do its work like a jackhammer breaking up cement.

While a preacher may be most comfortable with a single style, the preacher typically needs to be able to preach in a number of different ways. As Fred Craddock said vividly in a lecture, "We need a number of arrows in our quiver," such as inductive, deductive, narrative-story, conceptual, and imagistic. Thomas G. Long, a leading contemporary preacher, makes a similar point.

> It is important for those preachers who tend to design the sermon journey in a free-flowing, loosely connected way, with many side trips and scenic excursions into symbolic imagery, to depart from that form on occasion and to create a more tightly structured form for the sake of those in the congregation who travel better that way. Likewise, the preacher who tends toward the firmly guided sermon journey, with conceptual mileposts clearly marked, needs on occasion to supplement that sort of form with other, more fluid designs.[6]

In short, the preacher must be multilingual in homiletical form.

The preacher's approach for a particular sermon is not imposed *a priori,* but emerges from the encounter of the congregation (and the various subcongregations within it) and its various listener tendencies, the occasion (with its needs), the biblical text, the gospel, and the preacher. The preacher assesses which arrow has the best chance of striking the target.

Preaching Beyond Zarzuelas

By advocating that the preacher shape the form and expression of the sermon to facilitate communication with the congregation, we do not intend to suggest that the preacher compromise gospel content. The preacher hopes to help people understand the gospel with its promise and command as fully as they can in a given circumstance. Our purpose is to encourage the preacher to enhance the possibility for the hearing of the gospel in its fullness and force by consciously shaping sermons to account for the plurality of the listening community.

However, the preacher's efforts in this direction will be for naught unless the sermon has something to say. James Michener in his book *Iberia* speaks to this situation. Writing about Spanish music in the seventeenth century and the effects of the Inquisition, Michener says,

The more I listened to Spanish music the more I began to suspect that it failed because it lacked inherent seriousness; it did not direct itself to the major themes of life and thereby condemned itself to a secondary accomplishment. It could produce zarzuelas [brief, light musical playlets] but not operas or symphonies. The fault could not lie with the composers, for they gave ample evidence of their competence; it must have lain with the society in which they worked. Something quite stifling happened to Spanish intellectual life [in the seventeenth century] and it is reflected in the decline of Spanish music...The melodies remain, the rhythms, the technical competence and the brilliant orchestration, but the heart has gone dry.[7]

The public seemed to prefer, says Michener, "the brief and incidental to the sustained and generic."[8]

Michener's comments about Spanish music in the seventeenth century can be transferred to some Christian preachers in North America. Preachers sometimes become purveyors of homiletical zarzuelas when they (we) become fascinated with the technology of preaching but lose sight of the importance of theological substance. We can imagine ministers who could become so fascinated with the technology of adapting the sermon to the diverse congregations within the congregation that the preachers do not spend sufficient time or creativity in finding something important to say. Preaching must move beyond zarzuelas to a substantial theological agenda.

Sermons are great precisely when preachers have something significant to say. The fourth, sixteenth, and nineteenth centuries are three periods of Western history in which there were many great preachers. The preaching was vital because the preachers dealt with great themes: the evangelization of the Roman Empire, the reform of the church, the great missionary impulse. The great themes for the preacher today are quite different. Indeed, we can rightly criticize aspects of leading themes of our ancestors in these three signal centuries. When the church became confident of the state and other dominant forces in society, faithful witness was often compromised. The reform of the sixteenth century exacerbated the divisions in the church. The missionary impulse of the nineteenth century sometimes confused conversion to Christian faith with adopting Western culture. However, the point remains: preaching is powerful (and has far-reaching effects) when it deals with matters of importance in such a way as to make existential connection with the congregation.

The preacher whose heart has gone dry will be renewed by a generative theological vision under a fresh impulse of the Holy Spirit. No amount of tinkering with cohort-friendly modes of expression can substitute for theological dynamism. Nonetheless, when the content of the sermon is life-giving and engaging, the sermon has a better opportunity to make live contact with the hearts, minds, and wills of the congregation when the material is shaped to account for the diversity within the listening community. The preacher who uses a variety of baits likely will attract a variety of fish.

Four Approaches to Communicating with Listeners of Different Types

Every person and every congregation are unique. The data and perspectives that we discuss in this book are found in persons and groups in many congregations. Nonetheless, each congregation has its own particular combinations, peculiarities, and exceptions. Through priestly listening, the pastor can discover the distinctive listening profile of the community so that the pastor can incorporate as many listening orientations as possible into the designs of the sermons. Toward this end, the preacher might adopt one of the following four approaches. The preacher selects an approach based on pastoral analysis of the congregation and its needs on a given Sunday or during a particular season of the congregation's life.

First, the preacher may prepare a single sermon (or a series of sermons) with one particular group of listeners in mind. The minister shapes the sermon to speak especially to a target group. The preacher adopts this strategy when pastoral reflection on the congregation reveals that a particular group needs a specific message. Returning to the motif of the speaking center from the Introduction, the preacher can bring this group into the speaking and listening center of the congregation for the whole sermon.

For example, a preacher may shape a sermon so that it will appeal particularly to women who have a particular way of knowing. Some women, for instance, are silent knowers (as described in chapter 4). They lack confidence in their own capacity to receive and process information about the world. Hence, they remain silent. The preacher may design a sermon or series of sermons to help increase the confidence of such silent women in their ability to discern the divine presence and to make their own decisions in how to respond to the liberating movement of God.

Some readers may object that by shaping the sermon for a particular segment of the congregation, others will be excluded from the circle of those who can benefit from the sermon. We reply that listeners usually have enough flexibility that they can hear messages that do not correspond completely to their proclivities. They may experience a little static, but the sermon can certainly communicate. At this juncture, Fred Craddock's famous notion of overhearing may come into play.[9] Though not addressed directly, some listeners "overhear" the sermon, and, in the process, may find themselves drawn into it. Persons who did not arrive at worship with a question about the inspiration of the Bible may find themselves contemplating that issue as they overhear the preacher in conversation with the Bible class. Women who are not silent knowers may identify with silent knowers and join the movement toward liberation.

Second, for a single sermon, the preacher may conscientiously integrate several distinct qualities that enhance receptivity for distinct listening groups. The preacher would consciously include material that speaks to a range of groups.

For example, in the last part of chapter 3, we mention that a person is usually prone to take in the world through one of the following modes of perception: visual, auditory, or kinesthetic. While nearly all people include all modes, one mode usually predominates in a given person. Hence, the preacher can include material in a sermon that appeals to the senses of sight, hearing, and feeling. The sermon thereby has a good chance to connect with persons whose primary means of perception is visual, with those who relate to the world largely through hearing, and with those who are kinesthetic in their orientation. To take another example, in a multicultural congregation, as discussed in chapter 5, the preacher can explicitly name matters of race and ethnicity, and can provide basic information about the communities present. The sermon might celebrate the divine movement through each culture, help the various groups recognize how they enrich one another, and address the tensions within the congregation (and in the larger culture) that configure around race and ethnicity. Of course, regardless of whether a congregation is made up of persons of more than one race or ethnic background, a preacher is called to address racial and ethnic matters, both because they are points of tension and injustice in the wider human family, and because the reign of God inherently calls people who are different into deeper communion. The preacher who ignores such matters allows the silence of the sermon to reinforce racial stereotypes and divisions that are typical in aspects of North American culture beyond the church.

Third, over a season of preaching, the preacher may combine aspects of the two previous approaches and give attention to the full range of variables in congregational perception. While no single sermon would include material designed to speak to all listeners in their various modes of perception, the whole listening community would be included over several Sundays.

For example, in chapter 2, we describe characteristics of listeners in age cohorts: Builders, Silents, Boomers, and Gen 13. During Advent, the preacher might deal with the theme of hope as refracted through the Bible readings for Advent in ways that could be positively received by each generation. What are the hopes of each generation? How does each generation speak about its hopes? How do the hopes of the generations compare and contrast with Christian hope as expressed in the Advent season? How do their notions need to be reshaped according to core Christian thinking? The preacher can search for questions, issues, and figures of speech regarding Christian hope that have a good chance of being welcomed by each generation.

A fourth approach is to begin work on the sermon by focusing on the text and occasion and then to take the various listeners into account. Joey frequently follows this path. When preparing to preach at a regional gathering of the church, for instance, the material initially takes a leading role in shaping the sermon—the biblical text, the theme of the assembly and its purpose. Along the way, Joey pauses to ask *How will the listening groups at the assembly hear (or not hear) this sermon? Are some groups excluded? Will some groups feel that they received too much attention?* The preacher can then calibrate the material in the sermon to account for this aspect of pastoral analysis.

As every preacher knows, communication between pastor and people can transcend conventional homiletical rules. The response of the congregation to the Holy Spirit, the hunger of the listeners for a gospel word, or some other factor—any such factor can transform the poorest sermon into a moment of grace. A sermon that is theologically insightful, related to life, warm, genuine, and communicative can often be heard within *each* pocket of diversity that is discussed in this work. The most careful preparation cannot guarantee that the congregation will understand a sermon. Nonetheless, most sermons benefit from crafting that accounts for the characteristics of the different groups of listeners in the congregation. In any event preachers are ethically obligated to prepare as carefully as possible.[10]

By shaping sermons to account for differences in congregational perception, the preacher embodies an important theological point: the church is one. The pastor's homiletical approach is itself a witness to the breadth and depth of divine love as the preacher attempts to include as many as possible in the community of those who can receive and process the sermon. The preacher hopes that the congregation will be one and thus testify that God is one (Deut. 6:4). A multifaceted preaching program can help the congregation name (and become able to deal with) its own diversity. It can also help prevent the congregation from making idols of certain listener preferences.

Caveats

While the preacher can certainly help people have an opportunity to enter the world of the sermon by taking account of the tendencies of the listening community, this effort requires caveats. People are not trapped by the characteristics of the groups in which they find themselves. Belonging to a particular cohort does not completely predetermine how a person will respond to a particular mode of expression or to a particular sermon. Although people possess distinctive listener traits, a particular person can never be reduced to those traits as if the traits function mechanically to predetermine how a person will receive and process a sermon. A tendency is not a straitjacket, but an indicator of probability.

Furthermore, people do not always manifest listener traits in a pure way. A person often contains aspects of differing traits. For example, the authors of this book are Boomers by age cohort. Although we have many characteristics in common with other Boomers, we often relate to the church in ways that more resemble Builders (who are older, see chapter 2).

The configuration of listener traits in a particular person can change. For instance, we regularly see people who enter theological seminary at a level of faith development that James Fowler would catalogue as Stage 2 evolve into someone at Stage 3 or Stage 4 in response to the stimuli of the seminary. Changing life circumstances can prompt a change in listener tendencies.

People who share one trait may vary widely in others. For example, persons of the same age may have very different patterns of mental operation and contrasting theological worldviews. Each person is a collage with a unique combination of listener tendencies.

The fact that listeners fall into multiple categories at the same time can present the preacher with a dizzying array of possibilities for shaping the sermon: A European American, conservative, widow, Builder, who takes in the world visually and may be at Stage 5 in Fowler's trajectory of faith development. Does the preacher speak with her as a European American? a conservative? a woman? one of the least? a Builder? a Fowler Stage 5? as a person who is oriented to visuality? or some combination thereof? This woman represents the almost endless possibilities that combine in the different members of the congregation. The preacher cannot possibly take all configurations into account. Probably the preacher thinks of the sermon with persons with particular traits in mind on the basis of the intention of a particular sermon. A preacher may want to have conversation particularly with conservatives, or women, or Builders (or some combination).

Moreover, human beings often think, feel, and act in unexpected ways. A human being can transcend the limitations of many qualities. People sometimes choose not to think, feel, or act within their traits. For instance, a person who relates intuitively to the world may decide that a particular issue calls for a linear analysis. Sometimes a person responds differently to new circumstances without conscientiously deciding to do so. For example, a person who thinks in a linear fashion may get caught up in a sermon that is largely impressionistic or intuitive.

Thomas G. Long, a leading authority in the preaching community today, notes that preacher and congregation affect each other. "The preacher who speaks week in, week out, to a congregation is learning how to preach effectively to them, but they are learning also, discovering how to listen to this preacher. Over time, and under the surface, preacher and listener are gradually adjusting to achieve the best communication fit."[11] Factors such as sensitivity to life, specific experiences, education, moral commitments, and other factors, can manifest qualities that are often associated with groups other than the listener's natural one. For example, a member of the Builder generation need not inherently and in all ways manifest the characteristics of the Builders. A particular Builder's experience and education may lead her or him to be more like a member of the Boomer generation, at least in selected ways.

These observations emphasize the importance of Long's perceptive observations:

> Listeners *do* have diverse listening styles, and these *are* complex and not-fully-understood processes, but these styles are to be seen more as band spreads than single frequencies. In other words, while it is true that certain hearers may prefer to listen to sermons that are shaped in a particular way, may say that they get more out of a certain style of preaching, and may in fact find such sermons clearer and more compelling precisely because they are designed in a way that more or less matches their listening style, it does not follow that this is the only style of sermon they can "hear." If they are exposed to a sermon in an alien form, they may resist it somewhat, not like it much, or even reformulate it so that it fits more comfortably into their listening equation, but the fact of the matter is that they *can* hear it if it is not completely outside their range.[12]

The simple fact is that most listeners are able to receive and process a wide variety of communication styles. A preacher who has something significant to say in concert with the congregational context will often find people listening eagerly from across the various listening spectra. The preacher hopes to develop sermons that broadcast across a broad band.

Given the remarkable diversity of the listening community, a sermon never achieves complete communication with all members of the congregation. Nonetheless, a preacher can help the community have a good *opportunity* to enter into the world of the message. No amount of preaching skill can guarantee that the congregation will fully grasp the message as the preacher intends it. The preacher is called to shape the content and style of the sermon in the reasonable but not guaranteed hope that the sermon will intersect with patterns of human perception at work in the congregation on the Sunday that the minister preaches the sermon. This book aims to help people have an opportunity to receive the sermon.

2

Preaching and Different Generations

When Ron served as a pastor of a local congregation, he attended a Sunday school class party at which the class members reminisced about a previous minister.[1] The class was made up of persons who were older than sixty. One of the class members recalled that the previous pastor "always had a poem in his sermons, and I really liked that." Several of the participants nodded in agreement.

Ron had not used many poems in his sermons. But shortly after that class party, he began to include poetry in his preaching at least once a month. He is not a poetry aficionado, but he is acquainted with some poetry in the style of free verse. His favorite poet is W. H. Auden, so he made a point of citing Auden from time to time. However, no one said anything to Ron about the use of poetry in the sermons.

Later, a person in that class died. The family asked Ron to read the decedent's favorite poem as a part of the funeral: a piece in iambic pentameter by Helen Steiner Rice. Most of the class members were present when he read the poem at the service. After the burial, the class served a dinner for the family. Several class members thanked him for reading "that beautiful poem." One person even allowed that it must have been the first time that Ron had ever used a poem. A light went on: to this generation in this place, a poem is verse in iambic pentameter.

This incident illustrates the focus of this chapter. Each generation finds certain qualities of communication appealing, and other qualities less so. These qualities are related to the larger life journeys of each generation. Most congregations today are made up of persons from four generations: Builders, Silents, Boomers, and Generation 13.[2] This chapter explores how an awareness of generational qualities can help the preacher shape the sermon so that the sermon has an optimum chance to be received by persons in the different generations. For each generation, we outline the leading characteristics of the cohort. Along the way, we identify points at which the gospel correlates with that generation's preference. We also note points at which the gospel challenges generational styles and preferences. In the process, we call attention to qualities of preaching (including theological content and homiletical form) that enhance and frustrate communication with each generation.

A caution. The preacher must recognize that persons vary greatly within each generation. A cohort is not a monolith. Each generation contains persons with different orientations to receiving and processing communications, to spirituality, to priorities, to values, and to relationality. Some persons, in fact, are genuinely transgenerational. A preacher needs to identify the particular qualities of the generations (and their individual members) in the congregation. A pastor also needs to recognize that the characteristics of each generation are not frozen. A cohort's view of the world is affected while it lives. Therefore, a preacher needs to pay attention to changes in generations as they evolve.

Builders: The Institutional Generation

The Builders were born in the first quarter of the twentieth century (1901–1924). Because of their association with the Second World War, they are sometimes called the G.I. Generation, G.I. Joes. Tom Brokaw dubbed them "the greatest generation" because of the grace and power with which they lived through the Great Depression, World War II, and tumultuous changes in North American culture since the war.[3] The experience of limitation in the Great Depression and the even more anxious years of World War II were formative for the Builders' outlook on life. They came home from the war intent on creating a stable and peaceful world.

One of the primary ways that they sought to create a secure environment was through building social institutions that would stave off deprivation and violence, that would promote a sense of community, and that would provide for progress. For many Builders, the character of life in the presidencies of Dwight D. Eisenhower and John F. Kennedy represents the best of their personal, social, and religious hopes.

Toward the goal of helping their institutions create a secure social fabric, they work very hard in the home, in the marketplace, in the church, and in other institutions of which they are a part. They value constitutions, bylaws, and procedures because these are means through which the institutions mediate predictability. They respect careful management, attention to detail, and a friendly spirit.

The Builders have an institutional view of the church. To them, the church contributes to the stability of the larger social order by developing character and moral values. For instance, the neighborhood in which Ron lives in Indianapolis recently had a major racial uprising. The Builder pastor of one of the neighborhood congregations recommended an evangelism program to help get people into the church "to help settle down the neighborhood."

Builders want the church to succeed in the institutional terms by which success is marked in our culture: growth in numbers, financial solvency, influence in the larger society. For more than fifty years, Builders have been willing to sacrifice to help the church succeed. They are still willing to do so. The preacher can still appeal to the Builders on these grounds when appropriate to the church's nature and witness. The Builders are also interested in occasional sermons that focus on the institutional concerns of the church.

This concern for security is a double-edged sword for the preacher. On the one side, it can become a point of entry for the sermon as the preacher helps Builders discover how the gospel can create a secure world. On the other side, the security promised by the gospel results less from building stable, conventional social institutions than from the transformation of the social world. Indeed, Christians ultimately hope for the full manifestation of divine rule (NRSV: kingdom of God). This transformation calls for a social world in which all relationships, communities, and systems mediate God's unconditional love for all.

In order to make a meaningful witness, the church must give some attention to its organizational life. But the preacher must often remind the Builders that the church exists not for its own sake, nor to preserve the present social order, nor to "keep things quiet," but to point to the emerging dominion of God. The ultimate security that comes from divine rule sometimes calls for individuals, the church-as-community, and the wider social world to rearrange their values, priorities, and practices.

Builders do not inherently equate security with keeping the world exactly as it is. As a generation, the Builders are called forward by the desire to make the world a better place. Much of this improvement has demanded change. Consequently, if a pastor's message calls for change, they want to hear a positive vision of how things could be improved by making the change.

The twentieth century has been a time of remarkable expansion in science and technology. The Builders were raised to idealize science as opening the door to an unparalleled period of progress in human history. This progress was symbolized by the drive to end polio and other diseases. The General Electric Corporation typified the Builders' attitude with the famous slogan, "Progress Is Our Most Important Product."

Data from the physical sciences are particularly authoritative for Builders. The proverbial rocket scientist is one of their heroes. They accept the latest reports from the scientific world, and they have confidence that the sciences can lead us forward, particularly in medical discovery. The Builders also respect the results of the human sciences, though they are not as enamored of psychology, sociology, and the economic and political sciences as they are of physics, biology, and chemistry.

The preacher who seeks to persuade Builders that an assertion is worthy of belief will often find that Builders are convinced by scientific data. While they do not use the vocabulary of "progress" as much as they once did, Builders still want to know how a sermon will help them move toward a better life. This generation welcomes a sermon that shows them how its theme will add to the quality of life.

Not surprisingly, a few Builders take an uncritical attitude toward science and technology, assuming that if a development is technologically possible, it is desirable. The gospel challenges Builders to think critically about the degree to which a new (or lingering) scientific development is consistent with God's love for all and with God's will for justice for all. For instance, the preacher needs to help many Builders understand that the uncritical use of science and technology exacerbates aspects of the environmental crisis.

The Builders respond to challenge. As young people, they met the challenges of living through the Depression and conquering the Axis powers. The space program is one of the most potent symbols of the lure of challenge for this generation. When the Russians launched their satellite Sputnik (1957), the Builders responded by mobilizing an incredible array of resources (human, financial, technological) to meet the challenge and land a person on the moon before the Russians could. The Builders are still ready to rise to a challenge.

The preacher, therefore, can speak to them in the mode of challenge. In a sermon on financial stewardship, for instance, the preacher might challenge the Builders to increase their giving in order to help the church raise the budget so that the congregation can expand its ministries to their grandchildren.

William Strauss and Neil Howe describe this generation as "intensely left brained."[4] As a group, the Builders like logic, ideas, linear thinking, and propositional forms of communication. They regarded the Apollo 11 moon landing (one of their proudest moments) as "the embodied concretization" of the most distinctive faculty of the human being: rationality.[5] They like for a message to be clear and to have direct, practical implication for life.

Builders appreciate the arts. But they tend toward expressions that communicate directly and that get across a clear, hopeful message. Builders flocked to the musicals of Rogers and Hammerstein. These presentations touch a serious theme in a light and humorous way. A musical makes a point, but it does not usually search human experience with the insight, honesty, and poignancy of Shakespeare.

Many Builders, therefore, are inclined toward linear, propositional sermons. Builders do not crave sermons that make three points and end with a poem, but they do respond well to messages that clearly state a point (or points). They like sermons that are structured logically. Billy Graham is one of their favorite preachers. Graham talks about God in straightforward ideas. With a touch of elegance, Graham makes propositional assertions about God, sin, faith, the world, and a range of other concerns. He states clearly how he hopes the listeners will respond to the sermon. Graham articulates the benefits that will accrue to the listeners as a result of believing and responding. His stories function as illustrations that show the practical outcomes of the sermon's propositions for life.

Builders have a deep sense of loyalty and moral obligation to God, to their children, to the church, and to the larger community. They often respond positively when the preacher frames a message in terms of what they ought to do to fulfill their responsibilities. Builders appreciate practical guidance in how to carry out their responsibilities.

The preacher must handle this frame of mind with theological care. Builders' profound sense of moral commitment makes it easy for them to drift into works-righteousness. They can easily think that in order to merit God's grace, they must perform their obligations. Hence, the preacher must carefully set out the relationship between grace as unmerited divine favor and moral behavior as response to that favor.

While Builders brought forth their share of fundamentalists, the larger number of Builders tend not to be theologically doctrinaire. Douglas Alan Walrath reports asking a number of Builders, "whether they favor Southern Baptist prayer or Jewish prayer or Black Muslim prayer if prayer should be restored as the norm in public schools." However, Walrath's "question doesn't make sense to them." Most of them "assume that 'because we all believe in the same God,' our praying will be harmonious."[6]

The preacher may need to help Builders recognize that theological differences among the traditional world religions and the New Age spiritualities, as well as among different Christian communities, sometimes result in quite different views of Ultimate Reality, moral orientation, and social behavior and organization. Builders sometimes need help in coming to a distinctive understanding of the Christian faith and its imperatives. On the basis of a clear understanding of the gospel and its claims, then, the Christian community can enter into dialogue with other communities.

As children, Builders joined together in groups. In fact, their tendency to want to be together in gangs was, in part, responsible for their parents' founding youth organizations (such as the Girl Scouts and Boy Scouts) to channel their social energy constructively. As they grew older, they popularized sororities and fraternities and other forms of group life. To this day, they are joiners. Many of the Sunday school classes that they formed in the 1940s and 1950s are still vital centers of relationship. Class fellowship is often more important than the lesson. And class parties are often better attended than Sunday morning sessions.

Builders also respond positively to sermon themes about relationships. To be sure, some Builders are mostly interested in people who are similar to them (i.e., in values, culture, race, ethnicity, social class, education, national citizenship). The gospel challenges such Builders to move beyond their parochial arenas of concern to a gospel-sized vision of community. Frequently, the preacher needs to help Builders hear the gospel's call to enlarge their circle of concern.

The theme of relationships is connected to preaching in another way. Builders want to feel personally related to the preacher. The preacher who wants to receive a positive hearing by Builders needs to take the time to develop relationships with them. The preacher's most well-crafted sermons can fall on deaf Builder ears if the preacher has not attended their class parties, laughed at their jokes, talked with them in the parking lot, called in their homes, and visited them in the hospitals.

Builders are the first generation for whom a high school education became the norm and for whom college was a widespread dream. The G.I. Bill following World War II made it possible for a greater percentage of them to obtain a college education than any previous generation. Many Builders raised their children to assume that college would follow high school and that a college education would provide both economic security and life enrichment.

Builders' emphasis on education suits them well for teaching sermons.[7] They are often interested in the background of biblical passages, in the origins of Christian doctrine, in the history of the denomination (or congregation), and in its practices. Many Builders are willing to alter their patterns of thinking and acting when they learn that their previous ways do not measure up to the best of our current interpretation.

Builders respond favorably to sermons that have a positive tone. They are willing to recognize shortcomings and failures. Such honesty is sometimes necessary for progress. However, they do not want to dwell on the negative. Consistent with their general forward-looking spirit, they are motivated less by guilt and more by optimism and hearty cheerfulness. They want to be assured that they are on a promising track. And they want to know that despite their lapses, God is working positively with them.

When the gospel asks Builders to change, the preacher can often appeal to the fact that Builders have been leaders in change. When faced with new possibilities, they have cut their ties with previous patterns of thinking, behavior, and organization, and they have launched risky ventures that have proven successful. For instance, a preacher might help Builders reflect on the fact that they spearheaded the move from the old church (with its drafty sanctuary, cramped educational space, and no parking) into the new church building that has enhanced the community's Christian life and witness. The preacher can help Builders apply this can-do attitude to refashioning the life of the congregation for the new millennium.

The gospel sometimes calls Builders to repent of some of their preferences and to embrace fresh ways of thinking, acting, or feeling.

Instead of beginning the sermon with an overt attack on the Builders' preferences, the pastor may find it helpful to begin the sermon by naming the Builders' viewpoint and expressing appreciation for what that point of view or behavior has meant to Builders. Builders hear that the preacher understands them. This acknowledgment creates an atmosphere of trust and mutual understanding. The preacher can then expose the deficiencies of Builders. In the critique, the preacher needs to be careful to avoid caricature, to analyze the incongruities between Builder life and the gospel call in rational terms, and to explain how the change will bring about life improvement.

The Silent Generation: Bridge Builders

The Silent Generation was born between 1925 and 1942. The birthrate in the United States was lower for Silents than for any current age group. Evidently their parents were reluctant to bring children into the deprivation and uncertainty of the Great Depression. They are the smallest of the four living cohorts. The trait of being small in number represents one of the Silents' lifelong struggles. As a group, this generation is not as permeating a force in its own right as other generations. They have exerted significant leadership. But much of their energy is spent in responding to Builders ahead of them and to Boomers behind them. In comparison with other generations, they are relatively silent.

Their formative youth years corresponded with the return of Builders from World War II. Winning the war had been the dominant focus of the nation during their early lives. The G.I.s came home as heroines and heroes, powered by the vision of creating a stable world, with leadership skills honed in the service and with an unrelenting drive for education.

The Silent Generation was just enough younger, and just enough less mature, to be overshadowed by Builders. "Watching from the sidelines, they saw the nation celebrate thirtyish war heroes and indulge a new generation of postwar babies—and reaffirm a social order at once comfortable and impermeable."[8] As the postwar babies became youth and adults, Silents felt the national spotlight pass from Builders to Boomers. In a poignant observation, two researchers into this group say, "The Silents are the only living generation whose members would rather be in some age bracket other than the one they now occupy."[9] Some Silents continue to feel resentment toward Builders and jealousy toward Boomers. The church sometimes feels this tension.

Silents had their own war: Korea. But the Korean conflict did not result in the same degree of national recognition as World War II. Indeed, the Korean War was never officially declared a war. It did not result in a decisive victory. "Where George Bush's peers had conquered large portions of Europe, Africa, and the Pacific, Mike Dukakis's fought to a tie on one small peninsula."[10]

Builders took the lead in establishing the tone of the culture for the 1950s and 1960s. Silents initially saw life's purpose as "refining and humanizing the G.I.-built world."[11] They learned how to operate the scientific and industrial technology that emerged in the post-World War II boom. They also learned how to work within the human institutions that Builders styled. Silents patiently awaited their turn for top leadership, but many of them have been passed over and will never serve as the heads of the institutions of which they have been a part.

Silents made excellent assistants and associates for Builders. But the next wave of top leadership passed to Boomers, with only a few Silents becoming effective institutional leaders. Silents never produced a President of the United States, although they have given the nation a platoon of Presidential aides (e.g., Pierre Salinger, Bill Moyers, John Ehrlichman, Stuart Eizenstat, James Baker).[12]

A related frustration for Silents is that when they reached their prime, the world changed. In the late 1960s, powerful undercurrents began to shift the direction of our culture from the 1950s hegemony to a world that is more openly pluralistic, and ultimately postmodern. Many Silents feel that the world for which they had prepared not only unraveled before them but also unraveled with them moving into senior positions of leadership. The long-established churches, for instance, have declined in traditional measurements of institutional strength throughout the Silents' peak years: numbers of members, financial resources, power in the cultural setting. Their peak years have been given to presiding over continuously shrinking churches.

These developments alert the preacher to a motif that is important to Silents, especially as they move into the era nearing retirement. They yearn to believe that their lives and works have mattered to the human community and to God.

Although Silents have not, as a generation, exerted a lot of top leadership in their era, they have made distinctive and lasting contributions. They are contemporaries of Martin Luther King, Jr. As a generation, they are committed to justice in all aspects of the nation.

They have a deep, strong, and tender social conscience typified by the civil rights theme "Deep in my heart, I do believe, we shall overcome someday."[13] Silent women were the first to articulate and embrace the feminist movement in large numbers. Silents flooded the helping professions in the 1960s and brought public interest advocacy groups onto center stage in many communities. They regard a part of their public obligation as naming points at which the nation, town, church, other civic bodies, and individuals fall short of acceptable moral standards.

When the Silent members of the congregation hear sermon themes of justice, advocacy, and the public good, these emphases resonate with their sense of what is true and needed. Many Silents went to the South in the 1950s and 1960s in order to be a part of the civil rights movement. Many are still willing to work in behalf of creating a world that is fair. The preacher can help them act on this impulse by identifying specific actions by which they can translate their continuing desires for a just world into practical actions.

Silents emphasize dialogue and conversation as essential to the core of common life. Silents gave us "Nightline," the global style of town meetings, and the talk shows. They are skilled arbitrators, "mediating arguments between others—and reaching out to people of all cultures, races, ages and handicaps."[14] As one of their number says, "We don't arrive with ready-made answers so much as a honed capacity to ask and to listen."[15] This quality allowed them to bridge gaps when Builders and Boomers came into conflict in the 1960s and 1970s. They continue to be bridge builders as tensions between Builders and Boomers have become less public, more subtle, but still intense.

Silent theologians introduced the buzzword *conversation* to describe the character of doing theology. In so doing, they not only named an essential quality of theological method, but also canonized one of their generational characteristics. Silents who are not professional theologians appreciate sermons that have a conversational quality. By this, we do not mean that they want sermons in which multiple people actually converse aloud in the pulpit. But they want to have the sense that the sermon arises from a conversation, that the preacher is engaged in that conversation, and that the sermon allows them to become a part of the conversation. They want to know that the preacher has consulted all the parties who might contribute to forward movement in the conversation. As befits participants in any honest conversation, they want the others to be represented fully and fairly. Silents resent caricature, oversimplification, and the use of straw people in argumentation.

Silent people also listen for a homiletical word that opens the possibility for bridge building across races, genders, classes, nations, and cultures. The gospel's emphasis on reconciliation is especially welcome to them.

The Silent Generation also has a technocratic approach to life. They refined the corporate employee handbook. In Congress, Silents have been "a proven generation of bureaucratizers."[16] This rule-writing impulse is for the sake of regularizing patterns of common life that result in justice. They see regulation as the means by which to make due process the norm in daily practice.

Silents, then, have an innate sympathy with preaching that articulates a moral vision and details how Christians ought to put that vision into practice in specific situations. Silents know that life is complicated, especially by the many contingencies that can impinge on an idea, a feeling, or a situation. That is why they write such detailed corporate regulations. Consequently, they want the preacher to acknowledge the complexities in situations before the Christian community, and to take account of variations, exceptions, and other complications.

Many members of the Silent Generation feel considerable personal and relational pain. Justice, bridge building, and people helping have been their theme songs. Yet they have an unusually high incidence of divorce. Indeed, Silent legislators created no-fault divorce. A disproportionate number of their children have grown up in broken homes. And many Silents in midlife participated in the sexual revolution in ways that were quite disruptive of personal and family lives. Many Silents feel lingering guilt about these matters. They long to understand them from a transcendent perspective. In particular, they would like to know if God can help heal what their sexual experimentation has torn apart, and if God can relieve their guilt.

Joey also notices that many Silents are angry. Some of their anger revolves around the fact that they have been bypassed for leadership in many institutions. Some of it is focused on the fact that their agenda of justice has still not been fulfilled in North America.

William Strauss and Neil Howe eloquently summarize this generation, writing that the Silent Generation

lent flexibility to a G.I.-built world that otherwise might have split to pieces under Boom attack—and have helped mollify, and ultimately cool, the Boom's coming-of-age passions. Indeed, the Silents have been path breakers for much of the 1960s-era "consciousness" (from music to film, civil rights to Viet Nam resistance) for which Boomers too often claim credit. From youth forward, this most considerate of living generations has specialized not in grand constructions or lofty ideals, but rather in people, life-size people like the statues planned for the Korean War Memorial. Barbra Streisand's age-mates would like to believe that "people who need people are the luckiest people in the world." But, true to form, they have their doubts.[17]

The preachers who win a hearing among the Silents will likely be those who help the generation recognize points at which their lives cohere with the gospel and points at which the gospel calls them to be more just.

Boomers: Visionaries and Seekers

The Boomers were born between 1943 and 1960. They are called Boomers because the expanded birthrate during their natal years was dubbed the Baby Boom. They are the largest of the four adult generations. Like the Silent Generation, their numerical size represents something of their place in the national consciousness. At each phase of their lives, they have drawn disproportionately more attention and resources than other generations. Their sheer numbers, combined with their irrepressible force, have demanded that other generations reckon with them. Indeed, Boomers have been studied more than other quadrants of the population.

Boomers' childhoods were Edenic years, when it seemed that science, technology, and improved methods of education and parenthood were opening the door to a future of unlimited possibilities. "Leave It To Beaver" was a symbol of the world of their youth. Public schools and Sunday schools were bursting with children in record numbers. They developed a vision that the world could be made right. Their parents taught them to think for themselves. A mother of Boomers (who is herself a Builder) recalls, "We wanted our children to be inner-directed. It seemed logical to us that fascism and communism...could not really succeed except in countries where children were raised in very authoritarian families."[18] From the very beginning, Boomers were encouraged to learn how to make choices for themselves. This quality has become one of their lifelong themes.

A golden era seemed to lie before them. They became a generation of visionaries who wanted the outer world of behavior and achievement to correspond to the inner world of idealism. "Arriving as the inheritors of G.I. triumph, Boomers have always seen their mission not as constructing a society, but of justifying, purifying, even *sanctifying* it."[19] They conclude that nearly every institution they encounter needs spiritual overhaul.

As they entered into late youth and young adulthood, the war in Viet Nam became, for many Boomers, a symbol of the distance between the vision of a right, wise world, and reality. At the time of the war, Boomers were about equally divided between those who supported it and those who opposed it. (Boomers who went to college tended to be more opposed to the war than those who did not). Both groups of Boomers shared a common core: they opposed or supported the war on the basis of vision, albeit differing ones, of how the world could be made right.

Their protests against the war brought two Boomer traits into clear focus: a propensity toward confrontation and an urge for immediate change. Both Joey and Ron remember being a part of groups chanting, "What do we want? Peace! When do we want it? Now." Douglas Alan Walrath refers to this generation as Challengers.[20] They have an ingrained inclination to challenge persons, values, communities, practices, and systems to change so as to improve the quality of life. When they see the importance of change, Boomers have little patience for delaying implementing the change.

In the 1950s, most Boomers participated at least nominally in church or synagogue. However, from the later 1960s through much of the 1990s, many Boomers disappeared from church. Most generations take a break from church attendance in their late teens and early twenties, and then return to church when they marry and begin to have children. Boomers, however, have not returned in the numbers expected. Some left the church because it seemed impotent to bring about changes in a world in need of reform, from civil rights at home to the war in Viet Nam. Many Roman Catholics left because of frustration with the church's positions on such issues as divorce and abortion. Some left because the churches seemed spiritually impoverished.

Most, however, walked away from the church because it simply seemed irrelevant to them.[21] Participating in the long-established churches did not make a significant enough difference for them to attend and to support the church with their time, energy, and money.[22] The church did not offer a vision that seemed to Boomers to be distinctive. They could support their values and causes of choice without the hassle of institutional religion.

However, Boomers' relative lack of interest in the long-established churches does not mean that they are indifferent to matters of value and spirit. Wade Clark Roof calls Boomers "a generation of seekers."[23] Indeed, eight out of ten Boomers describe themselves as religious. They yearn for a vision that will allow them to understand life as a whole. They are in search of coherence between their inner and outer lives, between their guiding visions and the behavior of the world around them. In this respect, Boomers are a deeply spiritual generation. However, their spiritual quests take many different forms, and as often as not, take place outside the boundaries of the long-established denominations in which most Boomers were confirmed or baptized.

Members of this generation have always asked questions about the meaning of their lives, about what they want for themselves and for their children. They have continued to explore, as they did in the years growing up, but in new, and we think, more profound ways. Religious and spiritual themes have surfaced in a rich variety of ways—in Eastern religions, in evangelical and fundamentalist teachings, in mysticism and New Age movements, in Goddess worship and other ancient religious rituals, in the mainline churches and synagogues, in Twelve Step recovery groups, in concern about the environment, in holistic health, and in personal and social transformation. Many within this generation who dropped out of churches and synagogues years ago are now shopping around for congregations. They move freely in and out, across religious boundaries; many combine elements from various traditions to create their own personal, tailor-made meaning systems. Choice, so much a part of life for this generation, now expresses itself in dynamic and fluid religious styles.[24]

Characteristic of the way in which they were raised, Boomers "have to discover for themselves what gives their lives meaning," what values by which to live.[25]

Boomers who choose to return to the long-established churches in their middle years tend to do so for clearly articulated reasons.[26] Many Boomers want their children to be exposed to a core of moral teaching. A few Boomers are willing to be a part of a church if it results in increased family harmony; many have chosen churches that have strong programs for children and youth. Many Boomers return to church because they hope that its message will resolve their personal, and in many instances lifelong, quests for meaning. Boomers look for "something to believe in, for answers to questions about life. Feelings of emptiness and loneliness, whether or not they are articulated in this way, lead people in such pursuits."[27] Many, many Boomers return to church to belong to a community. To the Boomer, it is not a contradiction to want the support of a group while carrying out their often highly individual quests for personal meaning.

In the light of this profile, Roof identifies five qualities of congregations that Boomers will find attractive:[28]

First, Boomers seek "a place where things are done right." In their childhood years Boomers learned to desire excellence. They want to perceive that they are associated with top-quality factors in education, in family life, in the workplace, in the home, in relationships, in the products they buy. Boomers may disagree among themselves as to the standards that define excellence in a particular arena, but they share a yearning for quality. As they are becoming older and are encountering limitations, they recognize that they cannot always manage the best of everything. So they seek excellence in more restricted areas. For instance, Ron once spent the weekend with a couple who were serving a ministerial internship on a minimal salary. Late one night they pulled a package of very expensive, premium ice cream out of the freezer. "It costs a little more," one of them said, "but it's worth it."

Boomers take their striving for excellence with them to church. They want high-level programming for their children and for themselves. They expect for the service of worship to manifest the best qualities of its particular style, whether high church Episcopal, dignified but less formal Southern Baptist, or charismatically animated Assembly of God. The drive for excellence intersects with the sermon. Boomers expect the sermon to help them identify excellence in the realm of Christian faith. What are the best hopes of the Christian community for the world? for them? How do they move toward those hopes? Boomers also expect the sermon itself to be excellent. It should contain significant and carefully considered religious substance that relates to the lives of the Boomers; it should be crafted so as to be received clearly; it should be delivered in a warm and communicative way.

Second, Boomers seek a "church that doesn't whack you on the can." They seek a community that has a distinctive vision and distinctive standards, but that does not bully them and is not punitive. Boomers respond positively to a community that "recognizes freedom of conscience and relies less on fear. It is less authoritarian, and more democratic. It is a church with tradition, yet not closed to change."[29] They want the church to speak out for the poor, the homeless, and victims of injustice, but to do so in a way that honors the freedom of people to imagine different responses to those problems.

The preacher who would speak to Boomers, then, needs to be able to articulate the core of Christian vision with clarity. What is distinctive about the Christian way of interpreting the world? A Boomer hopes that preachers will speak their own convictions, but that pastors will also acknowledge the possibility of other interpretations. Boomers are quite willing for the pastor to criticize other viewpoints. In fact, in the interest of critical evaluation of the options before them, they often feel helped when the pastor does so. But they also want the preacher to acknowledge ambiguities and to recognize the possibility that other modes of interpretation may be commendable.

The preacher can draw on tradition. Many Boomers have come to believe the past contains treasures that can contribute to a viable vision for life today. They value tradition. They are open to a word from the Bible, from church history, from other sources in the past. Yet Boomers do not want to feel imprisoned by the ideas and practices and feelings of the past. The preacher often has an innate sympathy among Boomers when showing how the tradition can be rechanneled in response to fresh insights and discoveries. The great danger, of course, is that Boomers can so recarve the channel of tradition to suit themselves that their version of the tradition can lose continuity with what has come before.

Third, Boomers look for a congregation that "invests in people." They have practically no interest in the church as an institution. They are oriented to events and groups that are explicitly designed to help people develop their vision and make their way through life. Boomers particularly like small groups that are formed around particular issues or phenomena. The small group both addresses the issue and provides an opportunity for people to relate to one another. As the group deals with the common problem or interest, the people become a community of support. For instance, Builder women flocked to women's fellowship circles with prescribed curricula from the denomination. Few Boomer women are willing to be a part of such a group. However, Boomer women are glad to join groups that deal with issues relating to women in the new millennium.

The sermon seldom takes place in the warmth and relationality of a small-group setting. But the preacher who would speak to Boomers can take advantage of the Boomer focus on people by including stories about real people in every sermon. Of course, Boomers are most attracted to stories about Boomers. But they also like stories about people of other ages and from other times and places, particularly when those stories bring to life people who struggle with the same kinds of issues with which Boomers are struggling. Boomers empathize with such stories and struggles.

The preacher is likely to catch the Boomer's attention when the sermon deals in a significant way with an issue that relates to the lives of the people in the congregation. When Ron has made this suggestion to groups of clergy, several have initially objected, "That sounds like topical preaching. Such preaching was anathema to our seminary professors." Ron does think that topical preaching can make an occasional contribution to contemporary preaching, and there may be times when a topical sermon is just right for addressing a Boomer concern.[30] However, it is clear that the contemporary church also needs the steady nutrients of strong, biblical preaching. When it is possible to do so with exegetical and hermeneutical integrity, the preacher can relate the Bible (and the larger Christian tradition and vision) to the issues that are before Boomers. How does the gospel help Boomers make their way through midlife?

The latter observation may call preachers to adjust a significant aspect of their homiletical practice. According to a study by Joseph Faulkener of Pennsylvania State University, not many sermons today focus in a meaningful way on significant real-life issues. Preachers tend to pass on information about the Bible without showing its concrete significance for the listeners. Preachers take sideswipes at contemporary issues, but do not analyze them with care or explore their ambiguities and difficulties.[31] A pastor tends to use a contemporary issue as an illustration, but does not discuss the issue in depth. To attract the attention of Boomers, preachers need not abandon biblical preaching, but carry the hermeneutical movement forward so that the sermon offers the practical help that Boomers seek.

Fourth, Boomers want a church "where there's a lot of freedom in the basement." This architectural image has the sanctuary (the first floor) as a symbol of that which is common in the whole of the congregation and the basement as a symbol of multiple ways whereby people can relate to Christian faith. On Sunday, the community gathers as a whole in the sanctuary. Through the week, the community gathers in the many rooms in the basement in small groups according to the members' particular needs and interests.

Congregations that successfully reach large numbers of Boomers typically have a large cafeteria in the basement—"experimental classes, courses in the new spirituality, and groups of all kinds (Twelve Step, women's, quest, healing, Jungian analysis, peace and justice, support, sharing)." [32] Ideally, each group uses its particular focus as a port of entry for the gospel into the lives of Boomers.

The subject matters of the different groups that take part in the church's life can often suggest foci for preaching. However, a part of the preacher's work on Sunday morning is to help the congregation discover how the many different groups in the basement are essentially related in the Christian community. Indeed, one of the distinctive roles of the preacher in the midst of Boomer pluralism is to help the church develop an identity as a *community* in Christ.

This pluralism has dangers for both laity and minister. Boomers can neglect aspects of Christian life that are essential. They can pick and choose only those things that interest them and develop a personalized religion that loses touch with the breadth and depth of God reflected in historic Christian tradition. Pastoral leadership needs to encourage Boomers (and others) to expose themselves to an adequate curriculum to understand Christian faith in its fullness. Preachers, too, sometimes allow their own special interests to shape their preaching in a disproportionate way. A preacher who is fascinated by Joseph Campbell's approach to mythology can easily develop sermons that replay Campbell's themes week after week. Even if Campbell's viewpoints are helpful (itself a hotly debated point in today's Christian community), his version of mythology may not bring forth the entire gospel that is necessary for a Christian community to function optimally.

Fifth, Boomers look for a congregation "with a big heart." Many Boomers want to be part of a church that has compassion at its core (the big heart) and that actively helps people. Since the early 1980s, many Boomers have become involved in volunteerism. Roof describes the effects of this spirit in one congregation. "In more than forty lay ministries, parishioners, many of them boomers—volunteer their time and services to work with teenagers, pregnant girls, high school dropouts, jobs, housing, drug problems, alcoholism, overeating, elderly care, AIDS patients, and gangs."[33] Boomers often take a lead in the CROP Walk, Bread for the World, and peace with justice ministries. The energy of activism that characterized Boomers in the 1960s and 1970s has been transferred to more conventional arenas of service.

Many Boomers view such volunteerism as a matter of ethical integrity. The church's vision requires that they become involved in the human community beyond their immediate families. Such actions are important so that the outer behavior of their lives will adequately express the inner disposition. Many Boomers' quests have led them to believe that they are inherently related to other people.

Preachers can help Boomers recognize the connection between Christian vision and its call to witness in specific actions of compassion. Sermons can help Boomers deepen their sense of compassion. Pastors can identify opportunities for outreach that are available through the church and in the larger community.

Preachers can help the congregation see that Christian concern needs to be enlarged from the individual to the systemic level. Many of the problems that Boomers address through their individual actions (e.g., working in the homeless shelter, an afterschool tutoring program, or a job training event) are manifestations of larger forces in the social world. A particular act of compassion is of genuine help to the individual(s) who are affected, but does not typically change the systemic factors that feed the problem. Boomers need to direct some of their energy for compassion toward making systemic changes in our larger social world.

In addition, Boomers place a very high value on personal experience and feeling. As a college senior prayed at commencement in 1968, "We are eaten up by an intensity that we cannot name."[34] This characteristic was most public, perhaps, in Boomers' participation in the drug culture in the 1960s and 1970s. On one hand, drugs helped numb the pain of disappointment in government and in other social institutions. On the other hand, drugs enlarged their sense of psychic awareness. Most Boomers today discourage their children and grandchildren from using drugs. Nonetheless, Boomers are still deeply affected by emotive experience. Many of our Boomer friends seek a runner's high and its analogue in other endeavors. Boomers are drawn to groups, events, and writings that touch them in their interior lives.

The yearning for high-voltage experience is particularly noticeable in Boomers who left churches a generation ago and are returning. "They 'feel' the need for more excitement and sensation." Indeed, Roof finds that when they initially return to church, they seek to be touched in their emotive selves even more than they seek to clarify what they believe.[35]

This proclivity explains, in part, why the music in Boomer-oriented congregations is often emotionally touching. The lyrics are simple to the point of simplistic in many songs popular in congregations of Boomers. But the specific affirmations are not as important to Boomers as feelings of intimacy and mysticism that are stirred by the singing. In one song, for instance, people sing, over and over, a chorus that is almost mantra-like, "Emmanuel, Emmanuel." The preacher needs to help Boomers broaden their view of the nature and character of Christian singing. But the preacher's critique should begin from a sympathetic understanding of why such music is important to Boomers.

In addition to seeking a message that is forthright in its content, Boomers desire a sermon that has a strongly experiential element. A sermon on the faithfulness of God, for instance, would explain how God is faithful, and it would offer the listeners a moment in which, through the medium of the sermon, they experience divine faithfulness. For instance, the preacher might tell a story in which the experience of hearing the story is an imaginative experience of the faithfulness of God. However, Boomers do not want to be manipulated. The emotive dimension of the sermon needs to arise from genuine feelings. As a useful point of reference, a preacher with Boomers in mind might ask of the sermon, "What do I hope the congregation will experience in the course of hearing this sermon?"

Boomer spirituality comes with particular dangers. Religious individualism and loss of community can result from their insistence on choice and their desire for personal, interior experience. Boomers can be so tolerant of the views and actions of others that they are unwilling (or unable) to take a stand that is mandated by the gospel. The preacher must struggle against such reductionism.

Generation 13: A Relational Generation

Generation 13 is people born from roughly 1961 through 1981. The members of the generation, and interpreters of the generations, have not settled on what to call them, a fact that is related to their identity. The designation Generation 13 is derived from the fact that they are the thirteenth generation born since the beginning of the United States. Some writers refer to them as Generation X (drawn from the title of a novel by Douglas Coupland) because the X indicates that their character and contribution to the nation is still an *x* factor, an unknown.[36] Several Boomer authors describe them as "Baby Busters" because their generation appears to be a bust in comparison to the drive and energy exerted by the Boomers.[37] An authority on generational differences calls them "the disillusioned generation."[38] The authors of this book think of them as the Relational Generation because one of their permeating values is being in relationship with others. While this generation is still in search of a name, they do have distinctive characteristics that call for the church and the preacher to think about them in their own particularity.

Strauss and Howe provide a graphic image to summarize the experience of Generation 13.

> Imagine coming to a beach at the end of a summer of wild goings-on. The beach crowd is exhausted, the sand shopworn, and full of debris—no place for walking barefoot. You step on a bottle, and some cop yells at you for littering. The sun is directly overhead and leaves no patch of shade that hasn't already been taken. You feel the heat beating down on a barren landscape devoid of secrets or innocence. You look around at the disapproving faces and can't help but sense, somehow, that the entire universe is gearing up to punish you.[39]

Strauss and Howe explain, "That's how 13ers feel following the Boom."[40]

Two cultural factors are preeminent in the shaping of Generation 13. One of these factors is the emergence of postmodernity. Builders, Silents, and Boomers grew up in modernity, an era that began with the Enlightenment and continued in popular consciousness into the late 1970s (and still continues in the minds of some Builders, Silents, and Boomers). A hallmark of modernity was its trust that science and logical deduction could result in knowledge of universal truth. Mathematics could yield the solution. Scientists could arrive at the conclusion. Philosophers sought the first principles. Biblical scholars could speak of *the* interpretation of a text.

As Generation 13 was coming to consciousness, however, the assurance that the human family could arrive at universal truth gave way to the recognition that all statements of truth contain significant interpretive elements that arise from the interpreter's education, class, race, ethnicity, gender, and nationality. Generation 13 came to maturity in a culture that was pluralistic and relativistic in its attitudes toward certainty. Different (and sometimes contradictory) versions of truth existed side by side in the mall of human possibilities; people were free to choose which (if any) to follow. An upside of postmodernity is its spirit of liberation from dogma and its maximization of human freedom. A downside is a loss of confidence that life has ultimate significance or consequences. Many Generation 13ers have such a tolerant attitude toward differing viewpoints that they have little deep commitment to any one viewpoint.

The result of this attitude is represented in a high school Sunday school class that Ron was teaching a few years ago. The class was discussing why a person might want to be a Christian (in comparison with affiliating with another religion). One of the students (his son, then age 15, a last wave Generation 13er) summed up the class's attitude when he said, "Your religion doesn't matter. The important thing is to get along." Ron asked him what reasons he would give for having made a confession of faith, having been immersed, and now attending church and youth group. He shrugged his shoulders and spoke one of the sign-words of his group of 13ers, "Whatever." The answer did not fit the question. But whatever. It fit him and his classmates.

Where Boomers are driven by passion, moral vision, and a desire to make the world right, Generation 13 is more much more relaxed about its concerns. Generation 13ers care deeply about certain things, but they do not talk about them, or act on them, in the same way as their parents from the Silent and Boomer generations.

Postmodernity, in conjunction with Generation 13, poses two significant challenges for the preacher. When Builders and Silents see a preacher moving toward a pulpit, they innately accord authority to the preacher. However, the preacher cannot assume that a Generation 13er will assume that the Bible, the gospel, or the church has a claim that can be taken more seriously than other claims in the world.[41] The preacher needs to help Generation 13ers understand *why* the Christian faith can be important to them. Old-style apologetics (giving a propositional defense of the faith, using subtleties of logical reasoning) will not have wide appeal in Generation 13. As we note below, personal testimony and storytelling may be keys.

The other primary formative factor in the soul of Generation 13 is a widespread feeling of limitation. Throughout their lifetimes, the economic situation in North America has been declining, so that they are the first generation since the founding of the United States who can expect a lower standard of living than their parents have had. Someone coined the phrase "McJobs" to indicate the kind of employment for many Generation 13ers: jobs that Boomers considered degrading. Crime on the streets skyrocketed. The AIDS epidemic leveled many of them (and sobered many others with the fact that, as a friend said, "You don't get over AIDS.") Generation 13ers are more reserved in their sexual activity than Boomers, who reveled in sexual freedom and experimentation. The environmental crisis with its apocalyptic possibilities reached fever pitch in 13ers' formative years.

As children, they grew up through more divorcing parents than any other generation; 50 percent of the homes of Generation 13 children were broken by divorce. And as they observed, "Parents' things are always more important."[42] Andres Tapia summarizes an important trajectory in this generation.

> When the boomers were twenty-something, they were ready to save the world; busters feel they are barely able to save themselves. Survival is the goal. A composite statement of Xer frustrations might go like this: "Boomers had free love; we have AIDS. They had the War on Poverty; we have a trillion-dollar debt. They had a booming economy; we have downsizing and pollution." This is why "Die Yuppie Scum" has become de rigueur graffiti in Xer hangouts.[43]

Not surprisingly, many in Generation 13 think that America's "best days are behind us."[44] Generation 13ers tend to have a less well-defined vision of the future than Builders, Silents, and Boomers.

At the same time, Generation 13 contains another trajectory: people who have entered with gusto and savvy into e-commerce. A significant number of Gen 13ers have become millionaires and even billionaires through dot.com businesses. Money—tons of it—has come quickly and easily. For many, it has also disappeared in the same way.

Given the discouraging circumstances (at least as perceived by the Boomer authors of this book), the temptation is to suggest to the preacher who would reach Generation 13: offer them a word of hope. Help them see how the gospel can lead to a renewed tomorrow. However, Generation 13 has made peace with the idea of a limited future and is developing the skills and perspectives that will enable them to live in it. Their great point of optimism for the future is in personal relationships; they do believe that the quality of personal relationships (at least in their generation) will increase in future years.

In his fascinating book *Virtual Faith: The Irreverent Spiritual Quest of Generation X,* Tom Beaudoin notices that while Generation 13ers have not been drawn in significant numbers to traditional institutions of religion, they have their own deep spirituality, though it is mediated and expressed through the language and symbols of popular culture. Many lyrics and images that have nurtured this cohort have spiritual overtones. Beaudoin finds that Gen 13 typically turns to personal experience when they seek authoritative guidance in spiritual and other matters. They are aware of their own suffering and the suffering of the world, and they seek to understand its spiritual dimensions. They not only live comfortably with ambiguity but also insist that reality is inherently ambiguous.[45] This situation suggests that the preacher can engage in mutual critical correlation between the language, values, and experience of the gospel and those of Generation 13.

To be faithful to the gospel itself, and not so much as a strategy for reaching 13ers, the preacher needs to try to help this generation understand the gospel's eschatological vision. However, they will not respond to glib assertions about a rosy future. The vision that the preacher articulates must be realistic, respectful of the complexities with which 13ers live every day, and tested by the toughest, most skeptical questions that can be asked.

Indeed, one of the most noticeable traits of 13ers is skepticism that runs like blood through the arteries of the generation. As a group, they have not crossed the boundary from skepticism to cynicism. When greeted by a fresh possibility, one of their first reactions is to question it. Is this idea too good to be true? Who *really* profits from this product? Who is likely to get hurt in this deal? Indeed, the generational bumper sticker might well be "Question Authority." The preacher who would frame the gospel for Generation 13 needs to articulate *honest* (and not merely rhetorical) questions about the gospel message, the Bible, Christian doctrine, the Christian community, and the relationship of the church and its beliefs to the larger social world. At this juncture, the hermeneutic of suspicion can be the preacher's best friend as it helps the preacher expose hidden biases and tendencies, unspoken attitudes that cover falsehood and that support various forms of manipulation, even oppression.

Generation 13 has been greatly influenced by the electronic media. Next to being with friends, 13ers' favorite leisure activity is watching movies. They like MTV, which creates its message through images. This orientation has significant implications for preaching. Given Generation 13's propensity for movies and images, storytelling should play a prominent role in preaching for this generation. Generation 13 listeners have a particular empathy for stories of their own and stories of people who have struggled through adversity. Preachers who have been effective in reaching this generation have found that biblical stories, and especially stories about Jesus, appeal to them. Such preachers also find that Generation 13 responds positively to personal stories in which preachers openly discuss their own vulnerability and struggles.[46]

George Barna regards the Socratic dialogue as another style that is suited for this generation.[47] The preacher has a good chance of catching the attention of Generation 13 by asking honest questions and by creating a sense of the sermon as conversation.[48]

Generation 13 wants preachers to be authentic. And they want to know the full picture, no matter how disheartening. Dieter Zander, who started a highly successful congregation for 13ers in California and was on the staff of the famous Willow Creek Community Church in suburban Chicago, says this generation wants "to deal with the facts head-on. What they tell me is, 'Don't give me six easy steps to keep joy in my life. I know life is not easy.'"[49]

The preacher needs to be a full and honest human being in the pulpit. In fact, 13ers are often drawn more to preachers who can talk openly and honestly about the difficulties in their life journeys than those who trumpet the gospel as a formula for success. Furthermore, with Generation 13, preachers can raise probing questions about the Bible, traditional formulations of Christian doctrine, and Christian practice. Given their bent toward skepticism, Generation 13ers may interpret the absence of such questions as a lack of serious engagement among the gospel, the tradition, and the contemporary world. This generation is one with whom openness and straightforwardness are the paths of homiletical wisdom.

Concern for relationships with other people is one of Generation 13's most enduring attributes. This concern may be born from the "their own poverty of emotional connections" as they were growing up. Indeed, many grew up perceiving themselves as "alone."[50] However, in their late youth and early adult years, they discovered the importance of friends and of being related to other people. Compared to Boomers, Generation 13ers "are more emotionally sensitive and relational in character. They are more interested in developing and nurturing long-lasting, symbiotic relationships." They "sacrifice some of their time and energy to initiate and nurture meaningful friendships."[51] Indeed, Generation 13ers spend significantly more of their time with friends than do Boomers, and their favorite leisure activity is being with friends.

This concern with relationality coheres wonderfully with the biblical idea of corporate identity and concern to develop community, as well as with contemporary philosophical and theological notions of the interrelatedness of all people (and, indeed, of all things). Israel, after all, was a covenantal community, and Paul describes the church as the *body* of Christ. The preacher can use the focus on relationships as a natural point of contact with the gospel in two ways. For one, the pastor can help Generation 13 discover the relational nature of the church itself. In fact, 13ers may be able to help the church recover significant dimensions of the experience of community. For another, the preacher can help 13ers discovers points at which the gospel, the biblical traditions, and Christian theology and practice can help deepen the relationships that are so important to this young adult generation.

An interesting intergenerational twist accompanies the relationality of the 13ers. They resent Boomers. In fact, scholars who study generational relationships predict that the next great generation gap or generation war will be between 13ers and Boomers as the Boomers begin to assert their considerable force to corral national resources to give themselves a comfortable old age. However, many people in Generation 13 think of Builders as wise. The 13ers listen for how Builders made their marriages work, sacrificed for their children, and worked to build a stable and prosperous world. Many 13ers respect that which is old and proven. Hence, if preachers can present the Bible and historic Christian tradition as sources of wisdom for life, they may find that Generation 13 is unexpectedly sympathetic.

Given the postmodern ethos that shapes the consciousness of Generation 13, it is hardly surprising that they seek an approach to Christianity that is not dogmatic. They are particularly tolerant of other points of view.

Further, as Dieter Zander notes, "Busters are tired of being judged and pushed to conform."[52] Many 13ers have felt considerable pressure from Boomers to conform to Boomer values and practices. They feel the weight of Boomers' negative evaluations. Boomers, who are achievement-oriented and fired from within with unquenchable drive, communicate forcibly that they regard 13ers as slackers because of the latter's preference for relationship over accomplishment. They long for freedom from what they perceive as the misplaced condemnation of Boomers. Generation 13 will hear a genuine word of good news in the gospel's emphases on freedom, grace, and liberation from oppression.

Furthermore, as postmodernists, Generation 13 assumes that diversity is a positive value. They regard reconciliation among different races, ethnic groups, genders, social classes, and other dividing lines as enhancing the relational character of the world. They will respond positively to the gospel emphasis on reconciliation.

While the writer of Psalm 89 may not have had generational differences in mind, that passage still expresses the hope of the pastor who preaches to multiple age groups. "I will sing of your steadfast love, O LORD, forever; with my mouth I will proclaim your faithfulness to all generations" (Ps. 89:1). Knowledge of the leading characteristics of the different generations in the current church can help the preacher express the gospel so that each generation can hear the promise and demand of the gospel in its own language, and so that a generation's consciousness can be shaped by the gospel.

Even as we write and read, of course, a new generation is entering adulthood—those who have been born since 1981 (or so) that we have heard described as the Millennial Generation. The church needs *now* to begin to identify distinctive qualities in this rising group, and to learn both how to speak the gospel in the generation's language and how to help the newest generation speak gospel language. The oldest of them have already reached age twenty-one.

3

Preaching and Different Modes of Mental Process

John McKiernan, Ron's father-in-law, was a bomber pilot in World War II. After the war, he completed a graduate degree in mechanical engineering and taught engineering at a large state university before joining a major laboratory, where he worked on materials used in the first lunar landing. He has held every position of leadership in his congregation (some of them multiple times). He is an extremely disciplined thinker. He respects people, their diversity, and their gifts.

When Ron was visiting the in-laws' congregation one summer Sunday morning, the guest preacher said a few words about the biblical text and then offered a series of images (highly impressionistic in character) that were designed to make the hermeneutical connection between the text and the listeners. The preacher never stated the meaning of the sermon in a proposition.

Afterward, another member of the congregation effused about the poetic qualities of the sermon. "I have never heard such a wonderful sermon." John agreed that the sermon was beautiful. However, John added, "I got the point, but why didn't [the preacher] just say it?"

In these two reactions we get a thumbnail sketch of the major concern of this chapter. Researchers in the social sciences have discovered that people have different patterns of mental process. To put it in computer terms, different brains are loaded with different software programs. Different groups are "programmed" to prefer particular types of communication and to be less receptive to others. For instance, some people are more comfortable with linear, propositional patterns of thought, while others are more at home in poetry, image, and impression. These differences are not related to level of intelligence, but reflect the interior structures that people use to process data.

The minister can make use of multiple modes of preaching to have optimum opportunities to communicate with people who take in the world in multiple modes of mental process. No single homiletical style will do.

In order to draw out specific implications of this insight, we overview three bodies of research that focus on different ways in which people receive and process data about the world and themselves: faith development theory, the Myers-Briggs Type Indicator, and Neuro Linguistic Programming.[1] Each focuses on the process of human understanding from a different angle.[2]

Thomas Long criticizes the minister's use of such analytical systems as modern "astrologies" that provide the preacher with a false sense of confidence regarding what we can know about people and their ways of perceiving and making judgments. Long wisely notes that we cannot boil a human being down to a residue of predictable thoughts and actions. For each human being is "inescapably wild and full of wondrous surprises."[3] And, one should add, not so wondrous surprises. People, and the gospel, can transcend particular modes of mental processing. Human beings are not imprisoned by the traits of classification systems. Nonetheless, these theories often provide useful (if not imperial) clues by which to understand typical human patterns of perceiving.

A corollary. A preacher, like a listener, operates with particular preferences in mental operation. Some preachers incline toward linear, propositional patterns of thinking and speaking while others incline to more associative, imagistic, and poetic patterns. Preachers need to become conscious and critical of their own tendencies so that they can make optimum use of strengths and so that they can conscientiously make use of other forms of thought and expression that will enable the gospel to be received in an optimum way by people whose patterns differ from theirs.

Solid theological content can be expressed and received in a wide variety of ways. We believe that the gospel of God's unconditional love and God's call for justice for each and all can be communicated through all ways of knowing, all stages of faith development, all personality types, and all representational systems.

Faith Development Theory

Faith development theory gives an account of the ways in which people think. This theory focuses on *how* people think about faith. James Fowler and a bevy of researchers interviewed hundreds of people to identify the types of logic people use, the forms in which people conceptualize the world, the capacity for understanding the point of view of another, the sources of authority on which people draw, patterns of loyalty (family, tribe, nation), forms of moral judgment, and how human beings apprehend symbols.[4] Based on these categories, Fowler discerns six stages in which people think about faith. The stages are somewhat developmental in that the first three stages often unfold with age and life experience. By adulthood some people's patterns of apprehending faith change, while others do not.[5]

In each stage, people receive and process data differently. At a given stage, people are better able to receive and process certain kinds of information and experience than at other stages. At one stage, a person simply may not have the mental software to process data in a way that a person does in another phase. Such differentiations are unrelated to intelligence or theological orientation. However, as people evolve (even in adulthood) their structures for processing faith can sometimes change.

The preacher wants to help people at each stage understand the sermon.[6] To do so, the preacher can speak so as to take account of the different ways in which the congregation receives and processes communications. The preacher might develop elements within a single sermon to speak to persons at different stages. From time to time, a preacher may develop a sermon to speak to persons at a particular stage. Indeed, sermons can sometimes help people move from one stage to another. In sermons, preachers can encourage the congregation to become aware of the different ways in which people perceive the world. If pastorally handled, such awareness should help the members of the congregation understand why they think as they do, and how they can transcend the limitations of their stages of faith development.[7]

In order to take advantage of insights from this approach, preachers need to be aware of their own stages of faith development. Preachers tend to view the Christian faith, and to prepare the sermon, from the standpoint of their own development. Indeed, persons at particular stages may view their own stage as normative. Self-awareness will not only help preachers recognize why they think and preach as they do. Self-aware preachers can also transcend their own proclivities and work actively to understand the world and the Christian vision of persons at stages that differ from the preacher's stage.

A morally delicate matter comes into play. A preacher at one stage may find that preaching in a mode that is familiar to a person at another stage violates a preacher's fundamental theological conviction. For instance, a person at Stage 2 may require considerable direction as to what is right and wrong. A preacher at Stage 5 may hold the theological conviction that persons should think critically about significant issues for themselves. The preacher may have a theological aversion to telling a person what to think or do. Yet without such direction, persons at Stage 2 may not think that they have heard a real sermon.

In response to such conundrums, we suggest that preachers attempt to formulate their theological convictions according to patterns of thought that are characteristic of persons in other stages, but that honor the convictions of the preacher. For instance, a preacher might authoritatively tell persons at Stage 2 that they need to think for themselves on a particular issue. The preacher might outline a step-by-step method for thinking critically. The Stage 5 preacher would not think for Stage 2 people, but could provide a framework within which Stage 2 people can think.

Fowler claims that individuals from birth to about age two manifest "undifferentiated faith." At this pre-stage, infants and toddlers experience the world as a collage of experiences out of which they begin to develop their capacities for trust, mutuality, and autonomy. The transition to Stage 1 begins with the capacity to think, to use language, and to engage in ritual play, that is, to engage in differentiated actions.[8] The preacher's most significant responsibility to this listener may be to encourage the parents and other life-shapers in the child's world to try to create an atmosphere in which the infant and toddler can develop optimum capacity for trust and sense of self and in relationship.

Stage 1: Intuitive-Projective Faith[9]

This stage lasts from about ages two to seven. According to Fowler, this child cannot usually use formal logic, nor can the child connect events by cause and effect. Life appears to be less a connected movie and more a series of still slides. Lacking the capacity to see events, feelings, and behavior from another person's point of view, children derive their sense of right and wrong from adults. Right thinking, feeling, and behavior bring reward; wrong attitudes and actions result in punishment. The child tends to think of symbols and images as identical with what they represent. The real world and the imaginative world often coalesce in the mind of the Stage 1 thinker.

While we discuss children in more detail in chapter 6, we pause now over the question of whether children should stay in the sanctuary for adult worship (including the sermon) or go to a separate place for children's worship that is specifically designed to be age appropriate for children.[10] We favor the former. The contemporary notion of Christian practice suggests that people develop a Christian orientation to life on the basis of repeated activities in the congregation, such as participating in worship each week. Such participation develops an intuitive as well as cognitive orientation toward life with a Christian character. Indeed, such participation often encourages the development of a Christian heart, mind, and ethic more than enrolling in formal programs of Christian education. Hence, although children in worship may not think about the theological content of the service in the same sophisticated way that adults do, children still pick up attitudes and feelings, as well as some content, that orients them to the Christian worldview. They develop a "feel" for what it means to be Christian and to worship.[11]

For example, Ron and his spouse brought all five of their children to "adult worship" during Stage 1 of the children's lives. The youngsters often appeared to be only looking at books, drawing pictures on the attendance pad, or quietly enjoying a piece of gum. However, later they made comments that indicated something in the sermon got through. Typically, they would remember a story, and at home each pretended to be a preacher at some point in this stage. While such evidence is anecdotal, it suggests that at this stage, children may be more influenced by the sermon than adults sometimes suppose.

Children's faith development is tremendously influenced by stories and images.[12] We do not have the space to give detailed consideration to the widespread phenomenon of the children's sermon. We can, however, offer two observations.[13] One, the best children's sermon is often a positive, warm, strong story or image that encourages a trusting relationship with God, Christian community, and world. Two, children at this stage cannot always engage in comparative thinking. Many children's sermons ask children to compare God with an experience or an object. However, few children in Stage 1 are equipped with the cognitive ability to make the comparison. If the preacher wants to use an object with Stage 1 listeners, it is better to tell a straightforward story.

For instance, a pastor prepares a conventional sermon on a Bible passage that compares the strength of God to a rock. The point of the comparison is that God is strong enough to help us through situations that block divine intentions for the human community. Wanting the elements of the service to work together, the pastor sets out to develop a children's sermon on the same motif. The preacher is initially tempted to bring a rock into the sanctuary, pass it among the children, and ask, "How is God strong like this rock?" However, remembering that many children have difficulty comparing God with an object, the preacher instead tells the story of a teacher and a school class who faced a difficult situation. The teacher's inner strength helped the class get through their situation. The preacher points out that God works through strong people who use their strength to help children and other people. Whenever the children encounter such a person, they encounter God helping them. In the conventional sermon, the preacher refers to the children's story, thus helping both children and adults connect the two messages.

Stage 2: Literal Faith [14]

Stage 2 begins at about age eight. Most people evolve into the next stage in adolescence, but a few people remain at Stage 2 their entire lives. This stage is called mythic-literal because it is centered in the literal interpretation of the central stories (myths) of the faith community. The mind can use both inductive and deductive logic. Empathy–the capacity to see things from another person's point of view–emerges. These thinkers try to distinguish elements in stories that are literally true from those that are make-believe. Stage 2 thinkers are loyal to family or tribe. A primary goal is to follow the rules of life. Morality is reciprocal: you get what you deserve, and you deserve what you get. People at this stage seek clear statements of the true and the false.

At this stage, children and adults understand their lives not as episodes, but as a linear sequence in which events, ideas, and rules interrelate. Story becomes a primary means by which they interpret the meaning of their lives and the world. However, Stage 2 thinkers cannot usually step outside a story in order to reflect on its meaning. People at this stage anthropomorphize God.

The preacher needs explicitly to help persons at Stages 2 and 3 realize what they should get out of a sermon. These people listen for unambiguous statements of what they can believe and how they ought to act. Their confidence in such statements is buttressed when the assertions are supported by respected external sources of authority, such as God, Jesus, and the Bible. When such anchor-points are missing, the listener may discount the sermon's credibility.

Story is the primary means by which Stage 2 listeners order the world. Since to this hearer the meaning of a story is the story, the sermon needs to include the biblical story itself, or a story from Christian tradition or life. This listener cannot extrapolate easily from narrative content to its meaning; the person at Stage 2 will miss the point if the preacher presumes the content of the story and talks only about what people learn from it.

The Stage 2 listener does not have a highly developed notion of justice as a transcendent principle. Consequently, the preacher needs to help parishioners grasp how they will benefit (or be hurt by) their choices in theology and ethics.[15]

When developing a sermon for a predominately European American congregation on the vocation of the church to end racism and become a community in which love and justice shape all relationships, the preacher needs to define racism and state with absolute clarity that God condemns racism and calls for a community in which all people treat one another with dignity. The preacher needs to include two parts in the sermon for European American Stage 2 congregants. First, the preacher can help the congregation empathize with the hurt caused by racism to African Americans and other people who suffer under it. The Stage 2 listener will be positively impressed if the preacher has hard data to support the evil effects of racism on racial/ethnic peoples, including stories from such people describing their suffering. Second, the preacher needs to help members of the congregation at this stage understand how racism hurts European Americans, and how the end of racism and the emergence of a community of love and justice will be a help to Euro Americana.

Stage 3: Synthetic-Conventional Faith [16]

Stage 3 usually begins in early adolescence. For some people it lasts until early young adulthood (about age 20), while others never leave it. Most adults come to rest at Stages 3 or 4. This faith is synthetic in that people bring together (synthesize) concerns from different spheres. It is conventional in that it tends to conform to the faith community in which it is found. Synthetic-conventionalists tend not to step outside the beliefs of their community to examine the beliefs in a critical way. Much of faith at this stage is tacit. It is held very deeply, but uncritically.

The Stage 3 thinker still sees the world largely in polar terms (right/wrong, true/false), and value is still largely derived from an external source. The Stage 3 individual requires concrete directions. Thinkers at this stage understand metaphor and double entendre. As at the previous level, these thinkers understand themselves on the basis of the opinions of others; not surprisingly, a law-and-order mentality prevails. God is now described in terms of personal qualities directly related to the individual or community, such as friend, redeemer.

As in the case of the Stage 2 listener, the preacher needs to state the point of the sermon in clear, unambiguous terms, and to support the point with strong evidence and reasoning. These listeners most easily follow deductive sermons that contain propositions and linear thought. This observation goes against the grain of much recent, popular thought in the preaching community. Many preachers today are enamored of sermons that are inductive, indirect, and poetic, that are filled with stories that the preacher does not explain and that focus more on evoking feeling than in communicating ideas. The authors of this book confess that we are biased toward aspects of the newer approaches. However, the fact is that preachers who exclusively follow the newer trends will leave some in the congregation repeatedly feeling shortchanged or even frustrated.

Since the Stage 3 thinker has the capacity to begin to distinguish between literal and nonliteral elements in stories and other texts, the preacher can help this person to do so. The preacher needs to tell a biblical story fully and vividly so that members of Stage 3 can enter into the world of the story. The preacher can often help the Stage 3 listener imagine the world from the point of view of another by telling a story with which the listeners can identify and through which they experience the world as it seems to other people.

For example, in a sermon on wisdom crying out from the streets in Proverbs 1, with Stage 3 thinkers in mind, the preacher would want to paint a full picture of wisdom as a woman speaking out on the street as a prophet. The preacher would explain the concept of wisdom that permeates the wisdom literature and how wisdom comes to be personified as a woman. We do not literally think of wisdom as a female person, but understand the text as figuratively representing the fact that our encounters with wisdom are often so personal that it seems as though we are encountering another person. For the Stage 3 listener, the sermon might clearly list qualities of wisdom and folly, give examples of each, and call the congregation to embrace wisdom. The preacher wants to help the Stage 3 congregant picture clearly the wise life. Honoring the synthetic dimension of this stage of faith, the preacher can show how biblical wisdom helps the community integrate (synthesize) different aspects of life. Honoring the conventional aspect of Stage 3, the preacher can help the congregation recognize points of commonality between the worldview of wisdom and the worldview of the community. The preacher can use the security recognized by this conventionality as a base from which to help the congregants imagine how their worldview and community practices could be different as they incorporate other aspects of biblical wisdom. The sermon could help the Stage 3 community imagine how the world would be from an enlarged understanding of wisdom.

The transition to Stage 4—which many people make—often originates when people perceive contradictions between the authorities they have assumed to be true and other authorities. They are driven to make sense of contradiction. The preacher can help facilitate this transition by asking questions that that help those in Stage 3 question the adequacy of their worldview. When preaching on changes in contemporary worship in a traditional congregation, a minister could ask, "Why do some leaders in the church advocate new styles of worship (e.g., rock bands in church) while others do not?"

Stage 4 Individuating-Reflective Faith [17]

This stage usually begins in late adolescence or early young adulthood. For many people, it becomes the primary faith-orientation for the rest of their lives. It is individuating-reflective in that its holders are sufficiently individuated from the family or immediate community to reflect for themselves on what they will believe.[18] The boundaries of the good, bad, acceptable, and unacceptable are firm and explicit, but Stage 4 thinkers have thought for themselves about why they prefer these boundaries to others. Critical thinking begins in Stage 4, that is, self-conscious reflection on the strengths and weaknesses of various positions and selection of the option(s) that make the most sense.

People in this mode of cognition can now distinguish between literal and metaphorical meanings in texts and speech. Indeed, the Stage 4 person is willing to demythologize texts. The language characteristic of Stage 4 is propositional, analytical, and logical. The Stage 4 thinker is no longer a law-and-order moralist, but has a nascent sense of justice. However, the Stage 4 communicant still makes decisions with reference to the opinions of her or his primary community loyalty.

The sermon for the Stage 4 thinker is very similar to the sermon for the person who is in the mode of procedural knowledge in the next chapter. These persons want to think for themselves. At Stage 4, the listener is ready for a critical analysis of text, doctrine, situation, issue, practice, or feeling. This thinker wants to know the spectrum of interpretive possibilities and the strengths and weaknesses of each. This person wants to know where the authorities stand on each issue, but the Stage 4 communicant is willing to question recognized authorities and even to disagree with them.

At Stage 4, the listener is especially open to a sermon that articulates a clear, well-supported proposition with a direct, practical application to life. The individuative-reflective parishioner wants to separate the abiding dimensions of meaning in biblical texts (and other elements in the Christian world) from those aspects of the text that belong to a previous worldview. To the community at Stage 4, a biblical myth contains an outer wrapping of narrative detail that is expendable and an inner core of meaning that does not depend on the wrapping and can usually be stated propositionally. Stories and images in the sermon need to have a clear function, usually to support or illustrate the argument of the sermon. Stage 4 listeners like for stories to be explained so that they can get the point. They may regard an unexplained story as entertainment or filler.

For example, when preaching on the miracle story of Jesus' healing the bent-over woman in Luke 13:10–17, the preacher who seeks to communicate with the Stage 4 congregant could explain how miracle stories functioned in the ancient world, then review similarities and differences between the understandings of miracle stories in the ancient and contemporary worlds. The preacher could engage in a form of demythologizing by extracting from the narrative a point from the story that does not depend on the miraculous framework for its meaning. For instance, in this story Luke emphasizes God's restoration of women to full status in community. The preacher can ask, "Who are the bent-over women in our world? How is God restoring them to fullness of life in community?"

The transition to Stage 5 is frequently accompanied by the awareness that critical analysis cannot always account for the complexities of life.

Human existence is not always neat and tidy. Life has depths that cannot always be satisfactorily plumbed by critical thought.

Stage 5: Conjunctive Faith[19]

Not many persons reach Stage 5. When they do, they are usually in middle age or the golden years. As its name implies, it is a phase in which people conjoin aspects of their thinking about faith that have previously existed in separation, even in tension.

Stage 5 thinkers retain the critical edge of Stage 4 while recognizing limitations in critical thinking itself. Persons become cognizant of much relativity in their worldviews. These members are aware of the fact that human interpretations of the world are not detached and objective, but always include human biases and ingrained interpretive lenses. In this mode, the thinker can live with ambiguity and can accept paradox. The Stage 5 individual can enter vicariously into the experiences of others and can be deeply moved, even transformed, by such encounters. Authority at Stage 5 derives from the internalization of ideas and experience rather than on external sources. Loyalty is minimally determined by parochial boundaries, but is given to those causes that hold promise for the larger diverse community.

In contrast to the reductionistic attitude toward myth and story characteristic of the previous phase, Stage 5 thinkers can enter into the world of myth as myth, even while maintaining a critical perspective. The Stage 5 hearer does not require for a story or other text to be explained with an overt comment. This thinker recognizes that some depths of existence can only be adequately expressed in myth, imagery, poetry, and story.

Paul Ricoeur offers a practical model for dealing with these motifs in his three-phrase process of engaging a biblical text.[20] In phase 1, preacher and congregation encounter a text in the mode of *first naiveté,* that is, they hear the text straightforwardly. For example, when considering the transfiguration of Jesus, the community simply receives the text. In the second phase, *critical consciousness,* they raise the full range of critical questions about the transfiguration, such as, Do events like that occur? What did transfiguration mean in the first century? What did the various elements of the story evoke in antiquity? In the third phase, *second naiveté,* pastor and community revisit the story fully informed by their critical discoveries but now understanding the transfiguration metaphorically, as a story that discloses a new world to them. They participate in that new world by participating imaginatively in the story. Preacher and parishioners use the language of the story without interrupting their speech with explanatory phrases, but they understand that they are using the language figuratively and not woodenly. After the sermon, such listeners become aware of trans-figurative moments in the world around them.[21]

The sermon for people in this stage needs to be conjunctive. Stage 5 people want to know how the gospel helps them conjoin the many different aspects of life. A primary purpose of the sermon for Stage 5 listeners is to help them envision the inclusiveness of the gospel. They want to know how the Christian gospel relates to other religions and value-systems. The Stage 5 listener seeks a sermon that has a depth dimension.

For example, this listener will be troubled by the exclusive view of texts such as John 3:18, "Those who believe [in Jesus] are not condemned; but those who do not believe are condemned already, because they have not believed in the name of the only [Child] of God." The Stage 5 listener will want to think critically about this text in view of the claim of the gospel that God's love is universal and unconditional. As a matter of theological integrity, the preacher should do so, but also, for the preacher not to think critically about the text is to lose credibility with the Stage 5 listener.

The Stage 5 person can process a text or a part of a sermon on many simultaneous levels of conception and feeling. A preacher need not explain a story or a poem. In fact, the Stage 5 listener may find it distracting or diminishing for the preacher to state "the meaning" of a passage in propositional terms. Where people in Stages 1 to 4 respond most easily to a homiletic that makes its point clearly and directly, people at Stage 5 are easily drawn into a sermon that leaves them to ascertain their own conclusions.

For instance, the preacher could simply tell an extended story as the sermon. The Stage 5 listener will receive the story on its multiple levels and can process its significance without the preacher's compressing the meaning of the story into a proposition. Indeed, the Stage 5 listener will find such propositional summaries reductionistic and cheapening.

Christians in this mode will be drawn to a sermon that honors the complexities of a text and life. They are not likely to be seriously engaged by a sermon that oversimplifies. They want to know that Christian belief and practice demonstrate justice for *all.*

Because people at Stage 5 understand the relativities inherent in all claims and communities, the preacher may need to help people in Stage 5 sort out why it is important to belong to a *particular* community. Why should I be a part of the Christian community if the Christian interpretation of Ultimate Reality is only a partial interpretation? This aspect of Stage 5 thinking calls for the preacher to engage in a contemporary version of apologetics, that is, helping the congregation understand how they can understand the Christian faith in relationship to other religions (and people who have no religion) from a transcendent standpoint.

Stage 6: Universalizing Faith[22]

This stage, which usually occurs in mid- to late life, is so rare that most of us know only a handful of such persons in our lifetimes. This thinker perceives the interconnectedness of all things and the relativities of all knowledge and tribal loyalties. They are committed to compassion for all. They have a passion for justice, which they pursue with almost no regard for personal cost. Authority comes from an inner self that responds to the pain and brokenness of the world and will not rest until the whole cosmos is healed and at one. Gandhi, Martin Luther King, Jr., Mother Teresa, Abraham Heschel, Thomas Merton, and Dietrich Bonhoeffer represent persons who arrive at Stage 6.

In connection with earlier stages, we offer suggestions for shaping the sermon to help people at each stage receive it. In connection with Stage 6, the situation is reversed. The Stage 6 visionary is a kind of preacher to the human family. The local pastor and the congregation need to *hear* the person at Stage 6. Persons at this stage tend to be prophets. Their words tend to enlarge the vision of preacher and congregation.

Faith development theory calls for sermons that can speak with people at various points along the spectrum of faith development. The preacher who speaks only as a Stage 5 to other persons at Stage 5 is partially unintelligible to persons at Stages 2 and 3. If persons at Stages 2 and 3 never receive a sermon that is broadcast on their wavelength, they may well decide to tune into another homiletical station, or to turn off the Christian network altogether. If they receive a message on their own band, they may be willing to try messages on other bands.

Myers-Briggs Type Indicator

The Myers-Briggs Type Indicator was developed more than a generation ago to give practical application to Carl Jung's psychological theory of type.[23] According to the MBTI (as this system of interpretation is abbreviated), people relate to their interior lives and to the outer world according to identifiable mental habits called types. Researchers stress that people do not always mechanically follow their preferences. In fact, most people operate with aspects of all types; the preferences indicate the types that predominate in ordinary functioning.

The MBTI identifies a person's habits according to four indices: the direction people's energies flow, how people perceive the world, how people make decisions, and how people relate to the outer world. Each index has two poles, with each pole indicated by a letter representing that preference. (As explained below, these letters are E-I, S-N, T-F, and J-P). People are typed according to the pole toward which they tend in each of these four categories.[24] When all the preferences are combined, they result in sixteen different personality types. Combinations of letters represent these types, for example, ISFJ. In this part of the chapter, we concentrate on the implications of the four basic types for the preacher.

Preachers tend to communicate in patterns that are habitual for their own types. For example, an S (Sensate) minister tends to develop sermons that manifest Sensate characteristics. When the personality types of preacher and listener are similar, communication is usually enhanced. When the personality types of preacher and listener are different, communication is sometimes frustrated.[25] An iNtuitive (who appreciates poetry, image, and direction) listening to a Sensate (who prefers linear thought and expression) can think that the sermon lacks feeling and depth. A Sensate listening to an iNtuitive can think that the sermon lacks a point. Preachers who become conscious of the characteristics of communication in their own types, and the characteristics of communication in other types, can conscientiously enlarge their repertoire of homiletical approaches to attempt to communicate more effectively with persons in a wide range of types.[26]

How Energy Flows

What direction does a person's energy flow? Is it Extroverted (E) or Introverted (I)?[27] The energy of the Extrovert flow is energized by the world outside the self—actions, things, and speech. The Extrovert focuses less on ideas and more on actions and objects. This person does not think through an idea and then present it, but develops ideas while talking about them with others. Interchange with another person increases the extrovert's energy. The Extrovert likes creating ideas in a group (and may actually be drained by having to work alone). The Extrovert requires a lot of verbal affirmation in order to feel confident.

The Extrovert is most likely to be engaged when the preacher's physical presence embodies the sermon with vitality.[28] The Extrovert may lose interest in a preacher whose presence in the pulpit is flat and apparently unaffected by the sermon. This outward-oriented listener likes sermons that have a conversational character—a sense of give and take. They are more interested in hearing the preacher talk about the actions of the Christian life than about the ideas that power it. Extroverts are ready to hear about how the gospel affects people besides themselves. Extroverts often have natural sympathy with sermons that emphasize Christian mission; they want to *do* something. The Extrovert is drawn less to the sermon that has all the answers (and that presents them in a wrapped package) and more to the sermon that is actively wrestling with the subject matter. The Extrovert is ready to try out new ideas. In order to fulfill their desire to participate, some Extroverts might like to be a part of a feedforward group, in which they think with the preacher about the upcoming sermon, or a feedback group in which they engage in give-and-take with the preacher.[29] They want the preacher to help them think about the world beyond themselves. Extroverts do not require a systematically structured sermon with a packaged point. The preacher needs repeatedly to assure this group of God's good pleasure toward them.

When developing a sermon with the Extrovert in mind, the preacher can ask *What does this sermon call the congregation to do? How does the sermon invite the congregation to think beyond itself?* When preparing a sermon on the command of the Fourth Gospel to love one another (John 13:31–35), for instance, the preacher can help the Extrovert envision how to express love in the Johannine sense. The sermon can include stories of people who actively love one another. The way the preacher motivates the Extrovert to love is not so much by shaming the community for its lack of love as by affirming the community for the love it shows and by encouraging the community to extend such love more. In the weeks prior to the sermon, the preacher could locate some Extroverts and ask them to talk about how they understand, experience, and express love.

The energy of the Introvert flows inward and is energized by the inner sphere of ideas and concepts. The Introvert is focused more on ideas than on actions or objects. The Introvert thinks through ideas very carefully before verbalizing them. This church member likes to analyze the complexities in an idea, situation, or feeling before talking about them. Interchange with others is often important to the Introvert, but such interchange often leaves this person drained. (Many preachers who feel wiped out by preaching are Introverts). Where the Extrovert prefers oral modes of communication, the Introvert is more comfortable with writing. While working on a project, this person constantly asks questions.

The Introvert responds best to the preacher whose presence in the pulpit is quiet and reflective (but not dead). The preacher who is too energetic may turn off this listener. Introverted Christians enjoy listening to lecture-like sermons. Inward-oriented listeners want to know that they can count on the orderliness of the world; if asked to change, they want to be assured that change will not result in increased chaos. The Introvert listens for the significant ideas in a sermon and their systematic development. And the Introvert would like to arrive at a resolution. The inward-oriented listener is particularly interested in the interior experience of others. The Introvert's consciousness will be activated if the preacher can ask serious questions of the text and subject of the sermon.[30]

When developing a sermon with the Introvert in mind, the preacher can ask, *What does this sermon call the congregation to think about?* The preacher wants to deal clearly and seriously with important ideas. When preparing a sermon on the command of the Fourth Gospel to love one another (John 13:31–35), for instance, the preacher can help the Introvert understand the background and meaning of love in the Johannine sense. The preacher needs to help the Introverted congregation recognize the complexities inherent in the notion of love and especially of trying to express love in complicated situations. This listener would like to hear a story of the interior workings of persons involved in situations of loving one another. What did they think? What did they feel? What led them to act? Such stories need to embody the ambiguities and difficulties that are often a part of loving one another. Of course, the preacher would want to embody the sermon on love in a way that feels loving.

How People Perceive the World

How do people perceive the world? Is a person a Sensate (S) or an iNtuitive (N)?[31] The sensing person gathers data from the empirical world in a systematic, factual, linear way. This person takes in the world through the five senses and wants to have those senses engaged. The Sensate pays attention to the details of life and is impatient with a big picture that does not help people make practical sense of their everyday worlds. This person wants to know the rationale behind an idea or event. This person works steadily (even doggedly) at a task and is impatient with unexpected developments that throw the task off schedule or off target. Sensates like familiarity. The Sensate seeks precise answers to precise questions. This listener derives satisfaction from jobs that have a tangible result. Ron's father-in-law, John McKiernan, mentioned at the beginning of this chapter, is a Sensate person.

The ideal sermon for the Sensate is linear in character. The sensing listener is drawn to biblical texts and to passages in sermons that contain descriptive language that helps them see, hear, touch, taste, and smell. Sensates want to know the rationale for the position the preacher takes in the sermon. The Sensate wants to relate specific aspects of Christian faith to specific situations in which the congregation finds itself, and wants the preacher to point the Sensate to particular things that the believer can do to fulfill the point of the sermon. The Sensate can believe that the sermon's claims are true in the everyday, factual world of the listening community. Hence, the preacher can activate this listener's imagination with stories and images from the local community or from communities with which the Sensate can identify. The Sensate wants to know how to resolve contradictions and other complications to Christian faith. The Sensate Christian is not bored if the sermon follows a similar format from week to week.

When developing a sermon with the Sensate in mind, the preacher needs to be as clear as possible as to the major claim of the sermon and why that claim is believable. For example, when preaching on the apocalyptic return of Jesus (as a part of the end of the present age of history and the inauguration of a new world) as portrayed in the book of Revelation, the preacher who is thinking of the Sensate listener will want to state clearly the degree to which the preacher believes such an event will actually occur. Sensate congregants want to know why the preacher believes in the way advocated in the sermon. The Sensate would probably be open to a figurative understanding of language about the apocalyptic return of Jesus if the preacher explains why a figurative understanding is plausible.

The iNtuitive perceives the world in terms of possibilities and relationships. This church member does not think in linear sequence, but by association. The iNtuitive person is a visionary who is oriented toward the future and who can read between the lines of a text or a relationship or a situation. The N follows hunches that seem to pop into the mind from nowhere. They are often impatient with bean counters who lose the vision in a morass of details. Bursts of energy alternate with regeneration and brooding, which often gives the Sensate the impression that the iNtuitive is a slacker.

The ideal sermon for the iNtuitive is a vision that lures the imagination into the future. N types have their ears open for how the gospel can improve relationships in their immediate circles and in the wider human community. This listener appreciates a sermon whose various parts are related through association and not necessarily by means of conventional logic. The iNtuitive listens for the feelings and dynamics behind the text or issue under consideration and wants to know what preachers feel in their hearts. The iNtuitive comes alive when the preacher has a burst of energy in the sermon. The N types respond well to sermons that are open-ended and that leave them to finish working out the implications of the sermon. Impatient with routine, this listener warms to variety in preaching style.

The sermon for the iNtuitive listener is impressionistic, associative, and suggestive. Whereas the Sensate listener requires a precise propositional understanding of the topic, the iNtuitive frequently finds such thinking oversimplistic and emotively shallow. When preaching on the apocalyptic return of Jesus in the book of Revelation, for instance, the preacher who is thinking of the N congregant will not need to say, propositionally, what the congregation can and cannot believe about a literal interruption of history by the apocalyptic return of Jesus. The iNtuitive would likely find a sermon that focused on that question to be reductionistic. The preacher will likely want the iNtuitives to imaginatively participate in the imagery of the book of Revelation much as they would a poem or a novel. Of course, the preacher needs to provide enough historical and literary background for the iNtuitive to be able to imagine the world of the text in its historical and literary integrity. Along the way, the preacher can ask open-ended questions that open space for the N thinker to make connections between the text and the contemporary world, but the iNtuitive will be frustrated if the preacher explicitly makes too many of the connections for the congregation.

How People Make Decisions

How do people make decisions? Are they Thinkers (T) or Feelers (F)?[32] Thinkers make choices on the basis of objective, impersonal considerations. These people operate on the basis of logical analysis. They consider the causes of ideas, events, and situations. They think carefully and impersonally about where their decisions might lead. Impartiality and fairness permeate the T mind. The Thinker is more interested in ideas and concepts than in people. Thinkers seek to tell the truth; they are not always aware of the effects of their truth-telling on other people. When Thinkers reach a decision, they find it difficult to change their minds. These listeners tend to be brief and businesslike.

Critical analysis is at the heart of the sermon for Thinking persons. They make a make a decision about whether or not to endorse the content of the sermon and its possible implications for behavior on the basis of cold, rational analysis. Thinkers like biblical texts and sermons that articulate principles by which to make life decisions. They want to know where a subject originated, why it is important, the possibilities for interpreting it, the strengths and weaknesses of the different possibilities, and which interpretive options make the most (and least) sense. The Thinker wants a sermon to have a clear and articulate idea at its core. They want to know the intended outcome in thought and action of the sermon. The T listener can tolerate a high degree of difference of opinion with the preacher, with others in the congregation, and with the culture so long as the T believes that those with whom the T disagrees have given careful consideration to their viewpoints. The Thinker admires the pastor who preaches the truth, even when the truth goes against the grain of popular opinion and may even offend some people.

When developing a sermon for the Thinker, the preacher needs to articulate the decision that needs to be made, the criteria for making it, and the optimum outcome. For instance, when preparing a sermon on the topic of whether lesbian, gay, bisexual, transgendered, questioning or asexual orientations are a possible orientation for a Christian, the preacher who wants to communicate fully with the Thinker needs to clarify the decisions that the community can make regarding this issue. The Thinker wants to know how this topic is understood in the Bible and in the church's history and theology. The T congregant wants to know how people experience and understand gay, lesbian, bisexual, transgendered, questioning, or asexual persons today. In particular, the Thinker wants to identify the key pieces of data on which a decision turns, and how to evaluate those data today. The T listener wants to know the preacher's decisions and why the preacher finds that decision compelling. The Thinker feels free to disagree with the preacher (and to do so amicably) provided that the Thinker is convinced that the preacher has examined the data fairly.

The Feeler makes decisions subjectively, on the basis of personal perception, and with a high regard for how the decision will affect others. They are more oriented to people and relationships than to ideas.

Feelers value positive qualities in relationships with others, and they dislike strain and pain in relationships. Feelers will gloss over real differences among people in order to help everyone get along. The person with this personality characteristic is likely to go along with others in a group and to think that others' opinions are probably correct. The Feeler is often very chatty and finds it difficult to be brief and to the point. The Feeler also dislikes telling people unpleasant news.

The sermon for the Feeler is filled with people. In order to make a decision, this listener wants to know how people will be affected by the content of the sermon. The Feeler is likely to respond positively to a sermon that promises to help people have positive feelings. This listener is likely to resist a sermon that points in the direction of bad feelings and pain. A pastor can often help a Feeler make a decision by pointing out that one choice will increase unpleasant feelings and disharmony, while another choice will lead toward unity and happy feelings. The preacher can influence a Feeler's decision making by pointing out where most people stand on an issue. That fact alone has some sway with the Feeler.

When putting together a sermon that calls for a decision from Feelers, the preacher wants to help the Feeler understand how other people will be affected by the decision, especially how a decision will help other people feel better. If preaching on the issue of the degree to which the Christian community can regard gay, lesbian, bisexual, transgendered, questioning or asexual orientations as viable orientations, the preacher who wishes to commune most deeply with the Feeler will include significant and sensitive material in the sermon that depicts how traditional Christian condemnation of persons in sexual minorities has caused pain to them and to others in their world. Building on the discovery that Feelers like to have a sense of solidarity with community, the preacher can call attention to other people who feel similarly. The pastor should help Feelers recognize that a decision to support gay, lesbian, bisexual, transgendered, questioning, or asexual identity as possible orientations for Christians will likely bring them into conflict with some people. However, the preacher can help the Feeler see that the gains for the sexual minorities and for the wider community that come through endorsing multiple forms of sexual orientation are more important than the tensions.

How People Are Oriented to the World

How are people oriented toward the world? Some are Judgers (J) while others are Perceivers (P)?[33] The J is a planner who lives an orderly existence and who is comfortable when in control of events. They make lists and follow them. Judgers are very goal oriented. They like for assignments to be clear and definite. Routine increases their sense of creativity and freedom, whereas unplanned events and interruptions often disorient them. They seek closure in events, issues, and situations. The Judging personality honors values and standards, and is not likely to turn away from them. Not surprisingly, this person is immensely loyal. Judgers are very uncomfortable with ambiguity.

Judging listeners want to know how the gospel brings order, direction, and plan to life. The J hopes for a sermon that offers a specific goal with respect to the Christian life. The J wants a plan by which to implement Christian vision in everyday life. How can the sermon help the J plan? Judgers are most comfortable when they can sense that a sermon that is orderly and planned. They want to have the sense that the sermon has started somewhere and is making its logical way to a definite resolution. By the end of the sermon, they would like to have a list of items that are important for them to do.

Amos 5:24 declares, "Let justice roll down like waters, and righteousness like an ever-flowing stream." When preparing a sermon on this passage for Judgers, the preacher needs carefully to define justice (and righteousness, here a synonym for justice) and to specify the qualities of justice that must be manifest in a community. The J type wants to know how, in very practical terms, to implement justice in community and how the individual can be involved. Step-by-step, what must the individual and the community do in order to express justice?

Where the Judger is the model of organization, the Perceiver is more spontaneous and revels in making constant adaptations to life. Perceiving persons are open-minded and curious. They resist closure because they can always imagine new sources of data that might change their conclusion. They get energy from new experiences and they often find routine to be dull. They are extremely tolerant of differences of opinion and behavior. They want to understand issues, events, and situations more than to control them. The Perceiver frequently has difficulty making decisions and is quite comfortable leaving things open.

The Perceiver listens for how God is present and leading in everyday spontaneity. They appreciate themes in the sermon that emphasize tolerance, inclusivity, and the virtues of diversity. They do not like it when the preacher pushes them to make a decision, especially if they believe that not all the data is in. The Perceiver is willing to live with a high degree of openness to the various construals of truth in the world. Perceiving personality types like it when preachers are probing and curious, constantly turning over a text or a subject from a fresh perspective or in light of new data. They like variety in sermon topics and in homiletical form.

For example, when preparing a sermon on Amos 5:24 with a Perceiving community in mind, the preacher could explore various nuances in thinking about justice in the Jewish tradition and their various implications for different kinds of people. How would a particular notion of justice affect a European American suburban middle-class racist? a poor African American who lives in an urban ghetto? an Asian immigrant of high intelligence but limited immediate economic means who can barely understand English? The preacher might ask, "What are possible steps toward justice for each of these groups? What is gained and lost for the other groups when the community acts for justice for one group? Can we ever achieve a situation in which full justice is coming about simultaneously for each group? If not, what are possible priorities for taking steps toward justice?" The preacher may need to help Perceivers recognize that they must, at some point, reach closure. They must accept a notion of justice (recognizing that it may be flawed) and must take some steps (perhaps incomplete) toward realizing it in community.

Some Christian communities reflect the type makeup of the general population, but many congregations and denominations have qualities that particularly appeal to certain types.[34] For instance, "the no-frills, down-to-earth religious experience typical of Methodists and Baptists is more attractive to Sensors, for example, while the symbolic and liturgical styles of the Lutheran and Episcopalian churches have more attraction for iNtuitives."[35] Unitarianism, with its emphasis on rationality, appeals to Thinkers. Pentecostalism is a natural habitat for Sensing-Judging types.[36] Nonetheless, each group contains multiple types. When the preacher has the habits of the dominant group, the preacher needs conscientiously to include others in their homiletical styles. When listeners turn away from the message, the preacher can trust that the Holy Spirit is actively seeking other means by which to help the listener grasp the gospel and respond to it.

Neuro Linguistic Programming

Neuro Linguistic Programming (NLP) is based on research that finds that people represent the world and talk about it in one of three basic ways: visual, auditory, or kinesthetic.[37] All people operate with all systems, but each person has a preferred representational pattern. Preachers who are aware of these systems of representation and response can adapt sermons accordingly in order to help sermons include all representational modes.[38]

People Who Relate to the World Visually

For some people, the dominant function is visual (V). They take in the world through their eyes. They talk about the world in visual language. They are most attentive to communications that describe what the eye can see. They love word pictures. Such people create visual pictures on the screens of their minds, even when they are talking or listening.

The visual person prefers language that is derived from the world of sight. "I *see* what you mean." "This miracle story *shows us* a *clear picture* of God's love." To contact the visually oriented members of the congregation, the preacher can use language from the visual representational system. In particular, the preacher can create word-pictures that people can see. The preacher can also discuss conceptual aspects of the sermon in visual terms.

Seeing the preacher in the pulpit activates the Visual participant in worship. The pastor's appearance and mode of being in the act of preaching can be confirming or disconfirming for the visually oriented person. If the preacher's appearance and movement are consonant with what the preacher is saying, the Visual will perceive continuity and confirmation between the message and its visual representation. If the preacher's appearance and movement are dissonant with the content of the message, the listener is likely to greet the sermon with skepticism. The preacher who speaks of the peace that passes all understanding in a presence that denotes peace is credible, whereas the sermon's credibility is undercut when the minister speaks of peace but looks angry.

For example, when preparing a sermon on Elijah's confrontation with the prophets of Baal on Mount Carmel in 1 Kings 18:20–40, the preacher who is sensitive to Visuals in the congregation would paint the scene on the mountain. With the help of a Bible dictionary, the preacher could describe the elements of the scene, including the mountain; the dress of Elijah and its significance; the actions of the prophets of Baal, dancing and sacrificing their bull and cutting themselves; Elijah's rebuilding of the altar of God by replacing the twelve stones; the pouring of the water over the wood; and the climactic flash of holy fire that consumed the wood and the stones and that "even licked up the water that was in the trench" (v. 38). The preacher might even invite Visuals to "see this scene on the screen of your mind." When talking about the implications of the text for the congregation, the preacher would use the language of visuality: "Where do we see ourselves in this story?"

People Who Relate to the World Kinesthetically

For some people, the dominant function is kinesthetic (K). The "Kino" feels the world and talks about it using the vocabulary of feeling. In the literature of NLP, feeling has a double and often overlapping meaning. At one level, it includes visceral sensation (physical sensations of such things as movement, temperature, touch)—"I feel the weight of the world on my shoulders." At another level, it includes emotions. "The Sunday school class is very warm," that is, very friendly. The Kinesthetic listener is particularly attentive to communications that describe physical sensation and that engage the emotions.

The K person is likely to respond positively to a statement such as "What you are saying about God doesn't *feel* right to me." The K leader ends a meeting of the worship committee by saying, "I'll be in *touch* with you about the next steps." To include the kinesthetically oriented person, then, the preacher should use the language of visceral sensation and emotion. "Can you experience in your heart the world of the homeless person stretched out on the damp floor of the musty building?" "Do you feel God's love pouring down on you?"

In the pulpit, the pastor's person can invoke a Kinesthetic response. An animated pastor whose gestures and other body movements are consistent with the content of the message invites the Kino to believe that the claims of the sermon are true. A pastor whose animation is not consistent with the content of the message discourages the Kino from giving serious attention to the sermon. A pastor who speaks of God's love for the world and has body language that is warm, open, and embracing will seem more convincing to the Kinesthetic hearer than a pastor who speaks of divine love but whose body is motionless except for a few small, closed gestures.

When thinking about the Kino in the congregation for the sermon on 1 Kings 18:20–40, the confrontation between Elijah and the prophets of Baal, the preacher would describe what the people physically felt on Mount Carmel, such as the peculiar feeling of being on a mountain, the changing of the temperature over the course of the day, the texture of firewood, the water poured on the logs, the heat and brightness of the fire of God lashing down from heaven. The preacher would also describe the internal feelings that are generated by our encounter with the various characters of the story, and by the plot of the story. The text moves from Elijah's feeling of being the last of the faithful ("I, even I only, am left") to the desperation of the prophets of Baal as they appeal to their deity, through the suspense as Elijah prepares the altar with wood and sacrifice, to the intense awe that is generated by the theophany of the fire.

People Who Relate to the World through Auditory Means

For some people the dominant function is auditory (A). Auditory persons perceive the world, and talk about the world, in the language of sound. The A listeners are immediately engaged when they hear the preacher step into the pulpit and begin to talk. They are engaged even more when the preacher uses the language of hearing and talking.

For instance, after describing a difficult situation, the preacher might ask, "Do you *hear* that person's pain?" Or the pastor might orient the congregation to an important part of the sermon by saying, "I want you to *listen* very carefully now." The preacher might punctuate an important gospel affirmation, "This *sounds* too good to be true." The Auditory person might respond to a sermon by saying, "The main idea of your sermon *rings* true to me."

The preacher's voice is especially important to persons with an Auditory orientation. They respond positively when the preacher's voice is living and active and when the tone of the voice corresponds to the content of the sermon. If the preacher is speaking about joy, the Auditory member's confidence in the sermon is reinforced if the preacher sounds joyful. The Auditory listener is suspicious if the preacher speaks about joy but sounds bored.

When developing a message on the climactic confrontation between Elijah and the prophets of Baal (1 Kings 18:20–40), the preacher who wishes for the Auditory listener to participate optimally in the sermon will highlight the aspects of the text that contain speech and sound. The preacher will not just summarize the words that the characters speak but will actually speak them with appropriate dramatic expression and intensity, and will explain them so that the Auditories can hear the full reverberation that the language of the text would have had in the listening chambers of people of antiquity. The minister will also want to describe sounds in addition to speech that the people on the mountaintop would have heard, such as the sounds of the dancing of the Baalites (including their cries as they "cut themselves with swords and lances," as well as their raving), the pouring of the water over the altar, the crackling of the fire, the wail of the prophets of Baal being put to death. Furthermore, the pastor will invite A congregants to "listen for" the word that the text would "speak" to the contemporary community. The sermon will highlight auditory aspects of contemporary points of contact between the text and the world today.

Since the typical congregation contains people who operate out of all three representational systems, the preacher will typically want to include elements from all three systems in every sermon. Not only that, but with only a little extra effort, the preacher can include elements of taste and smell in nearly every sermon.

The three representational systems are in tension at one point. Visuals seek eye contact with the person with whom they are speaking. Kinesthetic and Auditory listeners sometimes prefer not to have eye contact with persons with whom they are communicating, particularly when they are under stress.[39] The preacher thus has a mixed responsibility when in the pulpit. On the one hand, the preacher needs to be available for eye contact with Visually oriented members. But the preacher risks losing Kinesthetic and Auditory congregants by trying to force eye contact when they do not want it. Of course, the pastor can take comfort in the fact that people who appear to be looking at their feet or staring past the preacher's head may be absorbing the sermon in their preferred representational system even though they are not giving the preacher the traditional signal (eye contact) of being involved in the sermon.

Relating These Three Modes

None of the three mental typologies that we discuss in this chapter provides a comprehensive understanding of how people process their experience in the world. Each analytical pattern focuses on selected aspects. However, we can see common themes and implications in several of the typologies.

The greatest point of commonality is that different groups of people think in different patterns. A pastor needs several homiletical approaches in order for different listening groups in the congregation to have optimum opportunities to enter the world of the sermon.

From their different perspectives, the first two bodies of research discover that the minds of some persons work in very logical and ordered ways, while others are more associative and spontaneous.

Some listeners can think critically, while others are largely receivers of the thoughts of others. Some hearers derive their authority from external sources (e.g., the Bible, Christian tradition, recognized leaders) whereas others create their own notions of what is authoritative and what is not.

Some listeners prefer sermons that are deductive. They want the preacher to articulate concepts and ideas and to spell out the implications for everyday faith and life. They are most comfortable when they know the direction of the sermon from the beginning. Some participants in the community want the preacher to explain a story or poem. Other listeners prefer communications that are inductive, even impressionistic. They want to work out the implications of a sermon for themselves.

Some people can understand language and other forms of symbolism at multiple levels. Others tend to process language in a literal way.

Some respond well when human feeling appears in a sermon, but others become uncomfortable. The latter often prefer to deal with ideas, while the former find ideas boring, or even insulating from the depths of life. Some people are prepared to make their own decisions—even when such decisions go against the flow of the crowd—while others are significantly influenced by the opinions of others.

Some Christians have an inclination to enter empathetically into the experiences of others and to see the world from the point of view of others. Another group of Christians has difficulty doing so. Some believers can live—and even thrive—in chaos and ambiguity. Others require a sense of security, including clarity about what is true and false, right and wrong. The former have the ability to see strengths and weaknesses in other points of view, whereas the latter tend to evaluate all viewpoints as either right or wrong.

Some people are naturally global in their orientation and loyalty. Others are more concerned with the tribal world. Some listeners light up when the preacher is visionary. Others want day-to-day principles and rules.

At the macro-level of sermon structure, the preacher can conscientiously use a variety of structures that appeal to different groups of listeners. For instance, some in the congregation respond very positively to narrative sermons (i.e., a sermon that relates a single story). A narrative sermon leaves other listeners wondering, "When is this extended introduction going to end so that we can get to the real ideas of the sermon?" At the micro-level of individual elements in the sermon (sections, paragraphs, sentences, turns of phrase) the preacher can often select content and language that are likely to be received positively by certain groups.

The preacher may prepare a whole sermon with the intention of communicating with a particular group of listeners. For example, the pastor might think, *This Sunday, I need to speak with iNtuitives. I will find a structure and develop the individual elements of the sermon especially for them.* Or the preacher might include material for different groups within each sermon, thinking, for instance, *I want to make sure that in this sermon, I have references for people who apprehend the world in visual, kinesthetic, and auditory ways.* The preacher decides on a particular approach for a particular sermon based on pastoral exegesis of the congregation.

These three patterns of analyzing human understanding do not contradict one another.[10] They examine human knowledge and communication from different standpoints. A woman could be at Stage 4 in development terms and operate out of MBTI type INTP with an auditory representational system. However, the preacher will seldom find it necessary to engage in such detailed analysis of listeners in order to make general use of the insights afforded by the different typologies. Through pastoral listening, the preacher can become aware of the predominant patterns in a congregation, and can conscientiously craft sermons to account for those patterns, while making sure that other listeners are included as well.

The three modes we have discussed are only three possibilities for understanding patterns of human perception. Ministers can profit from reflecting on how other ways of conceiving perception might help the preacher make the gospel available to a wide spectrum of listeners. For instance, Howard Gardner has popularized the notion of "multiple intelligences," that is, the idea that people know and understand not just in ways that are measured by conventional intelligence tests and academic exercises, but in multiple realms.[11] Gardner initially identified seven such realms: linguistic (verbal), mathematics (logical), spatial, kinesthetic, rhythmic, interpersonal intelligence, and intrapersonal intelligence. Although most people function at least minimally in all modes, an individual typically perceives most easily and fully in one, two, or three of these forms of knowledge. Conventional preaching appeals primarily to linguistic and logical knowers. The preacher can enhance the contact between the sermon and other kinds of perceivers by taking account of kinesthetic, rhythmic, interpersonal, and intrapersonal factors.

As we have frequently noted, the gospel is not a prisoner of the orientation or situation of the listener. The gospel can transcend and even transform listener preferences. However, with a little forethought and critical acumen, the preacher can help facilitate this process.

4

Preaching and Gender

A couple goes out for the evening. On their way home the woman says, "Would you like to stop for a cup of coffee?" Her husband considers and then replies, truthfully, "No." When they get home, he discovers that she is annoyed with him. "What did I do?" he says, throwing up his hands. He assumed that what his wife had asked was a real question. However, it was not a question. "Would you like to stop for a cup of coffee?" was an invitation.[1] In the words of Deborah Tannen, "Boys ands girls grow up in what are essentially different cultures, so talk between women and men is cross-cultural communication."[2]

Think of this problem in terms of preaching. Women, who make up more than half of most congregations, have likely spent most of their lives listening to male preachers speaking, in effect, a language from another culture. It is a masculine language in which almost every important figure, divine or human, is a "he." A half-century ago, the most frequently used illustrations were from Shakespeare, war stories, or Lincoln stories. These illustrations have mostly gone away, but we suspect they have been at least partially replaced with a successor: sports stories. Of course, women have learned of necessity to translate this masculine language into one that carries meaning for them. But it makes their religious task more difficult. And pleas for "more inclusive image systems" gain ground slowly (which, of course, is a military image).[3]

"The pulpit is a gendered place."[4] And for millennia, that place has been almost completely masculine. As preachers have strived to be more sensitive to matters of gender in preaching, they have sometimes faced a backlash from men. Not long ago Joey preached at a large church and was shaking hands after worship. A man approached him and said, "Well, you lost me after your first three words, preacher." Caught off guard, Joey could not recall his first three words until the man told him that the words were: "Sisters and brothers." "The proper thing for you to have said was 'Brothers and sisters,'" he said. "It's people like you who are driving men out of the church."

In the midst of this complication arises another. Most every congregation counts among its members gay, lesbian, bisexual, transgendered, questioning, and asexual persons, some "out," some "closeted." Some congregations are "open and affirming"; others are openly hostile; many are confused.

This chapter opens a conversation (and does not try to settle it) regarding issues in the relationship of gender and communication. We recognize that when we speak of qualities in communication that are associated with women and men, we are only referring to tendencies that are shared by many people in each gender. We are not reporting principles that apply fully to each and every woman or man. Individual women and men (and perhaps groups comprising women or men) often manifest traits that are typically associated with the other gender. In this area, as in so many others, each human being is a unique combination of qualities.

Our work in this area is hampered by the fact that most of the studies of gender in communication of which we are aware focus on European Americans in the middle class. More attention needs to be given to this phenomenon in other communities.

All this perspective serves as a reminder that two middle-class, heterosexual, European American males have written this book, which immediately places limitations on this chapter. We move forward by sharing thoughts prompted by *Women's Way of Knowing*[5] (a book written collectively by a group of women scholars) and Deborah Tannen's explorations into this subject in volumes such as *You Just Don't Understand.* We offer preliminary observations on ways women and men think and use language, and consider some impacts for the preaching of the gospel. We mention a predicament men face in our culture. We offer some similar comments from Christine Smith regarding preaching for lesbian and gay persons. And then we become quiet for a while and listen.

Women's Ways of Knowing

Mary Belenky and a group of colleagues interviewed 135 women in preparation for the influential book *Women's Ways of Knowing*.[6] They investigated whether women have distinctive ways of understanding themselves, of hearing and learning, and of expressing themselves. In a word, the answer is yes.[7]

The characteristics identified in the study are not all unique to women. Men share several patterns of coming to knowledge. While we focus largely on women's habits of knowing, we comment on differences and similarities with men.

Although women outnumber men in most congregations, relatively little research has made its way into homiletical literature to help preachers communicate in language and forms that take account of women's patterns of coming to knowledge and communicating.[8]

Two Ways of Talking about Knowledge

Before turning to the basic patterns by which women typically process communication, Belenky and her colleagues note that women and men tend to speak about knowledge in different language systems. Males tend to use visual language and to describe knowledge as illumination. A male might say, "I see what you mean." "I can picture what you are talking about in my mind's eye." In his writing and preaching, Ron frequently uses the expressions "view" and "viewpoint" for perceiving and opinions. The visual metaphor system suggests standing at a distance from that which is known. One observes the object of knowledge in a way that is relatively detached, even clinical.[9]

By contrast, women tend to speak of themselves and of knowledge in terms of voice. Having voice is fundamental because women have been silenced in so many arenas of life. To hear a voice and to have a voice break the prison of silence and demonstrate connectedness. "In describing their lives, women commonly talked about…'speaking up,' 'speaking out,' 'being silenced,' 'not being heard,' 'really listening,' 'really talking,' 'words as weapons,' 'feeling deaf and dumb,' 'having no words,' 'saying what you mean,' 'listening to be heard.'"[10] The vocal metaphorical system suggests connection, relationship, dialogue, and interaction between knower and that which is known.

A basic implication, then, is that the preacher's optimum homiletical vocabulary needs to include both visual and vocal language systems. Likely, male preachers need to be careful to include the language of voice in their preaching while women pastors need to make sure that they include visual language. This consideration extends to the selection of biblical texts as bases for preaching; over a season of preaching, a preacher should select texts that highlight both visual and vocal language systems.

At a deeper level, these two metaphor systems imply different qualities in the relationship of the knower and the known. Christians need to be intimately connected with God, other Christians, and the world. At the same time, Christians need to be able to transcend themselves and their situations so as to evaluate their situations critically and, if necessary, to modify their perceptions, feelings, and behaviors.

Patterns by Which Women Receive and Process Knowledge

The researchers discovered five basic patterns in which women receive and process knowledge. Women can move from one pattern to another. Indeed, from the standpoint of the gospel, it is often desirable to do so. Preaching can help women in each pattern grasp the gospel in ways that are understandable in their patterns of knowing. Preaching can also help facilitate women in the movement from one mode of knowing to another.

Silence[11]

Some women are silent. They are silent because they have not consciously learned that they can think and act as independent agents. They often feel that they are under the heel of arbitrary powers that seek to keep them suppressed. They tend to think that they have "a place" in the world; they feel pain when they try to leave that place. They frequently experience words as weapons that others use to "keep them in their places." Not surprisingly, many silent women experience disconnection from others and from language itself. Hence, they remain silent. When asked how she conceives of herself, one silent woman replied, "I don't know...No one has told me yet what he or she thought of me."[12]

The preacher is in a delicate relationship with the silent woman. Particularly if the preacher is a male, silent women may regard the preacher as oppressive. A minister may need to establish a pastoral relationship of solidarity with a silent woman before she can hear a sermon. Hearing a liberating word in a sermon may itself be the first step toward establishing a relationship that can help a silent woman develop a sense of voice.

The silent woman needs to hear that God knows her silence. She needs to know that God empowers her to speak and that God (and the church) hear her.

A preacher needs also to help the congregation to acknowledge the presence of silent women, to find ways to help them come to voice. Christian preaching also needs to help the community understand the factors in our culture that choke women into silence, and how divine leading can help recreate our social world as a place in which all can speak.

Received Knowledge[13]

This woman understands knowledge as receiving information from others. Women who receive knowledge have a positive sense of self and the capacity to act as an agent. They place a very high value on language, for language is a primary way that knowledge is transmitted. But they typically believe that others have more knowledge. The receiver's role is to listen to others. Receivers believe they have little to say.

Furthermore, most receivers have a dualistic view of knowledge. A statement is either right or wrong. Received knowers conceive of truth as a commodity that is passed, like a box, from one person to another. They speak in terms of "should" and "ought." Their attitudes and behaviors tend to follow the conventions of the community that has become the source of their knowledge. Indeed, "because women at the position of received knowledge believe that all knowledge originates outside of the self, they must look to others even for self-knowledge."[14] Receivers try to live up to the image that others have of them.

Some men are also received knowers. However, men generally are more rigid in their views of truth than women. Men tend to lecture as much as to listen. Women are usually better able than their male counterparts to identify weaknesses in the received versions of truth and to recognize the possible strengths in alternative conceptions.

Women and men tend to hold this position for a limited time, especially if they make their way into circles in which they are exposed to critical thinking (e.g., college). Many received knowers are prompted to move beyond this position when they confront competing authorities. At such a point, most received knowers recognize that all awareness cannot automatically be compartmentalized into neat categories of right and wrong.

In order to trust the preacher, the received knower needs to hear certainties in the sermon. If the receiver does not pick out a clear and certain word, the receiver will not regard the preacher as a real authority. In addition, the preacher needs to help received knowers take steps toward critical ways of thinking about God, Christian faith, their lives, and the world. In particular, the preacher needs to help break up false rigidities in the received knower's field of perception, and to help the receiver search for more adequate ways of dealing with the ambiguities and relativities that permeate life in the twenty-first century world.

The preacher might help in this transition by speaking as an authority (drawing on credible sources) who questions the authorities to which the received knower looks for guidance. For instance, on the basis of particular readings of selected biblical texts, some received knowers assume that women are to be subject to men in the home, in the church, and in the workplace. The preacher can often help such people question the adequacy of their understanding by interpreting the biblical texts differently or by questioning the validity of aspects of the texts themselves.

Subjective Knowledge[15]

The woman who has subjective knowledge feels independently capable of knowing. She is no longer passive, but is now an active subject who relies primarily on her own feelings and intuitions for her new perspectives. The subjective knower has a voice of her own and a sense of her personal authority. Of the 135 women interviewed by Belenky and her colleagues, almost half were subjective knowers.

What causes women to move from a pattern of receiving knowledge to one of subjective knowing? Typically, external sources of information no longer prove reliable. Failed relationships with men, particularly those involving sexual harassment and abuse, often create such a crisis of authority. The failure of previously trusted authorities, such as ideas, government, and managers in the workplace can also create crises. Educational settings can create such crises when teachers and learning events cause students to notice disparities between their received knowledge and other ways of speaking about a subject.

When old authorities have failed, women must actively locate other resources. Where do they turn? Subjective knowers have a hunch that their own experiences can serve as resources for knowledge. They cannot always explain why they make choices that they do, except to say that they "feel" right. They may even reject the opinions of recognized authorities (such as teachers, physicians, lawyers, scientists) in favor of relying on their own sense of what is right in a given circumstance.

As a part of the process of transformation, the subjective knower initially feels uncertain about her ability to trust herself. She usually tells the story of her transition to a person in whom she senses a nurturing quality and a kindred spirit. The companion is usually a woman (sometimes a mother, a grandmother, a friend, even a staff member at an agency), but it can be a sensitive male. The companion confirms the journey of transition.

Women report that the companion in life-transition is often the first person ever to listen to them. "By being given the opportunity to talk things over with a sympathetic, nonjudgmental person with similar experiences, a woman can begin to hear that maybe she is not such an incompetent, a dummy, or an oddity. She has experience that may be valuable to others; she, too, can know things."[16] The experiences of speaking and of being heard are essential to liberation.

The subjective knower needs to know that the preacher is listening to her. One of the clearest ways for the pastor to let the subjective knower know that she has been heard is for the preacher to include in the sermon stories of women with whom the subjective knower can identify. The preacher can also talk about the experiences of women who are subjective knowers. In our preaching classes, women are particularly drawn to stories of women who have felt unnoticed or devalued, or who have been involved in failed relationships with men. The preacher who uses such material in the sermon seems to say to women, "I hear your pain."

For women who need to make a transition from received knowledge about God and Christian life to subjective knowledge about such things, the preacher can function in two ways. First, the preacher can sympathetically lead the women into the presence of multiple Christian authorities who voice different interpretations of Christian matters. The preacher can often ask questions to help received knowers grasp the incompatibility of differing interpretations and the importance of resolving contradictions. For instance, in a sermon on Christian interpretations of evil, the preacher might ask, "Now, which of these ways of talking about evil seems right to you?"

Second, the preacher can function as an empathetic companion who can confirm the safety and significance of making the transition from one way of knowing to another.[17] In particular, preachers can tell stories of women who successfully have made the transition from received knowledge to subjective knowledge. Listeners are particularly encouraged when the preacher's own story models such a transition.

Procedural Knowledge[18]

Procedural knowledge results from established, self-conscious procedures for gathering data and coming to one's own perspective. Proceduralists particularly value knowledge that is gained from "objective" sources outside the self, though they also listen to voices from within the self.

Procedural knowers fall into two subgroups: separate knowers and connected knowers. Women tend toward connectional knowing, while men tend toward separated knowing.

The separate knower is aware of himself or herself as a distinct entity who exists separately from other selves. Knowledge itself exists as "bricks" of information or power. The separate knower's method (procedure) is to acquire knowledge by accumulating "bricks" of it. The separate knower evaluates the claims of the various sources of knowledge and accepts those that seem most persuasive. The separate knower tends to adopt the standards of the community for determining higher and lower quality knowledge. If the evidence demands it, the separate knower is ready to give up cherished preferences.

When listening to a sermon, the separate knower wants to know what the preacher has to say. This knower wants to take home a clear and identifiable brick, that is, a definite idea and its implications. Separate knowers want to know the sources (and their quality) on which the preacher relies. Separate knowers want to know the reasons why preachers are convinced that their sermons should be authoritative. Separate proceduralists will listen carefully to recognized experts. They insist that the preacher treat all contributors to the dialogue in a fair way.

Connectional knowing is the most difficult type about which to speak because it is of such a different character than any other type, and because its procedures are not as clear (and have not been studied as thoroughly) as other types of knowledge. A distinguishing characteristic of connected knowers is that they understand themselves to be connected to others. The procedure for gathering knowledge for the connectionalist is to be in relationship with another person. The relationship itself mediates knowledge.

In order to access the knowledge of others, the connected knower must share in that person's experience. Hence, the capacity for empathy is a key for the connected knower. One of the primary ways that women enter one another's experiences is through conversation that is informal, intimate, and self-revealing. They want to know the web of circumstances, feelings, and thoughts that are a part of coming to perception.

In such conversations, the experience of the other becomes a means by which the connected knower transcends her own experience. She discovers what life is like from the perspective of others in the conversation. Connected women tend to withhold judgment on the experiences of others in order to assess the degree to which another's experience might be valuable in coming to knowledge.

Connected knowing sometimes comes about through collaborative groups whose goal is to achieve knowledge by working together. Such a group works best when it lasts for a long time and people become sufficiently trusting to be deeply self-revealing and to question one another honestly. The hope is that the members of the group will help nurture their insights (even partially developed ones). Collaborative groups engage in criticism, but the criticism is in the context of connection. Through sharing of different perspectives and experiences, mutual questioning, and continuous engagement with one another, they expect knowledge to result.

The connected knower needs to feel a sense of personal relationship with the preacher. This connection can come about in part through the pastor's relationship with the connected parishioner in other areas of the congregation's life outside the sanctuary. It can also come about through the sermon as pastors reveal their own experiences and give evidence of empathetic hearing of the experiences of others. Indeed, for the connectional knower, experience is a primary authority. The absence of experience in a sermon causes the connected knower to wonder if the sermon is true.

The connectionalist would also like to sense a collaborative element in the sermon. John McClure finds that when the preacher meets with a group of people from the congregation as a part of the preparation of the sermon, the sermon can take on a collaborative quality. The preacher hears the people's questions, insights, and experiences, and voices them.[19] From time to time, the preacher may actually want to create a multivoice sermon that is a genuine collaboration (and not just a script that the preacher has prepared).[20]

Constructed Knowledge[21]

Some women (and men) construct their own perceptions of themselves and the world. They draw on intuition, reason, and the expertise of persons outside themselves. They are self-conscious regarding what they think, and why. They can transcend themselves, even as they can be passionately committed to the worlds that they have constructed. Knowledge is constantly in process as knowers evaluate and reevaluate their perspectives.

A distinctive feature of those who construct knowledge is their recognition that all knowers are affected by their contexts. Constructors contend that all understanding is influenced by the presuppositions of those who try to understand. All understanding is interpretive. These women respect a reputed expert when they can see that the expertise is well founded and when the expert acknowledges the complexity of the world (and the subject) as they know it.

Constructed knowers carry this desire to understand an idea or situation in its complexity into the moral arena. They recognize that few moral decisions are simple matters of right and wrong; moral decisions must often be made in the nexus of a complicated web of factors. Many moral decisions are thus relative: the chooser makes decisions that she judges to be relatively more helpful and less harmful than others.

Another distinctive feature of constructed knowers is their willingness to go outside the "givens" of present systems. If a present way of framing a problem is not yielding solutions, they experiment with other frames. The proceduralist, for instance, assumes the validity of the present structure of the church. Revitalization means revitalization of something like the present system. When faced with the lethargy and diminishment of the present church, the constructivist asks if the way in which the church is manifest ought to be reconceived.

Constructed knowers value a sermon that has the character of a critical conversation. Such knowers hope that the conversation will reveal clearly the claim of the sermon and the sources on which the sermon rests. These knowers further hope that the sermon will help them critically evaluate the claim of the sermon and its sources. Constructive thinkers particularly want to think critically about the ingrained interpretive biases in the preacher, in the church, and in the sources on which the sermon depends. As one of Ron's students said to another student, "Before I believe your sermon, I want to know who gets the payoff and who gets hurt."

In order for the sermon to ring true to the constructed knower, the sermon must acknowledge the complexity of the issues in the sermon. The constructivist is suspicious of sermons that offer simple perspectives on texts, doctrines, or personal or social situations. Constructive knowers would rather live with ambiguity and relativity than to make decisions on the basis of oversimplified analysis.

The Preacher as Midwife

Given these different ways of knowing, the preacher is a midwife who helps the congregation come to adequate understandings and perceptions of God. To do so, the midwife must prepare the sermon so that it will speak in the language through which different types of knowers can find themselves in the sermon. How then do preachers facing congregations that include people with all these different ways of knowing, preach effectively? One way is by talking with people to determine the ways of knowing that are present in the congregation so as to be sure to speak the language of the primary knowledge groups in the congregation.

The preacher can also speak directly with members of the congregation about patterns of communication that are received well and not so well. The minister who never asks people about sermons for fear of criticism may never learn what simple adjustments might make sermons more available and useful to certain people.

The preacher can also listen critically to the community. At an international gathering, for example, one walks up to a group and listens for a few minutes to ascertain what language is being spoken before joining in the conversation. Similarly, the preacher must be a listener. By listening to the people inside and outside church activities, the preacher learns their language. Asking and listening can provide useful clues to the preacher who wants people to be seriously engaged by the sermon.

Women, Men, and Language

The distance from brain to lips can be enormous. In addition to Belenky's ways of knowing, Deborah Tannen's work on women and men in conversation provides another spectrum of insight into how people communicate with one another, provided we continue to remember that specific women and men are often exceptions to Tannen's generalizations.[22]

Men tend to use language to establish status, while women use language to establish relationship, Tannen says. In a man's world "conversations are negotiations in which people try to achieve and maintain the upper hand...Life, then, is a contest, a struggle to preserve independence and avoid failure."[23] This observation is consistent with the observation of Belenky and her colleagues that men tend to speak of knowledge in relatively detached terms.

In a woman's world, however, "conversations are negotiations for closeness in which people try to seek and give confirmation and support, and to reach consensus...Life, then, is a community, a struggle to preserve intimacy and avoid isolation."[24] This observation, too, is consistent with the discovery of Belenky and her colleagues that women speak of knowledge in the language of "voice," which suggests that they associate knowledge with relationship.

Given these perceptions, we can easily recognize whose language is being used in the church when we speak of prayer *warriors,* stewardship *campaigns, victory* dinners, and even *personal* salvation. As Fred Craddock once said, tongue firmly in cheek, "Why, what's the point of heaven if you can't look over the banister and say 'Ha, ha, ha, ha, ha'?"[25]

Tannen calls attention to another dimension of communication that is important for the preacher when she asks, "Who talks more, women or men?" Following the stereotype, both men and women would probably say, "Women." But Tannen reports that study after study shows that men talk more than women. In meetings, in mixed-group discussions, in classrooms, in discussions after lectures, women speak as much as 75 percent less than men, and when they do speak, they speak less than half as long as the men.[26] Tannen reconciles the seeming contradiction by reference to what she calls *public* and *private* speaking or, in other words, *report-talk* and *rapport-talk.*

For most women, the language of conversation is primarily language of rapport, a way of establishing connections and negotiating relationships. For most men, talk is primarily a means to preserve independence and to negotiate and maintain status in a hierarchical social order.[27]

Speech, especially public speech, to many men is a chance to report on their place in the social order and to demonstrate that place by establishing the primacy of their thoughts and recommendations. The very act of reporting, of course, helps establish the person's place in the social hierarchy. For many women, speech is a way of establishing and maintaining relationship and developing community.

Following Tannen's model, women are at a disadvantage in church, where most of the language is public language and where much talk centers around the social ordering of community life through board meetings, positions the church should take on significant issues, financial decisions, and other such matters. One might even wonder if the marvelous contributions made by women throughout history in the discipline and ministry of prayer may be traced partly to the private nature of much prayer.

Drawing out the implications of these different perspectives for preaching is a delicate matter. At one level the preacher needs to speak in ways that include status and relationship, report and rapport, so that men and women both can hear the sermon in their own languages. In this vein, Fred Craddock recommends that preachers who prefer to preach "either-or" (read: *status*) sermons need to learn to preach some "both-and" (read: *relationship*) sermons. Why? Without making it a gender issue, Craddock says that "either-or" people need to hear some "both-and" because the Bible is "both-and," and "both-and" people need the affirmation they rarely get.[28]

At a deeper level, a language system is not value-neutral. A language system presupposes, validates, and even creates ways of being in the world that are consistent with that language system.[29] For instance, when I speak of the stewardship *campaign,* I invoke the perception that life is a military-like conflict; the stewardship campaign is a form of combat carried out in the congregation.

Speech that is typically male reinforces aspects of hierarchicalism, androcentrism, and individualism that work against the gospel's vision of an egalitarian human community of mutuality and support. The preacher who simply adds male language patterns to the sermon reinforces problematic aspects of the male worldview that are, in part, created and legitimated by that language. Pastors who self-consciously take up such language in the sermon need to use it to help men reframe their ways of thinking and speaking so that their thoughts and words help create a world shaped by the realm of God. The preacher may need to take up such language for the purpose of subverting its usual function in the world.

The language patterns of women are more congenial to the vision of life shaped by the reign of God. Many women innately speak in terms of relationship, connection, and community. Preachers, of course, need to see that such language in the sermon bespeaks community as conceived in the dominion of God.

Furthermore, since men have tended to speak more in public than women, thus giving the church a skewed picture of the world of communication, the preacher needs to make sure that a variety of voices are invited to the speaking center of the church, particularly women and others whose voices have been ecclesiastically marginalized. The fact of variety in empowered and empowering voices in the church is itself an embodiment of the realm of God, in which many different kinds of people are together in community in mutual affirmation and encouragement. Multiple voices help the church enlarge its experience and vision through encounters with fresh and challenging perspectives.

For persons, women or men, who may be struggling with voice and who decline the invitation to join the speaking center, the sensitive preacher may pick up on the problem and provide a voice for them. A man in a church Joey once served, a man well respected and admired by everyone, turned down the chance to be an elder again and again. When Joey finally asked him about it, he said that he declined because he was afraid of the elder's task of praying at the table. Joey suggested that they write some prayers together and then pray them out loud for each other. They did that together for a while until the man's confidence reached the level where he could stand next to Joey at the table and speak. This is not to indicate that this is an easy problem to solve, for women or men. Someone once wrote that the greatest fear of the American people, greater even than the fear of death, is the fear of speaking in public. Some people will never find a public voice, but they can serve in other ways and use their private voice effectively.

Preaching for Men

There was a time when to speak of "preaching for men" was to speak of preaching for everyone. When Wordsworth wrote of how difficult it was to "speak to men,"[30] he was not writing of a male-only audience. But times have changed, and so has our awareness of the differences between women and men. In the previous sections of this chapter, we compare and contrast women's and men's approaches to perception and communication. But we wish to say a few more things about preaching and men.

Prior to the 1960s in North America, roles and expectations for men were fairly well defined. Many boys grew up knowing what it meant to "be a man." The stereotype of that role was to "like football, be aggressive, stick up for the United States, never cry, and always provide."[31] These culturally defined roles and expectations drove many men into long hours at profitable but unfulfilling work, an inability to relate to family and others, depression, bitterness, and cardiac infarction.

However, possibilities for men are no longer as clearly defined as they were a generation or two ago. We find in Robert Bly's *Iron John*[32] and James Dittes's *The Male Predicament*[33] two ways of understanding male roles and expectations that are common in our culture today. Both Bly and Dittes use biblical characters to represent their thinking. This turn quickens our interest.

Bly is less interested in Jesus than in John the Baptist, the hairy wild desert dweller.[34] Bly encourages men to get in touch with the legendary "Wild Man" and develop their own "inner warrior." Bly urges men to "ride the wild horses." If necessary, in order to find authentic manhood, a man needs to leave behind things that inhibit his freedom and authenticity.

Dittes, on the other hand, chooses the Bible's two best-known Josephs for examination. He finds them startlingly contemporary in the way they respond to the predicaments they face. Joseph, the future husband of Mary, the mother of Jesus, is remembered as "the man who always did what was right."[35] Dittes reminds us that the most common image of Joseph in the church is that of the man in the Christmas pageant standing frozen and speechless behind Mary and the manger. Joseph had a dream of a normal life with a normal family. But other dreams got in the way. When he found his fiancée pregnant, he stood by her. He protected and provided for his unusual family, always doing the right thing.

The other Joseph, son of Jacob, and central figure of Genesis 37–45, was also a dreamer. He dreamed of greatness and then, after his brothers sold him into slavery, was led by his dreams to become ruler of all Egypt, subject only to Pharaoh. In Egypt, he was "dutiful prisoner, obeyer of authority, dispenser of authority—all the same thing, really."[36]

The two Josephs' stories are also, Dittes asserts, a story of American manhood: Joseph of Nazareth and Joseph of Canaan, forced into exile and thence into drudgery, dreamers become chore-boys. They did not (perhaps could not) transform their roles. But the hope for the Josephs and today's men is that they did not just tolerate their given roles; they lived vigorously and thoroughly into them. They accepted the unexpected and unwelcome intrusions into their plans, intrusions that put them in touch with a new destiny, undreamed of. And they claimed that destiny.

There are many permutations of these themes in today's culture. If one goes to a men's retreat in a long-established denomination, the "old-time" gospel songs and "rear-back-and-let-fly" preaching are often the norm. At many Christian male-only groups, such as Promise Keepers, men are urged to take back the authority they have surrendered to women.[37]

Based on these models, the minister might think that some sort of old-fashioned or authoritarian preaching is the best way to reach men. Preachers might think that they must appeal to the vestigial inner warrior in the men of the congregation. However, the pastor must ultimately ask, *Does such preaching affirm God's unconditional love for all and does it witness to justice for all; that is, does it encourage the church to develop as an egalitarian community of love and mutual support and to witness to that mode of relationship as a pattern for all communities?*

We recognize that sincere Christians answer the preceding question in different ways. Our theological assessment is that many such ways of communicating with men may sometimes work against the gospel. Old styles in singing and preaching often invoke nostalgia for a previous era in which the place of men seemed much more clearly defined than it does today. Such preaching sometimes discourages men from engaging the *contemporary* call of the gospel. Movements that reinforce the primacy of men in the household (as well as in the church and in the wider word) often actually reinforce patterns of hierarchy and domination that the gospel seeks to dismantle. The call to develop an inner *warrior* suggests that the man should relate to other people in the world as a combatant who seeks to defeat other people and take them prisoner. To live as John the Baptist did is often to give your all to a cause and wonder at the end if it has been worthwhile. We suspect that most men who ride the wild horses and live on locusts and wild honey are unlikely to find relief from the fears that haunt them.

The gospel calls men to recognize that other people are not subjects to be dominated or enemies to be conquered, but persons whom God loves unconditionally and with whom God calls all men into equal and supportive relationships. The preacher needs to help men develop a strong sense of identity and an agency, but an identity that is rooted in God's unconditional love for them, and an agency that serves relationships, households, and communities that embody the reign of God.

In the name of the gospel, the preacher may sometimes encourage men to have a disdain for boundaries, and to struggle against meaningless living. The vocation of the preacher, in relationship to men, is sometimes expressed in a paraphrase of Nelson Mandela, "We do not want our chains to be made more comfortable. We want them removed." In this spirit, the preacher may need to exhort men to be active agents of transformation in personal and social situations to help those situations adequately partake of the reign of God. In the power of the Spirit, men may need to throw off the chains of culturally limited roles.

At other times, the preacher may need to help men name and claim the roles in which they find themselves, chosen or not, and live creatively through them. A preacher does not want to encourage a male to be less than he can be, but a man's life circumstance may limit his options. However, the preacher can encourage men to respond as creatively as possible, even within limitations, to the possibilities that are available.

A key is to help men remember that they are not defined by conventional cultural expectations. A man may have a role, but the role does not control the man.[38] Men can transcend conventional cultural expectations. Some men, such as the Brooklyn dentist Joey met who chucked his role and became a sailboat captain in the Caribbean, abandon one role for another. But many men cannot. And to preach that they should toss aside their roles—husband, father, and companion— and go in search of the Wild Man could wreak havoc in households, civic institutions, churches, and Christian witness. Our perception is that most men need to grasp the full meaning in the roles they have while keeping an eye out for ways in which those roles can be adjusted to embody the reign of God.

A 1982 television movie, "Coming Out of the Ice," included Willie Nelson playing a man unjustly sentenced to a gulag in Siberia. One day another man asked how he could deal with such an unjust imprisonment. Nelson's character said something like this:

> I could spend all my time hoping that I'll get out someday, but the truth is I will probably die here. I could be consumed with bitterness about that, but what good would that do me? This is my life, the only life I have. And so I have learned to live this life, to appreciate things like the beauty of the taiga, the splendor of spring, the joy of a bowl of hot soup.

Pastoral sensitivity leads the preacher to know when to urge men toward revolution and when to encourage creative adaptation within circumstances.

Preaching for men is preaching for everyone: inviting courage for the day, offering hope for the morrow, grounded in and destined for the love of God, the vision of a world transformed by God's unconditional love and unrelenting will for justice.

Gender Orientation and Preaching[39]

Joey spoke to a group of pastors some years ago in Yakima, Washington, about gender-related issues in preaching. His lecture focused on gender in conventional heterosexual categories. After he finished, a woman came to him and said, "You have a very narrow understanding of gender, don't you?" He was caught off guard and kindly taken to school by this person, who reminded him that heterosexual females and males do not exhaust the manifestations of sexuality among us. Neither do lesbian and gay orientations. Some men and women are bisexual or transgendered. Others are questioning their sexuality, while still others describe themselves as asexual–feeling no sexual attraction. Gender orientation is much more elastic than he had indicated. Point taken.

The gay, lesbian, bisexual, transgendered, questioning, and asexual population (GLBTQA)[40] permeates North American culture and is found in almost every congregation. The preacher needs to take these individuals and groups into account both to help such folk understand the implications of the gospel for them, and to help the congregation as a whole become a community whose life testifies to the inclusivity of the gospel.

The response of the church to gay, lesbian, bisexual, and transgendered persons has historically taken one of three forms: condemnation, a call to change one's sexual orientation, or a requirement of celibacy.[41] The church has been much less aware of questioning persons and, hence, has not formulated as clear a response except to underline the primacy of heterosexuality. All three traditional Christian responses (condemnation, the call to change one's orientation, and celibacy) reject the legitimacy of other forms of gender pluralism. More confusion and pain are created when persons and congregations disapprove of such orientations but profess their love and support for individuals, such as Hal and Tom, who have been members of the church for thirty years.

A condemnatory approach to sexual minorities is generally grounded in two sources: Bible and culture. While we cannot rehash the extensive evidence and discussion regarding these issues, we summarize our thinking along these lines using the kind of theological thinking associated with liberalism in chapter 6:[42]

- The Bible contains only five definite references to sexual relationships between persons of the same gender (Leviticus 18:22; 20:13; Romans 1:26–27; 1 Corinthians 6:9; 1 Timothy 1:10). As far as we know, the Bible contains nothing about bisexual, transgendered, questioning, or asexual identities.

- The Bible renders a negative judgment on the sexual relationships between persons of the same genders.

- However, people in the biblical world did not think of sexual relationships between people of the same gender in the way many people do today. Increasing numbers of thoughtful, contemporary people understand multiple forms of gender orientation not simply as a behavior that people choose, but as an ingrained, God-given orientation of the self. Nor did people in the world of the Bible, or the post-biblical church, allow for gay, lesbian, bisexual, transgendered, and asexual persons the experience of stable, long-term, covenantal relationships in the way of many GLBTQA people today.[43] The experience of contemporary GLBTQA people in such relationships suggests that thinkers in the world of the Bible did not have a full enough grasp for the divine purposes of sexuality to be fulfilled in such relationships.

- In the world of the Bible and in Christian theology, the deepest function of sexuality is to embody a relationship of closeness, mutual responsiveness, and covenantal commitment that suggests, in miniature, the relationship of God and the world.[44] Indeed, sexual encounters can be sacramental; that is, they can mediate grace. This way of thinking is why the Bible sometimes refers to two people in a sexual relationship as "knowing" one another. Gay, lesbian, bisexual, transgendered, and questioning relationships can embody this function by expressing the deepest Christian understandings of sexuality.

Walter Wink points out that the Bible is pluralistic in sexual matters, and that our culture is as well.

> The crux of the matter is simply that the Bible has no sexual ethic. Instead, it exhibits a variety of sexual mores, some of which changed over the thousand-year span of biblical history. Mores are unreflected customs accepted by a given community. Many of the practices that the Bible prohibits, we allow [e.g. intercourse during menstruation, celibacy, exogamy, naming sexual organs, masturbation and birth control], and many that it allows, we prohibit [e.g. prostitution, polygamy, levirate marriage, sex with slaves, concubinage, treatment of women as property, and very early marriage–for girls, ages 11–13].[45]

Many people in the world of the Bible and in the history of the church regarded slavery as appropriate for people of faith. However, in response to broader theological reflection on the purposes of God for human life, the church no longer supports slavery. Just as the church has changed its mind on slavery, so the church can change its mind with respect to our past position that only one gender orientation is capable of fulfilling the divine purposes for sexuality.

Wink calls attention to an aspect of the scriptural witness in these matters that is still crucial to the church. "The Bible knows…a love ethic, which is constantly being brought to bear on whatever sexual mores are dominant in any given country, or culture, or period."[46] A question the church must face is the degree to which our attitudes and behaviors toward persons of all gender orientations reflect God's unconditional love for all persons and God's unrelenting will for justice for all persons–including GLBTQA people. The vocation of the church in our time includes witnessing to this claim through a love ethic in preaching and through embodying this claim in the life of the Christian community and in the larger culture.

Applying a love ethic to the culture's condemnation or ambivalence concerning GLBTQA forms of gender orientation has implications for the pulpit. At the very least, the preacher cannot remain silent. The preacher must help the congregation reflect theologically on these phenomena.

In congregations primarily made up of heterosexuals, preachers must decide whether to ease concerns related to the GLBTQA communities into the speaking center of the congregation in a gradual way, or whether to speak them immediately, directly, and fully.

Some congregations are uneasy with the very mention of the words "gay," "lesbian," and others from the sexual sphere under discussion. The preacher who is following an approach of gradually leading the congregation into conversation around these concerns might begin by helping the congregation become less anxious about simply hearing these words. Many people need to become comfortable enough with this language that they can use these words without having a visceral reaction that short-circuits their ability to have a meaningful encounter around these issues.

The preacher may need to help the community name the presence of multiple gender orientations in the congregation and in the larger world. Because many heterosexual Christians are unfamiliar with GLBTQA life, the preacher may need to help heterosexuals understand the terms *gay, lesbian, bisexual, transgendered, questioning,* and *asexual,* and the orientations to life that they represent. This approach may seem very basic and nonprophetic, but in many congregations it may make further dialogue possible, whereas confrontation could end the dialogue before it begins.

In churches where there is open hostility toward GLBTQA persons, preachers may take some comfort in the fact that people tend to be more relational than they are theoretical. People who will vote against becoming an open and affirming church may support people they have come to know and care about. In such cases, the preacher may be able to use the congregation's acceptance of a couple as a port of entry into the larger discussion.

Some congregations move easily, others with more difficulty. The preacher who introduces these matters needs to recognize that discussion of them may result in various fractures: church split, people leaving, pastor fired. We believe it is not wishy-washy to want to hold the congregation together, and it may be naïve to believe that every group of people can discuss such matters in a way that maintains the bonds of community.

The preacher generally sets the pace for engaging this question. He or she will need a discerning spirit for testing the times by asking, *What approach gives my community the best opportunity to enter into a faithful encounter with this topic?* She or he will also need a determination to embody the love ethic of Jesus.

Christine M. Smith has done groundbreaking work on preaching as a friend and not an enemy to persons of gay, lesbian, bisexual, transgendered, and asexual orientations.[47] Addressing methods and themes, Smith leads preachers to deconstruct the theological positions and cultural mores that have oppressed and silenced GLBTQA people. The preacher needs to call attention to the limitations of the Bible in furnishing direct guidance in this regard and to help the congregation recognize other resources for thinking theologically about these matters.

Beyond deconstruction, however, Smith urges preachers to lift up redemptive themes, such as creating a home place, the ever present power of grace, and resurrection. The church must become a safe space for persons with the full range of gender orientations. The preacher should assure GLBTQA persons that their status before God and in the Christian community is established by divine grace. The preacher can also assure the congregation as a whole of God's affirming presence in the community that affirms GLBTQA people. Not only can GLBTQA persons experience resurrection when they come into contact with such a congregation, but a congregation that welcomes such persons can itself experience resurrection.

At this point, a heterosexual preacher in a congregation composed mainly of heterosexual listeners may have a blind spot.[48] Many heterosexual preachers and congregations assume that heterosexuality is *the* standard mode of sexual expression, with other forms of sexuality as secondary, substandard, or even aberrant. Some ministers call predominately heterosexual congregations to welcome GLBTQA persons without asking such persons to change their sexual behavior or identity, but also without fundamentally changing the perception of sexuality in the congregation. Although the congregation accepts, and even welcomes, GLBTQA people, heterosexuals (and heterosexuality) remain in charge of the congregation. The preacher leaves the impression that heterosexuality is the norm. As one of our students said, heterosexuals often assume "that they know what the appropriate [sexual] boundaries are, make the boundaries a bit bigger, and then manage the diversity that they've decided to allow. They still hold the power to do the welcoming. In this system, [GLBTQA people] have to rely upon straight people for their welcome and their affirmation."[49]

The GLBTQA communities, joined by a growing number of Christians, insist that the gospel calls for congregations that are largely heterosexual to do more than simply welcome GLBTQA people. Congregations must do two things: (1) The Christian community must reconceive the very notion of normative sexuality to recognize that the full range of sexual expressions (gay-lesbian-bisexual-transgendered-questioning-asexual-heterosexual) are normal because all forms of sexuality are God-given. Many of us must surrender the idea that heterosexuality is the norm and that other forms of sexuality, while acceptable, are still not quite normal. (2) The Christian community must recognize that since sexuality is a gift from God, the identity of the church requires the presence of GLBTQA persons. The church does not just welcome such folk. If the Christian community in this world is to anticipate the great eschatological reunion of the fractured human family, the presence of such people is necessary. Indeed, the church is aberrant when it does *not* embody a community of gay, lesbian, bisexual, transgendered, questioning, asexual, and heterosexual persons.

Most pastors can remember sermons we have preached that might have been meaningful and grace-filled for GLBTQA folk. We can also remember sermons or talks that were not helpful, such as Jocy's message in Yakima. We can be grateful for helpful words, even those spoken unwittingly, and we can learn from experiences that were hurtful. The following excerpt from a sermon by Michael Piazza, entitled "The Gay Advantage," illustrates a homiletical engagement with a liberating theme.

> One advantage for gay and lesbian people is that if the fundamentalists are right about how people are saved, then gay people are the ones most likely to make it to heaven. What I mean by that is simply this. The current emphasis in conservative Christianity is that salvation is by grace alone and that you must be born again. No people have experienced new birth more fully than the man or woman who has spent years hiding in the dark, confining womb which society calls a closet. Whether we have come out to the whole world, or to only a few, or to just ourselves, being born again is an accurate description.
>
> I remember the frightening freedom I felt when I first came to deal with the reality of my own sexuality. Finally venturing out of the self-repression and denial and accepting the invitation to befriend myself as a homosexual created and loved by God. I remember thinking at that moment that if salvation was not by grace alone I was in real trouble. Other churches claim to hold that belief, but we are gambling our lives on it. The evangelicals sing "Just as I am, without one plea," but we believe it.[50]

Nobody does, or should, preach on sexuality every Sunday. But the issue of the church's response to GLBTQA people threatens to fracture denominations as slavery did 150 years ago. For heterosexual pastors to ignore the issue is to leave people bound by wrongheaded cultural mores and bad theological reflection. It is to leave GLBTQA persons without theological guidance in understanding their own situations and their place in the Christian community. To help persons to understand more clearly the foundations and damaging effects of homophobia, heterosexual privilege, and those church policies and structures that discriminate against GLBTQA persons can be a valuable aspect of the witness of preaching the gospel in this world Christ died to save.[51] To bring good news of grace, hope, and new life to bear on fear and anger is to help pave the way.

Recently, two persons have told us that the most difficult relational issue in churches of which they are a part is that of transgendered people. When a man whom church folk have known for years as Stan shows up one Sunday in a dress and introduces herself as Stella, many people simply do not know what to do or what to say. Transgendered folk may complicate matters by their awkwardness in their new mode of self-expression. As one woman said recently, "There is more to being a woman than learning how to walk in heels."

The pastor can be particularly helpful through dialogue with the transgendered person and, with permission, publicly announcing that the one people have known as Stan is a woman who wishes to be called Stella from this time forth, and then leading the way in acknowledging the transgendered person as a woman or man as the case may be. The congregation, as well as the transgendered person, experiences a certain awkwardness early in the new relationship. But the rewards of being the person one believes he or she was created by God to be outweighs that awkwardness and can lead to new feelings of self-worth and new experiences of Christian community.

Joey and Ron were at a professional society meeting in Oakland, California, a few years ago. One day we were invited to lunch at a downtown church pastored by a marvelous woman. Each table was hosted by a church member. At our table we were hosted by a lovely young woman named Patrice. She was very gracious and engaging. The pastor walked around to each table introducing the hosts. At our table she said something like this:

> One cold, rainy winter day about three years ago, I was working in the office when I thought I heard a knock on the door. No, I decided, it was just the wind. Then I heard it again and went to the door. When I opened it, I saw this shivering, drenched person who looked up at me and finally said, "I'm transgender. I'm a prostitute. I'm HIV positive. Does your Jesus have any room for me?"

It was a deeply touching story. The church knows the answer to that question, but we have to say it again and again. Jesus has room for all of us. And insofar as conventional attitudes toward gender close off that room for some but not others, we may be challenged, in Smith's words, "to deconstruct what appears to be the most fundamental of all human categories, gender."[52]

5

Preaching in Multicultural Settings

Almost thirty years ago, in his first position out of seminary, Joey found himself the associate minister of a downtown church. One winter Sunday an ice storm hit the town, leaving the streets covered with a half-inch glaze of ice. The senior minister having taken ill, it was Joey's responsibility to lead the evening service. Very slowly he negotiated the streets to the church, turned on lights and heat, and prepared for the service. He went to the chapel, waited, and waited, but nobody came Finally, he turned off the lights and heat, locked up the church, and started home. Few cars had ventured out that evening, and most of them were moving sideways and backward as much as forward. There was a hill on the main thoroughfare that he wanted to avoid, so Joey turned down a side street and continued until he saw something that brought him to a stop. There sat a little Mexican Baptist church, bright and cheery against the dark night. A number of cars were parked all akimbo in front, and when he rolled the window down, Joey could hear the music from the little congregation drifting on the air. It was a lovely and touching thing to see and hear. While one could not criticize those who chose to stay home that evening, one could wonder what the little church had that the big church did not, what drew people to the little church in spite of the weather.

That evening became the catalyst for Joey's becoming a pilgrim of sorts, one who would visit hundreds of churches over the years, from huge megachurches to tiny Christadelphian ecclesias, churches that were European, European American, African, African American, Asian, Asian American, Hispanic American, and Native American, among others; churches that were conservative and churches that were liberal; churches that were old, young, traditional, contemporary, charismatic, stodgy; churches whose worship lifted him toward heaven and churches whose worship made him so angry he had to get up and leave.

So many beliefs and styles. So many languages and worldviews. So many cultures. There was a time when cultures evolved in relative isolation. No more. In cities, and even in rural areas, we find different cultures living next to and among one another. One no longer has to go from one congregation to another to encounter multiple cultures. Today many pastors stand up to preach in congregations of once-majority Anglo Americans in which folk like those of that small Hispanic congregation are found in growing numbers, and Anglo Americans and African Americans may well be found in that once almost exclusively Hispanic congregation.

The preacher may look out on a Sunday morning congregation that no longer looks like the neighborhood where the church is located. Or perhaps the congregation has changed, and he or she sees a body that looks, thinks, and acts differently from the same congregation even a decade ago. It is not easy for the preacher to describe or define exactly what has happened. The catch-all term is that the church has become "multicultural." What does that mean?

What Is Culture?

One place to begin is by asking the question, What is culture? Definitions vary widely. There are historical, topical, behavioral, and symbolic definitions among many others. Definitions range from the simple to the complex. We can define culture simply as "learned experience," but most definitions are similar to this one: "The system of shared beliefs, values, customs, behaviors and artifacts that the members of a society use to cope with their world and with one another, and that are transmitted from generation to generation through learning."[1] Such definitions involve at least three components: what people think, what they do, and the material products they produce.

Eric H. F. Law's marvelous book *The Wolf Shall Dwell with the Lamb* reminds us that there is both external culture (the part we can see, taste, and hear) and internal culture, which consists of the unconscious beliefs, thought patterns, values, and myths that affect everything we do and see. Most cultural clashes occur on the internal, unconscious level—on the instinctual level where folk are not even aware of why they feel the way they do. Law's perspective suggests we might add what people feel and associate to the three factors of thought, action and products. It also means that culture has different degrees of visibility, so that a congregation that looks the same may still experience "culture wars" and strain with the proverbial six degrees of separation.[2]

In popular thinking today, culture is often associated with race, ethnicity, or geography. For example, we might refer to African American culture, Hispanic American culture, or Southern culture. People who speak of "multicultural preaching" usually refer to preaching in congregations made up of people from more than one racial or ethnic group. However, culture can also be associated with many other phenomena that may cut across racial, ethnic, or geographical designations, or may exist independently of them. For example, we might speak of culture associated with particular economic classes or jobs (such as blue-collar culture or white-collar culture, assembly line culture or management culture). Schools and businesses may have their own cultures. During the middle and late twentieth century, the General Assembly of our denomination, the Christian Church (Disciples of Christ), became a parliamentary culture whose life was centered around making decisions, passing resolutions, and otherwise conducting business in the fashion of Robert's Rules of Order. As the new millennium opens, efforts are underway to transform this culture into one of spiritual discernment. In the broad sense, almost all congregations are multicultural.

Multicultural is a more complicated word than it appears to be. Once associated with a "melting pot" assimilative understanding, it has hardened into what some feel is a new and perhaps unintended segregation. The term *melting pot* has itself disappeared, replaced in turn by *salad bowl,* and then *mosaic,* even *unmeltable ethnicity.* Some scholars suggest that assimilation still occurs in North America, albeit within specific ethnic groups: Anglo, Black, Hispanic, Asian, and Native American. But at the center of secular multicultural America, there is little to unite these groups.[3] Can the church succeed where the secular cultures have failed?

The history of the church has not been remarkable in this regard. Too often the church has treated cultures other than the reigning ones with contempt, operating with a slash-and-burn model. Charlemagne's evangelism, for example, was achieved by driving his vanquished foes through a river at sword point, so baptizing them into Christ.

In James Michener's epic novel *The Source,* he shares a dialogue on this struggle of the church. A Christian, a Muslim, and a Jew are discussing the relative merits and failures of their respective religions when the Jew says:

> The tremendously personal religion that evolved around the figure of Christ was all that He and Paul had envisaged. It was brilliant, penetrating and a path to personal salvation. It was able to construct soaring cathedrals and even more vaulted processes of thought. But it was totally incapable of teaching [people] to live together…The Christian discovers the spirit of God and the reality is so blinding that you go right out, build a cathedral and kill a million people.[4]

Blessedly, there have also been many thousands of dedicated souls who have submerged themselves with respect and affection in cultures other than their own, all for the sake of the gospel. In their doing so, the gospel has not been truncated, but made richer and stronger. One missionary to the Congo said this in 1924:

> I have long wondered whether we are doing right in introducing the white man's style of preaching in Congo. Have you ever watched the faces of the people when a native has been speaking in a palaver? And then contrasted the faces of those who have listened to you when preaching? Here is a test for you. Take a well-educated native who has been taught to preach on white man's lines. Let him preach, and then when he has finished, ask some of the women in the congregation to tell you what he has said. Then do this. At the close of a native palaver, ask any woman to tell you what any individual speaker has said. I think that in the first case you will find they have remembered very little, but in the second they have absorbed it all. Brethren, there is a reason.[5]

When secular society in the United States was dragged—kicking, screaming, and burning crosses in some places—into cross-cultural engagement, the church tended to lag behind. The old statement about 11:00 on Sunday morning being the most segregated hour in the United States is still heard with pain and with the realization that, by and large, it is still true. Early attempts at multiculturalism in the church were often paternalistic and assimilative.

We are still trying to figure out how the relationships among different cultures can best be informed by the gospel and make a gospel witness. In that sense, this chapter is a thought-experiment, a suggestion for process, rather than a prescription.

We believe the salad bowl model holds the greatest contemporary chance for success, because everything and everyone retain their distinctiveness while the different pieces support one another in a kind of community with respect for difference. Minority groups especially have soundly rejected the melting pot. And the mosaic model, forever frozen in place, ignores the ebb and flow of culture and offers little hope for positive change. Is the salad bowl model perfect? No. There is the danger that having been "tossed" into the salad, one may be "eaten" by the system. In several other respects it falls short of the dream of Jesus that we might all be one, even as he was with God. But no human model has reached the rarefied air of perfection. The communistic model of the early church was soon abandoned as impractical, and the "beloved community" of John the Evangelist and Martin Luther King, Jr., has yet to be realized.

There are few places, in fact, where the concerns of multiculturalism have come into more conflict than in communities of faith. Some churches have successfully mediated that conflict; most have not. Successful multicultural churches have strong magnetic and unifying factors that draw and hold large varieties of people together in community, churches in which one can see wealthy patrician bankers sitting comfortably in the same pew with recent immigrant laborers, and where butchers, bakers, and candlestick makers pray together.

The Roman Catholic Church, for example, has its strong enduring tradition.

People in Pentecostal churches are drawn together by experiences of the powerful activity of the Holy Spirit.

The primarily gay and lesbian churches witness for God's unconditional love and against a common oppression.

There are also other mostly nondenominational churches that gather around a powerful, charismatic preacher. The danger there is that such churches can become cults of personality, which do not survive the departure of the leader. Like comets, these churches and preachers often seem to come from nowhere, flame across the sky, and disappear.

Most mainstream Protestant churches have not had the success in becoming intentionally multicultural that the groups just mentioned have had. They lack a binding magnetic factor or, if they have one, it has become less and less a part of their life together, or disagreement has arisen about its meaning.

Many Presbyterians, for example, do not know anything about John Calvin and, if instructed about him and his theology, often do not like him.

A recent new church start among the Disciples of Christ thought about doing away with the Lord's supper, considering it tedious and uninspiring.

Southern Baptists, with their thoroughgoing grounding in scripture, have recently come to shipwreck over just how scripture is to be interpreted.

The exception to this trend seems to be those multicultural churches pastored by African Americans. James Forbes at Riverside Church in New York, Alvin Jackson at National City Christian Church in Washington, D. C., Jeremiah Wright at Trinity United Church of Christ in Chicago, and Cecil Williams at Glide Memorial United Methodist Church in San Francisco are examples. They are all dynamic preachers who preach an inclusive gospel that appeals to people across cultural boundaries. And the churches they serve appear to have an understanding of the gospel that embraces, even insists upon, people of various cultures relating positively in communities of support and witness to the kind of world they believe God wants and the ways that they believe God wants people to live together.

There are few, if any, European American preachers in the same league with those just named. Why is this the case? We can think of only two reasons. First, African American preaching is more appealing to European American people than European American preaching is to African American people. Second, minority persons, including pastors, are more skilled in relating to majority persons than the other way around. As noted church historian Justo González said to Joey: "I have had to deal with you, your language, your culture, your rules. I have had no choice. You, on the other hand, have not had to deal with me."[6]

Some of the issues that come into play in a discussion of multiculturalism have already been considered in other chapters, especially those on generation and worldview. We focus here more specifically on those differences among people engendered by ethnicity and language, realizing, as we shall see shortly, that these external traits of culture may not be as problematic as the internal and invisible ones. Forms and applications in the United States tend to group people as white (European American and others), black (African American and others), Hispanic (a variety of ethnic groups gathered under this linguistic designation), Asian or Pacific Islander (the broadest of all categories), or Native American (often called First Peoples in Canada). While this would be useless in places such as Bosnia, where widely different cultural groups look the same and speak the same language, in North America the differences tend to be somewhat more visible, either through racial-ethnic differences, different languages, or both. And because these differences are so readily apparent, people may be quicker to react to them based on learned prejudices.

In the week before this chapter was written, Joey was called to jury duty and sent into a courtroom with a panel of some fifty other potential jurors. Standing there facing them were four people behind two tables: two European American women and one Hispanic American male, all dressed in very nice business suits, and one young African American male dressed in a sweatshirt and jeans. After we were all seated, the judge welcomed us and said, "You may have already decided which one of the people in front of you is the defendant and asked yourself, 'I wonder what he did.'" The judge was correct in his assumption and correct in reminding us that this is not the way our justice system should work. But still waters run deep.

Resistance to Multiculturalism

The benefits of multiculturalism are manifold:

- It broadens and deepens our own limited and circumscribed experience, as individuals and as community.
- It prepares us for more effective and satisfying living in the real world of the new millennium as we better understand our own culture and better relate to others.
- It moves us toward that time when we shall all gather before the throne of grace to share in the joys of God together.

Multiculturalism nevertheless remains a challenge. The seminary where Joey works developed not long ago a program in globalization, an attempt to help our students experience the church beyond the local congregation, to establish relationships between our work and that of other seminaries in other countries. Joey was feeling good about this when he traveled to India. The first day he was there, at the United Theological College in Bangalore, he went to morning worship, and in the first prayer he heard, the Indian student petitioned God to "deliver us from globalization." Stunned, he soon realized that while globalization for him meant reaching out in friendship, learning from others, and moving beyond isolationism and xenophobia, for some others it meant cultural imperialism. It meant McDonald's hamburger emporiums in Tiananmen Square. It meant arriving at the top of the incredibly beautiful Karola Pass in the Tibetan hinterland and seeing a sign that read "Chicago Bulls are number 1." It meant Asians laboring in sweatshops to produce designer clothes for Americans. It meant thousands of Americans marching at a meeting of the World Trade Organization in Seattle to protest American jobs' being transferred to Asia.

The resistance to multiculturalism is thus lodged at least partly in the fear—no, the reality—that less powerful cultures will be swallowed up by more powerful ones. Half of the world's six thousand languages are expected to disappear in the next century.[7] As languages—and the cultures they bespeak—disappear, the world becomes a less interesting place. It is no surprise that resistance to the growth of global culture is strong. We have seen, for example, an interesting reversal in our approach to language in North America. There used to be a regional piquancy to the way people spoke, until "it fell victim to television's anemic homogenizing of our culture."[8] Now, however, particular ways of speaking, from Ebonics to Tex-Mex to inclusive language (which is not always inclusive), are making a vigorous comeback. And we are becoming more aware of the value of various dialects, such as Gullah and Boontling, which have become more than just curiosities. They tell us something about both their speakers and the rest of us. California has already become a state where a majority of the population are not European Americans, and Spanish is rapidly becoming the predominant language in major areas of the Southwest.

So again, we should recognize and appreciate those cultures different from ours. What, then, is the problem? There are three problems, actually. First, some cultural beliefs and rituals are difficult, if not impossible, to understand. Some of us are unable to understand why certain groups from India have no problem with wife beating and worse. Discussions with Indians have not solved the problem. Even when we speak English, it is as if we are speaking two mutually unintelligible languages and that we are somehow wired in different ways.

The second problem, following upon the first, is that we lack a critical approach to culture. Realizing the positive qualities of multiculturalism can lead to automatic uncritical approval of anything from another, generally non-Western, non-European culture. For example, there exists a deep-seated antipathy toward gays, lesbians, bisexual women and men, and persons who are transgendered, questioning, and asexual in many African and Hispanic subcultures. Rushing to embrace another culture may leave one in an awkward position of embracing values that go against the flow of the gospel. A true Christian multiculturalism would suggest that everyone has to change and that we are in error when we overemphasize our culture of origin to the exclusion of the transcending Christ.[9]

The third problem arises in the passionate defense or rejection of some cultural icon, depending on whether one is inside or outside that culture. One is told that he or she cannot understand a cultural matter, not because it is difficult or complex, but rather because of whom he or she is or is not. As a T-shirt says, "It's a Black [or Anglo, Latino, Asian] Thing. You Wouldn't Understand."[10] This is being written almost one year to the day following the tragedy at Texas A & M University on November 18, 1999, where twelve students were killed in the collapse of the huge bonfire that is part of the tradition of the school. In a sermon not long after the incident, Joey began this way:

> The tragedy at Texas A&M has riveted the attention of everyone I know. People far beyond College Station have been brought to their knees in sadness or anger or both. I cannot claim to understand or appreciate the various Aggie traditions. In fact, Aggies made clear in the aftermath that "If you're outside, you cannot understand; if you're inside, you cannot explain." I accept that. But I can watch and I can reflect. And it seems to me that at least part of the tradition and spirit of the Aggies has to do with being part of something larger than yourself.[11]

This is a good example of the internal culture about which Eric Law speaks, a culture grounded in association and feeling that is difficult both to explain and understand. Contending cultures, sometimes without reflection, ascribe to themselves the moral and intellectual high ground while belittling the other. The bottom line is this. If we are to love one another as Jesus commanded, and if we are to worship together, we must find some way to negotiate our differences and begin the slow and painful process of explaining, understanding, and changing.

Multiculturalism and the Church

Every church is multicultural—some intentionally, others unintentionally.[12] Some churches—generally urban, often small—are established specifically to give witness to a multicultural understanding of the faith. Other churches deny that they are multicultural. Operating on a "we win those most like ourselves" platform, some see their position as one not particularly philosophical, but rather practical, while others are intentionally exclusive for dogmatic reasons. In the former group, for example, are those churches in upscale suburbs that are 98 percent white-collar European American. They did not design their churches to be upper middle-class European American. That is just who walked in when the doors were opened. In the latter group are those who, for whatever reason, equate multiculturalism with sin. In the now-famous prayer offered before the Kansas Legislature in 1995, the Rev. Joe Wright prayed: "We confess, Father, that we have ridiculed the absolute Truth of your Word and called it 'moral pluralism.' We have worshiped other gods and called it 'multiculturalism.'"[13] S. T. Karnick follows this line of thinking when he writes:

> We know what is wrong: the culture. But we do not agree on how to make it right, because we have two radically conflicting notions of what is right. Culturally, there appear to be two, and only two, possible futures before us. One is the traditional, Judeo-Christian conception of society...The alternative today is multiculturalism.[14]

The Ayn Rand Institute's claim that "multiculturalism is racism in a politically-correct guise" exemplifies the extreme of this position.[15]

We deny the truth and even the possibility of all these denials, both practical and dogmatic, and return to our opening sentence: every congregation is multicultural. By this we mean that every congregation, no matter how much its members look "alike" and no matter how rigid its predominant theology, is composed of people who think and act differently, who have at least slightly different worldviews, who understand and use language in different ways. Granted, people tend to think of multicultural churches as multichromatic and/or multilingual, but we are writing to encourage the pastor who feels that she or he serves the most culturally identical congregation in existence to keep reading.

Many books exist on cross-cultural counseling, but there are few on multicultural preaching. It goes without saying that a counselor should take into consideration the worldview and the life experience of the client.[16] The same can be said for the preacher, even in an apparently homogeneous congregation. For example, consider the butcher, baker, and candlestick maker from the nursery rhyme of Mother Goose. They appear to be average, similar folk riding together in the "tub" of culture. One can, however, imagine the butcher and the candlestick maker having very different worldviews. The butcher may well have grown up poor and gotten to a good position and salary through sheer hard work. His take-home pay, however, is shrinking against his expenses. He sometimes wonders sarcastically why he did not become an orthodontist. He also feels increasingly insecure as markets downsize in accordance with cultural shifts. He feels the pressure of animal rights and radical vegetarian groups spearheading a cultural assault against a meat-eating public. He has over the years become politically and theologically conservative. The bumper sticker on his car reads, "I love animals. They are delicious."

The candlestick maker, on the other hand, may be a reconstructed hippie, a refugee from her privileged upbringing who helped shape the counterculture of the 1960s. Having rejected many of the values of her family and class, she views the butcher as no less than a murderer and his work as violent and bloody, killing God's wonderful creatures and stuffing humans with slow-killing fat and chemicals. Her work, by contrast, is about beauty and scent and light, and she has never used tallow in her candles or wood from live trees in her candlesticks. She does not own a car. She does not make much money or need much. She lives and works in a cooperative community. She is a vegan and does not vote, believing the political system too corrupt to be salvaged. She disdains the butcher, and the feeling is mutual. To him, she and her work are irrelevant at best, dangerous to the American zeitgeist at worst. They are both working people who, in times past, might have worked together against the establishment. But not now.

Picture now the poor baker, sympathetic to both yet caught in the middle, trying to hold them and the church together, the church where the three of them have just been elected as deacons.

You are their pastor. What can you say that will help these three people given into your care?[17] Ignore their experience and their worldview—and they will ignore the sermon.

Suggestions for Preaching

Whenever a congregation decides to engage multiculturalism intentionally or becomes aware of its unintentional engagement, problems and possibilities arise that the preacher can engage homiletically.[18] As we look at preaching from the perspective of culture, our suggestions fall into four categories:

1. The Preacher Teaches the Congregation about Its Multiple Cultures

If culture is "learned experience," then the role of preacher as teacher is critical. In his book *Creative Disarray,* Ronald Osborn surveys the twelve models of ministry that have functioned in the four centuries of the American experience (saint, priest, master, awakener, pulpiteer, revivalist, builder, missionary, manager, counselor, impresario, and teacher). He has made clear to Joey that the one he most expects to endure is teacher.[19] And how does this teaching preacher function?

> The mode of the Christian Teacher today differs radically not only from the authoritarianism of the New England Master but also from the persuasiveness of the nineteenth-century Pulpiteer. In a "world come of age," many persons resist persuasion by another; they want to find out for themselves. Rather than coming on as a glamorous partisan to argue a case, the Teacher adapts to the new situation by playing the role of the *discoverer,* the one who humbly guides us in uncovering a truth so that we "find" it for ourselves...Today's preacher teaches "as one without authority," raising questions, pointing to possibilities, hinting with stories, letting the hearer make the find—which no one else may really make for another.[20]

Even though preaching is not best seen as one knowledgeable person giving the answers to the assembled flock, Osborn still argues that the goal is the attainment of truth. Lucy Rose agrees with Osborn in rejecting both authoritarianism and persuasiveness as models for preaching. But she goes a step farther when she says:

> Contemporary insight into the limitations of language and realizations that old formulations of truth or the Word have excluded many people from the formative theological and homiletical conversations have convinced me that no "truth" is objective, absolute, ontological, or archetypal. The only way I can speak of "truth" is eschatologically.[21]

She goes on to say:

What is preaching all about if its goal is not the transmission of truth, an encounter with God, or congregational transformation? Preaching's aim is week after week to gather the community of faith around the Word in order to refocus its central conversations.[22]

The preacher seeks to promote the refocusing process by offering "proposals" that create space for genuine conversation and invite counterproposals.[23]

In the matters we have before us, such proposals might include the presentation of multiculturalism as fact, the naming of the different cultures present, and an offer of ways to help members of different cultures to understand one another, seeking to celebrate different cultures but also to name the differences and talk about them.

Consider this example. Some visitors show up at church. Their English is heavily accented, and their manners are different. Some members of the resident congregation avoid the strangers. Others want to reach out, but do not know how to go about it. In the next Sunday's sermon, the preacher tells the following true story. Some lunch money was stolen in a New Haven elementary school. Six children had access to the money, and they are shuffled off to the principal's office. As the principal addresses the children, he notices that one little girl will not look at him, but looks down at the floor. Assuming this to be evidence of guilt, he punishes her for the theft. Later, the principal learns that another child confessed to the theft and that the girl he "convicted" was raised in a culture where children do not look adults in the eye, but demurely lower their heads when addressed. Are her cultural "rules" wrong? Not necessarily. Would it make a difference if we took the time to understand her rules? Absolutely. How could we go about that? In telling this story, the preacher invites people to take some initial steps toward something very important that is present here and now.

The old hymn reminds us that "other hearts in other lands are beating with hopes and dreams as true and high as mine."[24] These other hearts are now not only in other lands; they are in the next pew. And the more we learn about one another, the more we discover that we are more alike than unalike and the more valuable our conversations become.

2. The Preacher Reflects Critically and Theologically on Culture

If culture is "how and what we think," then culture affects the doctrines and beliefs that provide the basis on which people hear sermons. Theology also affects (and should criticize) culture. The relationship is dialectical. Culture, especially as experienced in encounters with the other from different cultures, can help us see the arbitrariness and ethnocentrism of some of our theological statements. Good theology also helps us see the relativity and self-service of every culture. The preacher is constantly helping the congregation negotiate this spectrum. On the one hand, we need to learn from other cultures how they can help broaden our view of God and of what God is doing in the world. On the other hand, theology cautions us from absolutizing, even making idols of, our cultural mores, assumptions, and practices. This situation raises some difficult questions, such as how does a preacher from one culture suggest that qualities of another culture go against God's will? Here the conversational model is helpful, as opposed to a model of pronouncing prophetic judgment. But it is still a delicate matter to be handled with care.

How can a preacher speak so that persons across both small and large cultural divides are confronted with the promises and demands of the one gospel? The operative fear that accompanies this question is that in order not to be either incomprehensible or offensive to particular groups, we are reduced to a lowest common denominator gospel, one capable of providing neither change nor salvation. One might even say that the gospel is, by its very nature, offensive, "a stumbling block to Jews and foolishness to Gentiles" (1 Cor. 1:23). One remembers Fred Craddock's warning about preachers who, attempting to boil down a text or theme to manageable size, boil all the juice out of the message and end up preaching the stain in the bottom of the pot.[25]

Lawrence Hoffman has ably presented the other side of this question in his discussion of interreligious or common worship. He speaks of "prayers that hurt,"[26] prayers that exclude, for example, women or African Americans or Jews from the blessings of God. We might say the same thing about "sermons that hurt," not by prophetic judgment, but by exclusion. Hoffman suggests that people gathered in common worship have a marvelous opportunity for much more than watered-down lowest common denominator ersatz worship:

> To stand before God, united in our opposition to injustice and violence, committed to rescuing the planet from despoliation,

and joined in remembering victims of violence whose blood cries out to us all from the earth, is surely no light thing. Avoiding prayers that hurt creates a service of the highest (not the lowest) common denominator: and that is something indeed.[27]

Does Hoffman's approach to interreligious worship also speak to multicultural Christian worship? Kathy Black thinks so. She suggests that meaningful multicultural worship emerges from a process of sensitive negotiation among the various cultures that gather for worship.[28] Two problems remain. Negotiating prayers and other liturgical acts may be easier than negotiating sermons. Further, Black did a study that focused on intentionally multiethnic congregations. We want our study also to engage those mainline churches whose congregations look "alike" and who would not believe themselves to be multicultural.

Here are four suggestions about "negotiating sermons" in multicultural situations. First, one of the casualties of contemporary ministry is the "just visiting" pastoral call. We may make an initial call in a new pastorate and then call on prospects and new members. But otherwise, time, energy, and necessity limit calls to hospital and crisis situations. The multi-job family means few people may be at home during the day, and many do not want to be bothered in the evenings. However, short prearranged visits at home and work can be very rewarding, for pastor and people. Most people enjoy having you see where they work and what they do if your visit is brief and does not interrupt business. Furthermore, in home visits, seeing how the living space is arranged and how family members relate to one another can tell you much about their cultural values. Such home and work visits also tell you a great deal about how your sermons are going to be heard and processed and may suggest themes, texts, and methods.

Second, preachers need to be more proactive in generating feedback from sermons. Most preachers tire of the "enjoyed your talk" responses while shaking hands at the back of the church after service, but they fear inviting more reflective feedback because of the criticism that could arise. Other preachers can even anticipate the criticism that might emerge, but do not want to make the effort to deal with it. After we have established our methods of sermon preparation and delivery, and after we have grown comfortable with a theological model, we are loathe to examine them, not to mention change them. Nevertheless, sermon feedback can rejuvenate our preaching, and we should welcome it.

Third, while it is difficult to describe good preaching, one factor is a constant. Good preachers read and protect time for reading on a variety of levels. George Hamilton Combs, a noted preacher in the first half of the twentieth century, wrote in his autobiography: "It may be said that 'much study is a weariness of the flesh' and that 'of making of books there is no end.' Even so; but better that the preacher be weary than those who listen to him, and while to bookmaking there is no end, there is certainly a quick end to the preacher who doesn't read books."[29] As traveling preachers, we frequently are ushered into the pastor's study before church while the pastor attends to Sunday morning details. One of the sad sidelights to that experience is that we can almost always tell from a quick perusal of the pastor's library precisely when he or she graduated from seminary. How? Because that is when the books stop. Help from some of America's best preachers and homileticians on building a good preacher's library may be found in *Best Advice for Preaching*, edited by John McClure.[30]

Another useful approach is to ask Brian Wren's question, "What language shall we borrow?"[31] And when language that is comfortable is language that hurts, we suggest that it give way to new ways of speaking and understanding. As Hoffman says,

> There are those who object in principle to common worship. They find it inauthentic, trivial, or worse. Casting around for a biblical image, they charge worshipers in common with uttering pure Babel...I, on the other hand, prefer as my text, Exodus 12:38. When the Israelites left Egypt, "a mixed multitude also went up with them" (RSV). Surely the exodus is the way to freedom, a road we travel still. And we...are the "mixed multitude."[32]

Hoffman's "mixed multitude" is a good response to those who fear the "Babelization" of society. Preachers must become multilingual if they want to be heard in multicultural churches. This may mean making the effort to become at least minimally conversant in the "languages" of those in the parish: youth, Hispanics, African Americans. People can speak English, for example, and not understand one another. Joey's sojourn in French West Africa, where he picked up not the language of the Sorbonne but bush French, left him better able to understand the French spoken in Niger than the English spoken in parts of Nigeria. It was a matter both of dialect and of metaphor.

We live in a world of languages. We function fairly well jumping from one world to another in secular conversation: "Ciao, amigo. Whassup? Not much." But when we move to religious language, the problems multiply. First, we may find ourselves using archaic or outdated language that has lost its meaning for most people today. One scholar spoke of his experience leading a conference at a fundamentalist school. The faculty members there were well-trained scholars, up-to-the-minute in their academic disciplines. But when they switched into religious language, they were suddenly in the middle of the nineteenth century. Words such as justification and psychopannichism are of little innate interest to most of today's people, important and natural as they are to a scholar. If a preacher needs to use such language, the preacher needs to explain and vivify it.

Furthermore, we may find that meanings often shift between languages and/or generations. Joey will never forget serving as a chaperone at a teenage dance during his first pastorate. One girl asked him if his fiancée was "cool." He replied, "Oh, yes, she is very cool." The teenager was impressed. It was not until much later that he learned that what he had really been asked was whether or not his fiancée smoked dope. Some of the most powerful and painful examples of this problem with religious language occur in Barbara Kingsolver's brilliant novel *The Poisonwood Bible,* which tells the story of a hard-shell missionary who takes his wife and four daughters to the Congo. He had little use for or facility in Kikongo, the indigenous language, and consequently butchered it almost every time he used it, making his theology sound ridiculous and offending his hearers at the same time. One of his daughters makes the following observation:

> It is a special kind of person who will draw together a congregation, stand up before them with a proud, clear voice, and say words wrong week after week. *Bandika,* for example: to kill someone. If you spit it out too quickly, as the Reverend does, it means to pinch back a plant or deflower a virgin. What a surprise it must be to the Congolese to hear that brave David, who intended to slay the mighty Goliath, was actually jumping around pinching back plants, or worse.
>
> Then there is *batiza.* Our father's fixed passion. *Batiza* pronounced with the tongue curled just so means *baptism.* Otherwise it means "to terrify"…
>
> "*Tata Jesus is bangala!*" declares the Reverend every Sunday at the end of his sermon. *Bangala* means something precious and dear. But the way he pronounces it, it means the poisonwood tree [a deadly plant].[33]

Saying words wrong is not just the province of chauvinistic missionaries. It happens in church every week. When all the language and imagery of a sermon are masculine, many women have trouble connecting; when the concerns of "family" are always at the speaking center, single persons can become discouraged; when everything about the church—preacher, people, culture, worship—are old, young people can quickly tune out and, as soon as they can, go out. The preacher must learn to use the concepts of the people who are present for the sermon.

Preaching effectively to the "mixed multitude" also requires preachers to deal creatively and gently with James Fowler's assertion that "truth is multiform and complex and must in its richness, ambiguity and multi-dimensionality be approached from at least two or more angles of vision simultaneously."[34] One thinks of the question, "What is the next letter in the series A-B-C-D-E-F-G?" Most people would say, "H." But musicians might well say, "A." There is often more than one way to look at things, and in a multicultural setting, these ways may or may not be vividly apparent. Different approaches to theology, music, the degree of emotion appropriate to worship, and so forth are evident and often seen as competing with one another for primacy. When it comes to preaching, some people have never listened to evangelistic, soul-winning kind of preaching, while, for others, there is no other kind of preaching.

If the congregation is going to survive as a multicultural community, such matters must be negotiated. This certainly does not mean that anything goes. Nor does it mean that we must accept a lowest common denominator approach to being church. What it most likely will mean is that out of these negotiations new understandings will arise, different from any of those with which we began. These new understandings will lead to different approaches to worship and other aspects of our life together. The result is "a new kind of Christian identity," one that grows specifically out of the engagement of the local context with gospel traditions.[35]

How can the preacher accomplish this without preaching either a watered-down gospel or one unintelligible to many of her or his people? Fred Craddock once described preaching as "looking up at a snow-capped peak called the text, while running around the bottom trying to get a better look."[36] Taking this approach a step farther, we might suggest preaching from more than one of the cultural vistas on that run. Thus, the preacher says, "From here we can see this, but if we move around to this side, we have a different perspective, a different view." One is not necessarily right and the other wrong. In fact, inviting people to look at a text or theme from a perspective new to them may be energizing. We know of no better example than the story of the prodigal son. From whose perspective do we preach: the son's? the father's? the elder brother's? the fatted calf's? It makes a difference. It also makes a difference when one preaches this text to those whose family structures are strong, those whose family structures are weak, and those whose family structures have collapsed.

Perichoretic Preaching

One useful way to describe this suggestion is to borrow a word from the ancient church by way of George Cladis. He tells us that John of Damascus, writing in the seventh century C.E., described the relationship between the three persons of the Trinity as "perichoresis," which is a kind of circle dance in which the persons move around the circle in a way that implies intimacy, equality, unity yet distinction, and love.[37] Perichoretic preaching could function in two ways. First, it could invite a variety of people to be involved in the dialogue leading to the sermon.[38] Second, the sermon might move around the theme or text, stopping to provide views from various perspectives. The preacher might look at the subject of the sermon from the perspectives of different cultures in the congregation. Even should the preacher end up sharing her or his preference for a particular view, others will feel that their perspectives have been taken seriously and not ignored.

There are some nonnegotiable issues, but not as many as some want to make out. One new multicultural church start adopted this position: "Jesus is the Christ, and everything else is up for grabs." Well, that is a beginning. Even such seemingly irreconcilable issues as abortion have some common ground. Most people can agree on the need for fewer abortions and can hope together toward a time when no one becomes pregnant who does not want to. When the preacher and/or people see one viewpoint as right and the other wrong, or at least not mutually able to inhabit the same space, then two options remain. The issue can be put into that box labeled "awaiting more light" and left for a while to mellow, or people can see how far the envelope can creatively be pushed toward a resolution without congregational rupture. There are very, very few issues that require people to take leave from one another. The vast majority of congregational schisms have occurred over petty, insubstantial issues. And that in itself is wrong.

There is more to perichoretic preaching than perspective for perspective's sake. It can give insight into the one who preaches and those who listen. In a playback session after a sermon, a professor said to a student from India, "You kept dancing around the subject. Why didn't you just come out and say what you meant?" The student smiled and said, "That's not our way. You Americans are so brash and blunt in the way you say things. You go straight to the point without giving people time to prepare themselves for it. You think it's 'getting to the heart of the matter.' We think it's rude."

Before leaving this concern, we need to reaffirm that the negotiation that leads to a new Christian identity will not be achieved without considerable pain. People tend not to respond well when that with which they are familiar and comfortable is taken from them. Joey's father bought a baseball glove for him when he was twelve. It was a MacGregor, Willie Mays model, and it was beautiful—a leathery tan color that weathered to a beautiful golden brown. That glove and Joey made a lot of miles— and catches—together, through Little League, PONY League, high school, college intramurals, and then, with the pocket retrofitted for softball, many a church league game. They caught a lot of flies and dug out a lot of grounders. Whenever Joey came back from Africa or New York or someplace else, the glove was always there, like a puppy, ready to play. Every time he slipped his hand into it after a long absence, there was a momentary burst of surprise and joy. It felt good. It fit him, well, like a glove. Later, in his athletic dotage, he used it mostly to play catch with his son.

One day Joey and his son were playing in the yard when Joey was called to the phone. He laid the glove on the bumper of his pickup truck. The call was a minor emergency. He ran out, hopped in the truck, and drove off. Hours later, he remembered the glove, and ran back to the truck. Of course it was gone. He tried everything: traced his route several times, talked with neighbors, placed an ad in the paper offering a reward, but he never saw it again. A friend of thirty years, lost in a moment's forgetfulness.

Finally, resigned to its loss, he began to search for another one. Of course he wanted one just like the old one. He tried on dozens. But his search was unsuccessful. Gloves are different now: bigger, elongated, awkward, and very expensive. As Joey returned discouraged from one of his trips to various sporting goods stores, his son, missing their baseball time together, asked if he had had any luck. He shook his head and walked on, but heard his wife say to their son, "And he won't find it, because he's looking for something that no longer exists." She was right. The next day he went out and bought a glove on sale that was as different from his old glove as it could be: a big, black, intimidating Wilson, Tommy John model. It is a great glove. He will never forget the old one, but the new one will take care of him and his remaining baseball days quite well.

Multiply this loss a thousandfold and you have some sense of the pain, frustration, and anger people feel when a loss hits them at the level of their faith, that which they have believed and lived by, sometimes for many years. The hope here may be found in what Robert Bellah calls the

> faith of loss—a relinquishing of some familiar, understandable, and previously treasured knowledge or meanings or assumptions, and a discovery that the world does not then fall apart but is somehow even more deeply meaningful than it was before.[39]

When changes are made in worship and preaching to invite more people to the speaking and listening center of the church, the preacher has three responsibilities to those who are forced to endure unwanted change: (1) reassurance that they and their beliefs are important to the preacher and the church, (2) demonstration that the emerging new identity of the church will be good for everyone, including them, and (3) finding places where they and their gifts can be creatively involved in the life of the "new" church. Otherwise, they will leave.

In the same way that various models of perichoretic preaching can keep the preaching ministry fresh and interesting to both preacher and different listening groups, attention to the "faith of loss" in preaching can help to assure that no one gets left behind when the new train leaves the old station. To use another metaphor, Jesus said one does not put new wine into old wineskins, or the wineskins will burst (Mt. 9:17). A parishioner came to Joey once when the church was contemplating a change in worship and expressed his position laconically: "I'm just an old wineskin." Well, we do not wish to contradict Jesus, nor are we oenologists, but we suspect his saying referred to completely refilling an old wineskin (probably poorly cured) with new wine. We doubt that adding a little new wine to an old wineskin would result in catastrophe. Similarly, a complete turnover of change in church could overwhelm a "faith of loss" position that a more moderate pace might engender. The "mixed multitude" of the congregation does not always sprint together toward the promised land. Sometimes the congregation seems a ragtag quibbling bunch bent on self-destruction. But, as Leslie Weatherhead said a generation ago, "The Church often stumbles, often errs, often does silly and even sinful things. The only thing it can't do is fail."[40] If the church is of God, it ultimately cannot fail.

3. The Preacher Helps the Congregation toward Multicultural Worship

If culture involves not only what we think but also "what we do," then culture affects liturgy, the way we do our worship and preaching.[41] In one seminary African American students lobbied to have a piano brought into the chapel so that they could worship with the music that was most meaningful to them. The school organist argued against it. When told that the African American students' music was more congenial to the piano than the organ, the organist said, "Then we need to teach them to appreciate sacred music." That was a painful moment for everyone. It did, however, help us to realize that all of us, especially those who are a part of majority cultures, tend to have rather narrow, tightly circumscribed views of reality that do not easily admit other views. We believe our definition of "sacred," for example, to be normative, when it is not. What it does represent is assimilation at its starkest.

One phrase appears in almost every religious advertisement, be it radio TV or print media: "Join us." This seemingly innocuous phrase may, for some, have a poison pill in it. "Join us" can mean "join us in our shared journey toward God." It can also mean, "join our cultural understanding of the shape and route of that journey and become like us." It then becomes something most of us dearly wish to avoid but finally cannot: an issue of power.

Eric H. F. Law provides us with an approach to this problem, one that is modeled after Pentecost. He suggests that Pentecost has always been interpreted as a miracle of the tongue ("they were all filled with the Holy Spirit and began to speak in other tongues" [Acts 2: 4, RSV]), when it is at least as much a miracle of the ear ("each one heard them speaking in his own language" [Acts 2:6, RSV]).[42] Law proposes that the miracle of the tongue was for the powerless, bringing them, in the language of this book, into the speaking center. Conversely, the miracle of the ear was for the powerful, to help them listen and understand. Both miracles were required to make the Pentecost experience complete:

> This implies a bridge-building strategy that requires two different approaches from the different cultural banks. On the one end,

the church needs to teach the white middle and upper class to listen…On the other end, the church needs to encourage people of color to gather in communities of their choosing. In these communities of faith, they are encouraged to find their own identity and strength…Then, the church needs to give them a platform to address the whole church.[43]

This "Pentecostal" approach to worship marries well with Hoffman's idea of the worshiping community as a "mixed multitude." The mix of voices and ears cannot be ignored by the preacher. It is one thing to bring various people to the speaking center. It is another to train ears to hear them.

People do not want to have their cultural realities challenged. But Law reminds us that Jesus calls us to do just that, to go against our instincts. "Take up your cross and follow me." Who wants to do that? Those who are serious about following Jesus.

Speak, preacher. Listen, people. Speak, people. Listen, preacher.

Look at how this works with one text, Mark 5:24b–34, Jesus' healing of the woman suffering from a perpetual hemorrhage. Joey's history with this text had been academic. He avoided it when he could. When he could not, he had always preached it from a certain distance, having no real grasp of the woman's situation. Then one day a friend spoke to him of her recent hysterectomy and the physical and cultural suffering that had led up to it. Men have always considered menstruation a kind of pollution, she said. It was a "woman" thing and not for public discussion. My menstrual period, she said, was never-ending. I was bleeding to death and I could not even talk about it! Joey's conversation with this woman was followed by a conversation with a pastor of a mostly gay and lesbian congregation. The pastor recounted how, at a recent Bible study, they had been looking at this text when one of the members said softly, "This was a *blood* disease." The conversation stopped as everyone pondered the text from a new and contemporary perspective. This text is now more vivid to Joey than ever before and not because of any achievement on his part, but rather from listening to people whose experience has been different from his.

4. The Preacher Leads the Congregation into Multicultural Mission

We come now to the last of the four aspects of culture: "what we make." Anthropologists use this to refer to the tools and artifacts of a culture. We could certainly consider church architecture under this rubric, but that is not our primary concern in this book. Of course, architecture does affect preaching, but others will have to write that story, save two brief suggestions below. Our concern is for the goals or hoped-for products of preaching. Phrased another way, what is it that the church "makes"? We begin our answer by saying: a community. What kind of community? That beloved community that seeks to represent, as best it can, the eschatological community we find in the book of Revelation, the gathered "saints from every tribe and language and people and nation" (5:9), one community in all its particularity.

Then, reducing the particularity to a personal level, the church "makes" servants of God who are part of something larger than themselves. Jesus tells a story about a young man who thought that getting was better than giving. So he said to his father, "Give me my share of the property." But though he got what he asked for, the end of his adventure was hunger and loneliness and a place among the swine. So he went home and said, "Father, I have sinned against heaven and against you. I am no longer worthy to be called your son. Make me as one of your hired servants." His first request, the one that led him to the pigsty, was "give me." His last request was "make me" a part of a community. This request brought him a ring for his hand and shoes for his feet.[44] But more importantly, it brought him grace and peace.

There are multiple lessons from this parable. The vast majority of people are communitarian in nature. They cannot thrive apart from others. Alone, they can sink into loneliness and depression. So getting together in communities, especially communities of faith, is a good thing. The only problem is that getting together for community's sake, for the sake of getting together, rarely lasts. For there is also a fractious side to our nature, which eventually drives us apart if there is not a strong reason to stay. That reason is mission. We come together and stay together in order that we might do something together that we cannot do alone. Community is a by-product of mission rather than the other way around.

Churches cannot do everything on the mission front. Those who try are doomed to ineffectiveness. One creative response is for a congregation to be generous givers to the denominational outreach program to help with the abundance of missional causes and then choose one cause, need, or mission in which members will intensely invest themselves, personally and congregationally. There will need to be substantial agreement about this choice or call. Those not engaged by it may feel left behind and leave. Here are two examples of churches' taking on a local mission:

- a rural Presbyterian congregation who decided that no person in its county would go hungry
- the Madison Avenue Christian Church (Disciples of Christ) in Covington, Kentucky, which took upon itself a special ministry to the mentally handicapped in its community

How can the preacher in the multicultural church help the congregation that is unclear about its mission? Here are some suggestions.

First, he or she can preach on issues that matter in multicultural settings. For example, Jung Young Lee mentions five feelings of Jesus that are very much present in our world today, especially among marginalized people: rejection, humiliation, alienation, loneliness, and nothingness. Lee then encourages us to help transform these into feelings of acceptance, humility, and the "allness" one finds in God.[45] Preachers take note. Lee is here speaking of Law's internal forms of culture. He also has interesting suggestions about external forms:

The essence of a marginal God is suffering love, symbolized by the cross. We are bearers of the cross: centralist people bear a beautiful cross, while marginal people bear a rugged cross. The centralist Christ wears a crown of gold, while the marginal Christ wears a crown of thorns.[46]

In solidarity with the marginalized in her or his congregation, the preacher might make gentle suggestions about the accoutrements of worship. Would Jesus really use gold communion ware? What are some options? Let those who have them share what serve as chalice and paten in their culture. Similarly, Michael Mata writes the following:

The environment of a "truly" multiethnic congregation affirms the diversity of the congregation. For example, room décor. Signage, bulletin boards, etc. would reveal a diverse congregation even if you didn't see the people.[47]

Then the preacher might make proposals concerning an approach to determining a missional focus for the congregation, one that would involve as many people as possible.

William Sloan Coffin once said, "It is pointless to expect a suburban church to act like an inner-city congregation,"[48] Telling such a congregation to sell its beautiful building, give the proceeds to the poor, and meet in homes and storefronts for worship may be profoundly Christian. But we suspect the result would be the termination of the pastor and hardened resistance of the church to any future suggestions about radical mission activity. The pastor should give his or her people the best chance possible to be God's servants as faithfully as they can. To demand that they do what they will not do may allow the preacher to go down in flames with her or his Christian purity intact, but it will not help staff a work camp in Honduras, stock a food pantry, provide a safe place for young people to gather on Saturday night, organize English and Spanish courses, find ways to help homebound folk feel more a part of the life of the church, and more things that the people might do if motivated.

While multicultural preaching can be quite challenging, it can also be energizing as preachers help communities. To be sure, preaching in multicultural communities (and preaching to help communities become multicultural) can involve significant risk. Nevertheless, such preaching can help congregations embody the multicultural reality of the reign of God. Multicultural preachers will seek to do the following:

- facilitate the central conversations of the church around issues of multiculturalism by naming these issues in sermons
- help the congregation find its new identity while honoring and affirming the inevitable "faith of loss" that will occur in transition as a congregation ceases thinking of itself as one culture and recognizes its multiculturality
- listen to the people to whom they preach to honor their fears and to help them envision the gospel qualities of a multicultural church and world
- be sensitive to "saying words wrong" and preaching "sermons that hurt"
- move beyond the "one size fits all" sermon toward perichoretic models that will engage texts and themes from more than one perspective
- keep the mission of the church outward into the multicultural world for which Christ died

6

Preaching and the Least of These

Picture a preacher we will call Jim. While climbing into the pulpit one Sunday morning, his eyes are drawn to five people, perhaps because they are all sitting on the back row. One is a woman who has been one of the stalwarts of the congregation for years. She is now descending into Alzheimer's. Her smile is no doubt sincere, but her eyes are vacant, and Jim knows she will understand little if anything of what he says. Her husband, sitting beside her, looks tired. Folks in the church have been loving and helpful, but mostly they are sad about her and concerned about him.

Sitting not far from them is a man Jim has never seen before. His clothes are frayed, but he is not unkempt. Has he been too long down on his luck or too long out on the road or both? Jim wonders what kind of need or memory has brought him here today. What value, if any, will the sermon have for him today? Will he get to talk with the man after church? What will he say? Will the stranger ask him for money? What will he say in response? Will he invite the man back? Or will the man be gone before Jim can get to him, never to be seen again? Probably.

The fourth is a tiny white-haired widow who is always there, but rarely has more than two words to say to him. Jim visited her—once—but they did not have much to talk about, and he has not found his way back. She is a member, he thinks, but she has never made a pledge in the stewardship campaigns or attended any church functions other than worship. She just puts her dollar in the plate as she always has and keeps coming to church as she always has. What will she think of the sermon?

The fifth person is a ten-year-old boy, sitting with two friends on the back row, where ten-year-olds congregate—too old for children's church, too young to defy parents and skip church altogether. Many of the children who sit through his sermons pay Jim scant mind. But this boy frequently looks at him. What is he thinking, Jim wonders. And how is the sermon, couched in adult rhetoric, useful to him, if at all?

Jim remembers how some homiletician had told him years before that he should prepare his sermons with a specific person in mind. Well, he never had any of these people in mind when he prepared his sermons. He prepared his words for the movers and shakers, for the biblically literate, for the theologically inquisitive. He prepared them for various listening groups in the church: the women, the men, the liberals, the conservatives, and so on. But he did not prepare them for these five people and others like them, those who live—often alone—on the margins of the congregation or beyond them. They are "the least of these." Looking around, he sees that there are others in the congregation like them, and he does not know what to say to them.

We have suggested, with Clement, that homiletically "we need a variety of baits, owing to the variety of fish." No one homiletical style or method best (p)reaches (to) everyone. In this chapter our concern is how the good news can be heard by those who, for one reason or another, are unfamiliar with the foundation on which the Christian enterprise and Christian preaching stand; those who were familiar with it but have lost the ability to reflect on it; and those who are both familiar and reflective, but who have been consigned to the silent margins of the church. We will consider the following persons and groups: the stranger, that generally silent minority composed of children and older adults, the poor, and those who are physically or mentally disabled.[1]

The Stranger

"I was a stranger and you welcomed me" (Mt. 25:35). The idea of the stranger and the appropriate Christian response to that stranger is deeply embedded within our faith, so deeply that we often ignore it. Jesus himself, in Albert Schweitzer's words, "came to us as one unknown, without a name."[2] And Christians have often affirmed that "God comes to us in the guise of the stranger."[3]

However, our response to the stranger is often, at best, ambivalent. *Hostel* and *hostile* have the same Latin root. And while we exhort folk, with Paul, to "extend hospitality to strangers" (Rom. 12:13), we also instruct our children to "never talk to strangers." William Shea has written that the stranger has always been a focus of the tribe, "which takes the stranger to be at once a threat and a promise, both fascinating and fearful."[4] The Christian tribe is seldom different. That unknown person sitting in the pew is both threat and promise for the congregation: future board president or rabble-rouser or both? This one who is unknown is also fascinating and fearful for the preacher. How will this one hear what I say? Will the message be helpful or not?

On any given Sunday preachers look out at a number of strangers and pilgrims, people they do not know. These include a variety of visitors and perhaps inactive members who have been to church so rarely (or not at all) that preachers draw a blank when they look at them. The visitors may be friends or relatives of people in the church, other folk shopping for a church home, or simply drop-ins, people who saw the church when driving or walking by and decided to go in.

The members of the congregation will quickly size up visitors based on looks, clothing, demeanor, voice, and so forth. Are they possible candidates for membership in the church or those that, while we will be Christianly polite to them, we frankly hope we shall not see again? People in many churches will say that they want "new blood" in the church when what they really want is "fresh blood," people like them to do the work of ministry so they can rest on their laurels. Some churches, especially those downtown in great urban centers and those in resort and vacation areas, may well have more visitors on a given Sunday than members. So how does one preach to those one does not know?

The authors of this book are professors who have not been pastors for a long time. They do most of their preaching as guests, which means they have become traveling preachers. The vocation of traveling preacher is one they take seriously.[5] There are both benefits and drawbacks to the vocation. Traveling preachers often find themselves up against a set of expectations they had not foreseen. The people were expecting a different kind of preacher or sermons on a different theme. Sometimes one travels to another town and church thinking the task is to preach only to find something else bubbling under the surface. There lies the real need: the pastor and people are at odds with one another, and they need someone from outside with whom they can talk. Living in airports and strange pulpits can become very tiring. There are benefits, of course. People almost always treat their guests with genuine kindness. Furthermore, sometimes a word from outside can be heard in a way that a familiar word cannot. And finally, if the sermon or sermons go badly, one can always get back on the airplane and go home to plan the next trip. So it is that we feel a deep sadness for the lament of the great preacher W. E. Sangster, "I am a traveling preacher unable, by reason of sickness, either to travel or preach."[6]

The largest problem for the traveling preacher is neither fatigue nor criticism. It is standing before a group of people whom you do not know. One does not know their backgrounds, their journeys in faith, their needs, what they expect from and how they hear preaching. This can lead to misreading, not only of texts, but also of people and occasion. So how do traveling preachers preach? As best they can. Most understand that within the widely varying interpretations of the good news are core questions and affirmations that engage people on a primal level. Further, most realize that sermons must not just sit there, but move, must not just be heard, but also seen. So they try to craft their sermons so that people can see what they mean and make the journey of the sermon with the preacher. Furthermore, most traveling preachers take steps to get to know, at least on a surface level, those for whom they will be preaching. Some work is done in advance, with telephone, e-mail, or letter communication with the pastor or other host. Traveling preachers look forward to meals with church people and to visiting with them on Sunday mornings in church school classes, in the halls, or in the sanctuary. We have never much cared for the sort of grand entrance into worship that many pastors like, where they process into the sanctuary like Miss America. We often walk into the sanctuary before worship to visit with people. The pre-service handshakes and greetings are just as important, if not more so, than those that come after the service.

What traveling preachers have learned may also be of help to parish pastors. A few minutes in the sanctuary before worship gives you the chance to meet people you may not know and learn things that will help you communicate better with them during and after worship. A chance remark about loneliness may lead the pastor, within the parameters of prayer or sermon, to mention that "some of us may be feeling lonely this morning" before sharing good news about the presence of God and the community of faith. Another suggestion: when there are strangers in worship, the preacher can make an attempt to visually include them within the world of the sermon. Looks that linger tend to help people realize that you know they are there, that you care about them, and that this message and the good news it brings are for them.

When we look at the sermon itself in relation to the stranger among us, there are several things to say. First, consider that the preaching event is a compound of text, Spirit, sermon, preacher, audience, occasion, and other factors. We do not have control over all or even most of these factors. And we cannot prepare the message for those we do not know who may or may not come to worship.

Or can we?

We hope our people will grow in faith and in their knowledge of the Christian story. But in a postmodern world we can no longer assume a level of knowledge when we preach. So accessibility to the message is an important issue, both for regular attendees and strangers. This is not a matter of "dumbing down" the message. It is, rather, working to make sure that the message is clear, vivid, and compelling; that the language and imagery are accessible; and that the theological affirmations are concrete and useful.

Second, Calvin once said that the pastor is responsible for the eternal souls of everyone given into the pastor's care. That is an exceedingly intimidating affirmation. And it has come back to us on those occasions when, for whatever reason, we preached a really lousy sermon, then had a parishioner who had been in church that Sunday die the following week, and finally we had to shake our head and lament the message we gave the deceased to take before the throne of grace. God have mercy!

Fortunately, God does, and we may have been too hard on ourselves. But the presence of the stranger does serve to remind us of the singularity and the immediacy of the sermon. Any given sermon may in fact be the last sermon someone will ever hear or, for that matter, that we will ever preach! Certainly it may be the only (or last sermon) some people will ever hear us preach. Preach a series? Sure, but remember that each sermon must stand on its own with its own timely word. For many of the listeners, it will be the only one of the series that they will hear.

Many preachers have one or more questions they ask themselves after they have prepared their sermons, questions such as *So what?* Perhaps it would be useful to us, to our regular folk, and to the stranger to ask, *If this is the last or only sermon someone is to hear, will that be all right?* If the stranger returns, perhaps even becomes part of the congregation, so much the better. But if we never see the stranger again, perhaps the word we sent with him or her will be of use in the journey.

A caveat here: What we have just said does not imply that each sermon should contain everything the preacher knows about the Christian faith. When theological students preach in chapel, generally only once in their seminary careers, one of the temptations they must struggle with is that of trying to say everything instead of saying one thing. There is a difference between bringing a complete load to your hearers, which is desirable, and bringing the whole load, which is not.

Next, we need to remember that strangers are not all cut from the same cloth. Some are travelers or vacationers who cannot let Sunday morning pass without being in church or who enjoy visiting churches in other cities. Churches in places such as New York and Washington, D.C., often have more visitors than members in worship on Sundays. Churches in other places, such as Florida and the Rio Grande Valley of Texas, see their congregations more than double during the winter months with the arrival of snowbirds from the north.

Some strangers are searchers in quest of meaning for their lives or with some great need they hope to have met. One couple whose daughter was killed in an automobile accident told of going from church to church looking for help. Some strangers are drop-ins who just happened by and came in out of curiosity or folk who for some reason had an inkling to go to church this morning. For these people this hour of worship is crucial. If something sparks, if they are engaged by the worship, they may well be back. If not, they will not be seen again.

Finally, there are the vagabonds, wanderers, homeless ones who may come into church for very basic reasons—a place to be warm, a cup of coffee and a doughnut, a smile, a word of hope. All these people come with different needs and problems. Being the church for them may involve the pastor and people in a variety of ministries, but the first need is for the compelling reassurance of God's unconditional love.

As one person pointed out to us, what we have written in this section makes a strong assumption: that those about whom we have spoken have made the effort to get to church.[7] We agree. That makes a difference. These persons otherwise unknown to us have opened the window to themselves by themselves. Those we encounter in secular settings—in hospitals, in prisons, or at a gospel mission where they are required to listen to a sermon before they can eat—may not be so inclined. They may be angry at the world, the church, God. They may not willingly listen. We still feel the content of our message is the same: the vivid description of how much God loves all of us in spite of everything. We preach this core message again and again in the hope that one day it may slip through the cracks in a wall of distrust and anger.

The Silent Minorities: Older Adults and Children

"Religion that is pure and undefiled before God, the Father, is this: to care for orphans and widows in their distress, and to keep oneself unstained by the world" (Jas. 1:27). The New Testament's specific concern for widows and orphans becomes a symbol for the church's broader concern for older adults and children. These persons, central to Jesus' ministry, often exist on the margins of congregational life, present but powerless, the figurative or literal "widows and orphans" of our time. They are often unable to support the church or the preacher with much in the way of leadership or finance. Sometimes their faces tend to blur together under blue hair or cowlicks. The neglect of these marginalized persons may indeed be benign—we are all so busy—but it is neglect all the same.

In any event, a significant change in perceiving the relationship of the marginalized to the church and its mission has taken place. For a long time, the church spoke of its ministry *to* the marginalized (represented here by the silent minorities). From this perspective the church did things *for* them. In recent years, the church has begun to speak more and more of the ministry that such persons contribute to the mission of the church. The church witnesses not *to* them but *with* them, and recognizes them as agents who can help the church renew its life and witness.[8]

To place these persons at the speaking center requires at least three sensitivities from the pastor. First, remember that yours may be one of the few caring voices they hear in the course of the week. All of us have been in line at some store behind an older person talking with a harried clerk just for the sake of a bit of human contact, a kind word or two. At the other end of the generation gap we find children, trying to grow up in an increasingly impersonal world. We watched a film in church a generation ago called "Cipher in the Snow." It was based on a true story about a boy who asked to get off a school bus one snowy morning. He took several steps, fell over into the snow, and died. There was apparently no medical reason for him to die, but also no reason for him to live. One teacher investigated and found that the boy was in everyone's mind just a cipher, a zero, a faceless nobody. The film was unforgettable.

We know now that life for the young is even more complex and complicated than it was then, and the need for caring voices is even greater. In the same week that this is being written, a seventh-grade boy, whose mother was in the office talking to the school principal about a bad grade, walked to his locker, took out a handgun, walked into the restroom, and killed himself. The bad grade, hardly crucial in the larger scope of things, seemed like Mount Everest to him, and he saw no way around it.

The second sensitivity requires openness to the experience of those who have been marginalized. William J. Carl, Jr., has edited an excellent book called *Graying Gracefully: Preaching to Older Adults,* which deals with preaching to older adults. It is filled with vivid and useful suggestions. We mention only these thoughts from Walter Burghardt while recommending the book to everyone. Burghardt begins by quoting Henri Nouwen:

> Our first question is not how to go out and help the elderly, but how to allow the elderly to enter into the center of our own lives, how to create the space where they can be heard and listened to…Thus care for the elderly means, first of all, to make ourselves available to the experience of becoming old.[9]

Burghardt then reflects on Nouwen's words:

> Once preachers have allowed the aging into their own lives, have opened themselves to the experience of aging (whatever their age), have listened as if their own lives are at stake (as they indeed are), then the actual preaching is far less fearsome.[10]

If becoming old ourselves is part of the process of bringing those often marginalized older adults into the speaking center, can it also be said that reaching out homiletically to children and teenagers requires us to make ourselves available to the experience of being young? Or to paraphrase Nicodemus, can we be young again? Absolutely.

Once Joey had been invited to conduct a preaching mission in a local church and had arrived well in advance of the Sunday evening service. The pastor saw and grabbed him, told him that the youth sponsors had not showed up that evening, and asked him to take the youth group for an hour. Joey asked the young people what they wanted to do and got no response, so he announced that they were going to talk about preaching. After the rolled eyes and groans settled down, they had a great discussion. He came away feeling that young people often feel left out of the larger life of the church. It seemed to him that they have a relatively narrow window of accessibility. Many of them are physically adults and emotionally children. They do not like sermons that are over their heads, nor do they like preachers talking down to them. The position of preacher is not one for which they automatically feel respect. They do not like sermons that are long, boring, or heavy with judgment (who does?). They prefer sermons that deal with relationships, meaning for their lives, and the future. The one thing about which they were in unanimous agreement : "If you want us to listen to you, then listen to us sometime." In other words, allow them into the speaking center. Fair enough.

One final sensitivity is called for. Attention spans may shrink toward the extremities of life. Both the young and the old may wander in and out of the sermon. But that is all right, because they seem to be present for what they need to hear, for the stories that call forth or help create their own memories, for the affirmations that help them feel loved and included. Preachers who make themselves available to the experiences of those silent ones on the margins of the church will not only have better, more useful things to say to them, they will also be heard.

Once, when asked about preaching, Martin Luther explained his approach:

> Complicated thoughts and issues we should discuss in private with the eggheads. I don't think of Dr. Pomeranius, Jonas or Philip [Melanchthon] in my sermon. They know more about it than I do. So I don't preach to them. I just preach to Hansie or Betsy [referring to his children].[11]

He exaggerated a bit, we think, but his concern for simple, clear, vivid language may be why Luther remains readable today.

Some children leave worship for children's church before the sermon, but many, especially older children, do not. Every preacher has had the mysterious experience of surveying the congregation while preaching and noticing a child whose eyes are fixed on him or her. The child strains to understand what is being said and, if the words do not register, the child has no compunction about yawning or looking away. We may not be able to perfectly emulate Luther—we cannot imagine pitching every sermon at a five-year-old level—but we can make attempts to be inclusive of children in our preaching.

As Carolyn Brown writes: "children can worship meaningfully, using traditional forms, *if* they are learning the meaning of these forms, and *if* the forms include content that reflects *their* lives and concerns as well as those of adults."[12] In the sermon, then, we can make sure that at least one central story or illustration in the sermon is available to people across the spectrum of age, from children to older adults. That story may be all they hear, but it will help them to understand more about the faith that belongs to them as well as to others.

The Poor

"The poor have good news preached to them" (Lk. 7:22, RSV). Part of the reason for the early church's concern for widows and orphans was that these people were often locked into poverty. Concern for the poor has been part of the Christian ethos since the beginning. Jesus was a poor man.[13] Born and raised in humble surroundings, Jesus "had no place to lay his head" as an adult. Because of its beginnings, "the church is tied by *inborn vocation* to indigent and suffering humanity."[14] Down through the centuries, however, this vocation has often been minimized, forgotten, or ignored.

One minister, learning of our project, said that the hardest block to overcome in the way we relate to one another in church is not age or gender or any of that other stuff: it's money. Well-to-do churches and church folk often see the poor and dispossessed as a bother, deserving of their status, and placated with handouts. During the Middle Ages there existed an annual Feast of Fools, often presided over by a Lord of Misrule or a Boy Bishop. The feast parodied the sacred rites and customs of the church. However, this burlesque, like American minstrel shows, demonstrated that the participants–children and the poor–were not to be taken seriously during the rest of the year.

In recent years, the church has paid a steep price for its benign–or sometimes malignant–neglect. Not long ago, at a conference for preachers, the subject was the decline of mainline Protestant churches. Speakers put forth various rationales, from normal cultural swings to the vacuity of liberal theology. The inimitable David Buttrick changed the direction of the session when he arose to say, bluntly, "The mainline churches have declined because they have abandoned the poor."[15] One might also say that the church that excludes the poor excludes Jesus. Or, conversely, "through knowing the poor better, the church knows its divine founder and Lord better."[16]

In the Introduction, we included socioeconomics as a labeling and often divisive factor in the church. Here we look at possibly the most visible manifestation of that: poverty. Neither of the authors have pastored in urban ghettoes or in other churches where the majority of parishioners lived below the poverty line. So we depend on the wisdom of others in talking about preaching in the churches of the poor, be they storefront mission stations, or house churches determined to include the homeless, or old churches from which the wealth has departed. Our experience is with those downtown and neighborhood churches that always had poor people in them and where the relationships between people of different means was frequently awkward.[17]

Church planners often do not consider that some young people cannot join the youth group at a theme park or go to church camp because of the cost. Some families cannot attend the all-church retreat. Some people do not feel they will be accepted at church because they do not have the proper clothes. Some cannot get to church because they do not have a car. When church folk have to ask every time there is an activity at church, "Who is going to pick up Minerva?" both the folk and Minerva can get tired of it. Others do not feel comfortable in some churches because of their practices, their programs, even their architecture. Writer Eddy Hall says that price tags on fellowship and study materials can exclude people. And so-called "scholarships" for these things can be hurtful rather than helpful. He suggests that all activities of the church should be by donation, with the understanding that everyone is welcome whether they can pay or not.[18] One pastor in a church that welcomed all people modified the typical post-offering prayer by saying, "Bless, O God, the gift, the giver, and the heart that would have given."

How can the preacher help instead of hinder the full welcome and participation of the poor into the life of the church? Tex Sample, writing about hard living people, says that they do not like preachers who are always after money, who holler at you, who make you feel bad about being in church, who make you feel uncomfortable.[19] How shall the poor have good news preached to them? Here are three suggestions.

First, the sermon must not be couched in language that cannot be understood by the people. Preachers fresh out of seminary and proud of their newly acquired theological patois are often guilty of this. One such preacher finished his first sermon in his first church and was shaking hands at the door when a woman said to him, "Well, preacher, I think I know your favorite text." Puzzled, the preacher said, "And what might that be?" "Feed my giraffes," she said as she walked out. Charles Spurgeon, who preached to overflow crowds of rich and poor in London, said it this way in 1857:

Why did John Bunyan become the apostle of Bedfordshire, and Huntingdonshire, and round about? It was because Bunyan, while he had surpassing genius, would not condescend to cull his language from the garden of flowers, but he went into the hayfield and the meadow, and plucked up his language by the roots, and spoke out in words that the people used in their cottages. Why is it that God has blessed other men to the stirring of the people, to the bringing about of spiritual revivals, to the renewal of the power of godliness? We believe it has always been owing to this—under God's Spirit—that they have adopted the phraseology of the people, and have not been ashamed to be despised because they talked as the common people did.[20]

Preachers need to remember that the worship of mainline churches, with its scriptural texts, prayer books, and hymnbooks assumes a literacy that not all people bring with them to church. The preacher would do well to consider if those who cannot read well, do not know many or any Bible stories, and are unfamiliar with the doctrines of the church have a chance to hear good news preached. If not, it is the preacher's job to find oral and visual ways to make that hearing possible.

The second suggestion concerns hermeneutics, especially the preacher's approach to the corporate nature of faith and her or his interpretation of what it means for us to be created in the "image of God." Enlightenment individualism has tended to personalize our understanding of *imago Dei:* "I" am created in the image of God. It is not far from this belief to the assertion that the indigent are not. David Buttrick goes so far as to say that "personalist preaching, in offering models of personal salvation, actually fosters a neglect of others, particularly of socially disadvantaged others."[21] We would prefer a softer phrase, that preaching on personal salvation alone can foster such neglect. The perils of individualism are not overcome by simply being concerned about other individuals. As Enda McDonough puts it:

A deeper shift in consciousness is demanded whereby I think primarily in inclusive "us" terms rather than "me" and the "others" terms or in exclusive "us" and "them" terms. When the unity of humanity begins to be thought and felt and acted upon, the real locus of the divine image becomes evident to us, the human race as a whole, and its historical members at any particular time, taken both in their irreducible individuality and in their unbreakable unity. Until that kind of image of humanity prevails, humanity as image of God will be partial and fragile.[22]

The helpful preacher will enable his or her congregation to understand that they are more than a collection of individuals; they are the body of Christ. We will march into the new Jerusalem together or not at all.

The third suggestion returns us to a theme that is central to the Second Testament. The synoptic Jesus proclaimed a radical change in the social order and often used a theology of reversal in his preaching: "The last will be first" (Mt. 19:30), "Those who humble themselves will be exalted" (Lk. 14:11), "Those who try to make their life secure will lose it" (Lk. 17:33), and "Blessed are you who are poor, for yours is the kingdom of God" (Lk. 6:20).[23] Concern for the poor formed such a large part of Jesus' preaching that to ignore it or to trivialize it into "be a little less greedy" messages leaves us with a truncated gospel. When Jesus' life and work are seriously engaged, then everyone, whether their poverty is economic, political, psychological, or spiritual, can meet the poor man Jesus, who is one of us. Consider the old hymn:

> My Master was so very poor,
> A manger was His cradling place;
> So very rich my Master was,
> Kings came from far to gain His grace.
> My master was so very poor,
> And with the poor He broke the bread;
> So very rich my Master was,
> That multitudes by Him were fed.[24]

But these sentiments are hardly limited to the church's past. Consider a recent popular song by Joan Osborne, who asks, "What if God was one of us, just a slob like one of us?"[25] In each of these songs, there is hope in the affirmation that we are not alone, and no better news for the poor to hear and then bring to the speaking center of the church than this: Jesus is one of us.

Physical and Mental Disabilities

"Even these may forget, yet I will not forget you. See, I have inscribed you on the palms of my hands" (Isa. 49:15–16a). God will not forget those who suffer. Unfortunately, we often do. And even when we are mindful of them, we often do not know what to do or say. Joey was talking with a group of pastors at a conference in North Carolina when one of them told the group about a beloved woman in his congregation who had been struck with a progressively debilitating illness. She had moved from cane to walker to wheelchair. The church had supported her and kept her constantly lifted up in fervent prayer. They had held healing services, anointed her with oil, done everything they and the pastor knew to do. In spite of her illness, her faith had remained strong. At this point the pastor said: "Why should I not walk up to her next Sunday, lay my hands on her and say, 'In the name of Jesus, I command you to stand up and walk'?"

All were stunned to silence for a moment. Joey knew that a great deal was at stake in the question, but he had no slick, easy answer. Slowly, he said something like this:

> If you do, I assume one of two things will happen. One, she will be healed, which will be wonderful for her and everybody else, except perhaps for you. She will have a burden lifted; you will have one imposed. The lines of those wanting and expecting healing from you or from God through you will be immediate and long. Two, she will not be healed. What if, in response to your command, she tries to stand up and cannot? Could that damage her "still strong" faith? Could it damage yours? The rest of the congregation's? What would I do in your situation? I would pastor. I would pray. I would plead. But I do not think I would command. Perhaps my own faith is not strong enough or my understanding of the healing ministry is too shallow. Or perhaps, as Jesus said, one should not put the Lord your God to the test.

They had a good long conversation together after that. Joey never heard whether the pastor "commanded" the healing or not. Since that time, he has come to realize, with the help of Kathy Black and Nancy Eiesland, the difference between "healing" and "cure" and the importance for the church of disabled persons' having access to "the speaking center."

> *Cure* is the elimination of at least the symptoms if not the disease itself. *Healing*, on the other hand, has many meanings attached to it. Consider the phrases "healing presence," "healing moment," and "healing service." Each of these images elicits a sense of peace and of well-being, but they do not imply cure.[26]

Joey wishes he had made that distinction in North Carolina. Jesus sent his disciples out to preach, to teach, and to heal. When the church became institutionalized, the healing ministry largely disappeared, to be replaced by rituals such as unction.[27] The contemporary interest in recovering this ministry has frequently substituted cure for healing, and while it has certainly done much good, it has also given rise to much quackery.

We refer readers to Kathy Black's valuable book *A Healing Homiletic* for ways to bring persons with physical disabilities and psychiatric disorders into the speaking center. She engages issues of blindness, deafness and hearing loss, paralysis, chronic illness, and mental illness. In the next few pages we offer some reflection on the problems of mental retardation and various forms of dementia, including Alzheimer's.

An interesting novel by Laurie Devine called *Nile* is set, appropriately, in Egypt. The story contains a mentally disabled child named Batata. At one point the following dialogue takes place between a Muslim and a Jew:

Long ago Abbas had decided about Batata. "The boy is special. A special child. Batata is one of heaven's favorites. The house is blessed by him."

"Blessed?"

Abbas patiently explained it to Baruch. "Most people–men, women, children–live out their lives as we do. A few are good. A few bad. Most in between, *nuss wi nuss.* Allah gave us our minds and our hearts. And sometimes–and sometimes not–we use them well. But there are some who are so dear to Allah that He keeps their minds with Him in Paradise, so that all we see here on earth is what remains. A body without a full mind but with a pure heart. In the villages we call such blessed ones saints. We revere them, we care for them, and we learn from them. In my village there was one such man. It was said he ate only straw and mud. He tore to shreds whatever clothes we gave him. He was a holy man, and we honored him as a saint when he died–too young–because Allah wanted him home. The women visit his tomb now to ask for special favors. Batata, too, is one of heaven's favorites. Praise Alla–*el-hamdulillah!*–for giving him to us."

Baruch lifted his glass in a toast to Abbas. He thought of the asylums he had visited in Europe and of the deep shame associated there with mental illness of any sort. *One of heaven's favorites.* The more Baruch learned of Egyptians, the more they moved him.[28]

This description of Batata has a certain charm. But Kathy Black points out the danger in such an approach, whether the mentally disabled person is seen as angel or devil, blessed or cursed. In either case, the result is that most people stay away, not wanting to become involved. No one wants to get involved with a "devil" and most people see "angels as a little too beyond their reality as they deal with the daily struggles of life."[29]

Jean Vanier has a more creative approach. Vanier says that "the particular suffering" of persons who are mentally disabled, "as of all marginal people, is a feeling of being excluded, worthless and unloved."[30] To overcome that feeling, one needs both to live in community and to make a contribution to that community. Vanier, founder of the l'Arche communities for the mentally disabled, affirms with Paul that every person has a gift to share. Vanier names some remarkable gifts found at l'Arche that most of us rarely consider: the gift of listening, the gift of discernment, the gift of wonderment, the gift of the grandmother, the gift of animation, the gift of availability, and the gift of the poor.[31]

> One of the most precious gifts in a community is to be found among the people who cannot assume important responsibilities. They have no ability to organize, inspire, look ahead or command. But they have very sensitive and loving hearts. They can recognize people in difficulty straight away, and with a smile, a look, a flower or a word, make these people feel that they are close to them, carrying their cross with them. These insignificant people are at the heart of the community and carry its extremes as well. They carry the people who are discontent, who are blocked toward each other, who are envious or who disagree radically. It is the love of the hidden people, which keeps the community united. The leader brings unity through justice, but these loving people are creators of unity just by being who they are. In their tenderness, they are artisans of peace.[32]

One of the tasks of the preacher is to call forth the gifts of his or her people, not just the more visible gifts of leadership or exhortation, but also the less visible gifts Vanier describes. Part of the work of worship is celebrating the gifts of God.

In tandem with that, no member of Christ's body should feel her- or himself ungifted by God. The Madison Avenue Christian Church in Covington, Kentucky, has been recognized for ministry with the mentally challenged. These people share in the music ministry of the church, help lead worship, and involve themselves in various service projects of the church. Pastor Mike Delaney pays attention in his sermons to verbal and nonverbal communication. He tries to help people feel words, not just hear them. And he always arrives early for worship to greet everyone, including those who are developmentally disabled. One of the issues for many of these persons has to do with safety: "Is this sanctuary a safe place for me?" Through the warmth of his personal contact, he tries to assure them that it is.

Most of us have assumed that the people who have sat in our congregation staring vacantly at us when we preached could hear what we were saying but could not process our words, that there was no way to reach them with a useful and hopeful word. Many of us have since learned differently. Those who work with Alzheimer's patients remind us that the patients lose their memories backward from the way they gained them. The earliest memories are the most enduring. As one pastor said to me, "they may not know me, but they know God." They also remember Bible verses and hymns from childhood, which, if one thinks about it, is yet another reason for the religious education of children.[33]

In a series of lectures on ministry with Alzheimer's patients, Denise Dombkowski Hopkins suggests that the church make provisions for patients to attend church services as long as they possibly can and hold up the familiar symbols of the faith to help patients stay in touch with God. Familiar word-symbols in prayer and sermon can also give both strength and hope. She cites Perry LeFevre:

> the fragile and dependent elderly, even those who are confused and senile, have not lost all center. To be a center is *not only* to give but to receive, and those who can not yet give—the newborn child, or those who can no longer give…give in their receiving, by being open to caring love.[34]

They become care-receivers instead of caregivers, but they are still an important part of the caring ministry of the church.

How are they then called into the speaking center of the church? Samuel Balentine, echoing Nancy Eiesland, mentions one way, saying that the word of God "must be articulated from the standpoint of the victim, not the onlooker…Otherwise, there will only be room in church for Job's friends who are too eager for intellectual explanations of suffering."[35] On a trip to Jerusalem a minister walked through the garden to the Church at Gethsemane. On the wall of the church was a prominent sign that read "no explanations in the church." He said that was one of the stranger suggestions he had ever seen, but in this case we believe it to be true. We receive and affirm; we need not explain.

During the five years Joey's mother suffered from Alzheimer's, it was as if the opposite of what Abbas said of Batata were true. God had not kept his mother's mind in heaven when she was born. But there were times during those last years when it seemed that while her body remained here, her mind had gone on to heaven before her. In what was an otherwise miserable experience for her and us, there were a few times when one could see through the apparent vacancy to an almost angelic expression, and sitting quietly next to her was like sitting very close to heaven. Some dismissed that experience as silly sentimentality. Perhaps it was. But we submit that a clinical explanation of disintegrating ganglia in the brain is not nearly so much comfort as a window though which one catches glimpses of eternity.

Robert Davis, a Presbyterian minister, wrote a book with the help of his wife while he was slipping into Alzheimer's.[36] Davis said that he knew that his mind's assurances of God's promises and presence would cease, and then, he said, "I must rely solely on those who love me to keep me close to the Father by their prayers, and to reassure me with songs and touch and simple words of scripture."[37] He goes on to say, "Be gentle with your loved ones. Listen to them. Hear their whispered pain."[38] As Alzheimer's patients fall into silence, the pastor must bring the prayers, the songs, the simple words, and the whispers into the speaking center. A final thought: Davis asked his congregation to remember him the way he had been before. We can testify that this is difficult. It is hard to get beyond those almost grotesque last pictures we have of a demented loved one. So it occurs to us to add something to what Davis said. Remember him the way he was before *and the way he will be after.*

What does this have to do with preaching? Just as in funerals we sometimes speak to the one who has gone on before as though he or she were present with us now as part of that great cloud of witnesses, Joey sometimes found himself speaking to his mother as though she were mentally sharp and responsive, confident that that part of her which had gone on before could hear him. Can we do the same thing in church? The person with dementia in front of you *is* here in more than their present confusion. They are here in their most brilliant past and their most stunning future. Speak to them as they are. Yes. But bring also both memory and hope to the speaking center.

"God will remember, even as the patient with Alzheimer's slowly forgets."[39] And that is our hope.

A final group to consider in this section are neither mentally handicapped nor mentally ill. These are the people who might simply be called quirky, who seem to be wired in a different way from the majority of folk. They may wear strange clothes, especially hats. They have peculiar interests, which often emerge in Sunday school classes, whatever the subject for the day may be. They may frequently change chairs in class or worship, interrupt class or worship with what appear to be off-the-wall comments, and have other odd mannerisms. And yet it is clear that these people love church and are almost always there. Their faith is strong, if not systematic. While there tends to be a high acceptance of and concern for these people in rural communities, there seems to be a low tolerance for quirkiness in the cities and suburbs. Such social misfits and/or deviants from the cultural norm are often seen as threatening to the stability of the mainstream church culture. Those who occupy the positions of power in the church are loath to allow too much quirkiness into the speaking center.

For the challenged, the ill, and the quirky, the presence of the preacher is of paramount importance. The words of the sermon may not connect, but an inviting presence does. And this is where we need feedback. We may work hard to hone the words of our sermons, but we are often unaware of the presence we are manifesting in the pulpit. Some of us frown when we concentrate, presenting a different emotion than we actually feel. Some of us drop our sentence endings, yell to add positive emphasis, punctuate the message with annoying mannerisms, and sometimes even preach as if we do not believe what we are saying. An inviting presence helps make the message inviting, especially to those who may not be able to process all the concepts being expounded in the sermon.

In summary, the groups and situations we have described in this chapter may call for different approaches at different times, but we believe there is common ground, some things that preachers can do to help bring the least of these from the margins to the speaking center of the congregation.

Remember that the preacher's presence is as important as his or her words. Greet people warmly. Speak in a caring voice and visually include people in the sermon. As for the content of the sermon, assure everyone that God loves them and that God remembers, even when we forget. Be open to the experience of others in the message and make it available through clear thoughts and vivid images. Remind listeners that God has not left anyone ungifted, that we all have gifts we can use for God. And make sure that each sermon, while not presenting all of God's good news, is in and of itself a good and clear word for Jesus Christ.

7

Preaching in a Congregation of Conservatives and Liberals

Christians are deeply divided on how to interpret many issues today faithfully. For instance, Christians disagree on the role of women in the home and in the church. Should women be submissive to their spouses? Is it permissible for women to be ordained? Is God's will closer to policies recommended by Republicans or Democrats? Should Christians take a particular position on prayer in the public schools? Must one become a Christian in order to be saved? (Christians even hold different views on the meaning of salvation.) Is abortion a possible Christian option? Can a gay, lesbian, bisexual, transgendered, questioning, or asexual orientation be compatible with Christian faith?

In the important book *Culture Wars,* James Davison Hunter points out that many of the church's internal disagreements in such arenas are part of a larger culturewide struggle between two competing moral visions. On the one hand, orthodoxy seeks to shape culture in the United States around authorities that are external, clearly definable, transcendent, and largely unchanging. Progressives, on the other hand, seek for the values and practices of the culture to respond to the spirit of the contemporary age; the community should adapt its views of the good and the right in the light of new insights in the physical sciences, in the social sciences, in values, and in faith. In Hunter's graphic image, proponents of these polarizing tendencies are currently waging a war

149

to "define America."[1] The primary battlefields are family, education, media and the arts, law, and electoral politics.

The church is deeply implicated in the cultural conflict that Hunter identifies, for the church attempts to represent the character and will of ultimate reality. Indeed, the church has representatives on both sides of the culture wars precisely because Christians come to different conclusions about who *God* is and what *God* wills in specific situations.

Christians come to different conclusions about how to think and act because their differing theological methods and positions lead them to different conclusions. The same congregation (especially in a long-established denomination) often contains people who operate out of different theological presuppositions and who come to different—even contradictory—points of view.[2] A single pew can become a battlefield in the culture war when a conservative person sits next to a liberal communicant.[3]

In this chapter, we consider how the preacher can prepare a sermon that takes account of the *theological* diversity that is a part of most congregations in the long-established denominations today. Although Hunter introduces the terms *orthodox* and *progressive* to describe the two major tendencies in the church's current diversity, we use the more familiar designations *conservative* and *liberal.*[4]

After commenting on the unsatisfactory nature of the terms *conservative, liberal,* and *moderate,* we sketch the folk and formal lay theologians found in most congregations. In the heart of the chapter, we describe the large framework within which this discussion takes place: how Christians come to interpret God. We identify the main characteristics of conservative and liberal ways of reaching the knowledge of God today among European American Christians in the long-established denominations. Along the way, we consider approaches the preacher might take in order to speak a word that has a likelihood of being taken seriously by both conservatives and liberals.

We cannot offer a homiletical formula that will magically allow the preacher to mesmerize conservatives and liberals alike. However, preachers can incorporate several qualities into the sermon that increase the likelihood that both conservatives and liberals will give the sermon a serious hearing.

Both the authors of this book tend toward the liberal end of the theological spectrum. However, we respect conservative perspectives and believe that we can describe the essence of conservatism.

Cautions in Using the Terms
Conservative and *Liberal*

We use the terms *conservative* and *liberal* to designate the two ends of the theological spectrum. However, we use these designations with reluctance; they derive from the political arena.[5] They are neither indigenous to Christian community nor necessary to it. Because of their origins in political life, they tend to discourage dialogue and to encourage polarization and confrontation.

People who hear and use these expressions often respond emotionally, to the point that they suspend critical thought. Noncritical reactions to ideas, events, and feelings are contrary to the gospel and the needs of the times, both of which call for people of different theological views to be in critical conversation with one another in search of the fullest understanding of God's purposes that we can reach.

The terms also oversimplify the plethora of theologies and theological methods in the formal theological scene today.[6] Five major theological families are currently prominent—evangelical, pentecostal, postliberal, liberation, revisionary.[7] While theologians within each of these families have much in common, the differences within each family can be immense. The language of *conservative* and *liberal* does not always help nuance differences among (or within) the various theological families. Nonetheless, as Charles W. Allen observes, regardless of their problems, a lot of people use the terms *conservative* and *liberal* as convenient shorthand expressions.[8]

We avoid the designation *moderate*. Many North Americans like to think of themselves as moderate. They deliberately avoid extremism in search of a middle way. Few North Americans are zealots; they like to partake of the virtues of both conservatism and liberalism while avoiding the excesses and mistakes of each.

However, it is extremely difficult to stake out a moderate position in theology. When push comes to shove, most people who call themselves moderate lean more toward one end of the theological spectrum than the other.[9] We agree with Charles R. Blaisdell, editor of a collection of essays on these matters, "The moderate position is just too muddy."[10]

Lay Theologians: Folk and Formal

In most of the congregations that Ron visits as a guest Bible study leader or preacher, he finds two groups of laity with respect to theological method and position. One group he calls folk theologians, and the other formal theologians.

The folk theologians usually include both folk conservatives and folk liberals. These people have conservative tendencies and liberal tendencies, though neither group has been exposed to formal training in these matters, nor have they reflected systematically and critically about them. However, as Delwin Brown points out, a person or a congregation may be influenced by a tradition even when the congregation is not familiar with that tradition. Ideas, values, practices, and feelings are often transmitted without conscious intention from place to place and from generation to generation. People develop intuitive sympathies with conservative or liberal categories.[11]

Folk theologians frequently derive some of their sympathies from their childhoods. While they gathered some of these childhood inclinations from the formal teaching of the church, they likely acquired quite a few from previous generations of folk theologians (often heavily edited by local tradition).

Some folk theologians pick up cues from the wider culture. Conservative Christians, for instance, take in conservative clues from various media in which conservative Christian witness is prominent. A person who tunes into a religious radio or television broadcast, or who picks up a paperback book on a spiritual subject at the supermarket is likely to encounter a conservative Christian view. Given the widespread media coverage afforded the so-called Christian right in the last several years, it is not surprising that many laity assume that conservatism (sometimes political and economic, as well as religious) is the Christian way.

Some people arrive at their preferences as a result of their own thinking about what makes sense to them. For instance, early in Ron's college career, Ron decided to study for the ministry. Shortly after he told his family, his mother confessed privately that she "just couldn't see" how a fish could swallow a person and vomit that person up after three days. His mother had never heard of the categories of conservative and liberal and their formal characteristics, but she thought as a liberal (at least on religious matters).

Some people do not so much think their way into positions, as have intuitions or feelings about what is right and wrong. They operate day by day on the basis of hunches about what is true and false.

The teaching and preaching of the church, of course, influence many people. However, many members get their perspectives on Christian faith in bits and pieces—a Sunday school lesson here, a sermon there. They are seldom exposed to Christian faith in a systematic way. Their Christian vision often resembles a patchwork quilt in which some of the pieces do not match.

The preacher can help folk theologians become critically aware of the actual sources of their views. The preacher can help members name the sources from which they draw their opinions and assess the strengths and weaknesses of those sources. Many people are not aware that what they have unconsciously come to regard as historic Christian truth is really an idea that they picked up at the hair salon or from the host of a radio talk show.

Folk theologians are often more than willing to sort through the sources of their knowledge of God in order to make use of the ones that seem most reliable and to exercise caution in their use of ones that seem less well warranted. Most Christian folk theologians are less interested in being conservative or liberal than in being faithful to God and to the best of their human understanding.

Folk are often grateful to discover larger and deeper wells of Christian perspectives from which to draw. In a particularly dramatic example, Ron was leading a Bible study in a stale church basement. He first rehearsed the traditional exegesis of the text and then sketched an alternative way of understanding the passage. As he finished the alternative, a woman on the back row stood up and burst out, "I always wanted to believe that way. But until this moment, I didn't know it was possible." The revisionary exegesis deserved more reflection than a single burst of acclamation, so the group talked at length about the strengths and weaknesses of the two exegetical possibilities. But the memory of the woman's face (combining insight, anticipation, energy, and relief) continues for Ron as a reminder of how change, even transformation, occurs amid folk theologians.

In addition, in almost every congregation that Ron visits, he is greeted by a small group of theologically sophisticated laity. In some combination of the following, they have developed a self-conscious theological position: they have listened to thoughtful Christian teachers, read substantial literature, and carefully thought their own ways to distinct conclusions. Formal lay theologians understand why they think as they do and why other modes of Christian interpretation are unpersuasive.

Ron's uncle, now of blessed memory, was a case in point. A county judge and a doctrinaire conservative, he spent several summer vacations taking classes at the Moody Bible Institute in Chicago, a conservative institution. By the time he combined his summers at Moody with his independent reading and the many conferences he attended (not to mention his immense intellectual powers), he was at least as theologically sophisticated as his pastors, albeit they were more toward the liberal end of the theological spectrum.

A preacher often finds natural communion with the formal lay theologians who share the preacher's theological mind-set.[12] They can become some of the preacher's most attentive listeners and may even bring the pastor's attention to materials that can be of use in preaching.

What happens when the theological orientation of the preacher differs from that of a formal lay theologian and leads to substantial disagreement on matters of importance? In the optimum situation, preacher and lay theologian can converse about the nature and seriousness of their differences and can learn from one another. We have nearly always found that such interchanges help both pastor and congregation member to understand the viewpoint of the other, and to reflect more deeply and carefully on their own standpoints.

If preacher and formal lay theologian cannot reconcile their viewpoints, they may take a cue from many seminary faculties and other manifestations of the church in which persons of different viewpoints exist in the same community. They agree to disagree, but to do so agreeably.[13] They continue to listen to one another, to challenge one another, and to offer alternative points of view. If the lay theologian is articulate in public settings, a disagreement with the pastor could become an ideal occasion for pastor and lay theologian to model creative dialogue among those who disagree in the quest to identify divine leading.

Along this line, Richard Lancaster, a retired liberal pastor of Meridian Street United Methodist Church in Indianapolis, reports a comment made in good spirit by a parishioner who was a conservative formal lay theologian. "Dick, we try to keep you from going over the theological speed limit." Pastor Lancaster engaged conservative perspectives thoughtfully and seriously. Because of the care with which he handled conservatism, conservatives listened intently to his criticisms. He spoke not as a loose gun shooting at caricatures, but as one who had a sympathetic understanding of the conservative system. The formal conservative lay theologians took his preaching seriously in part because he took them seriously.

Once in a while, differences in theological viewpoint immobilize a congregation. Indeed, a church can become a fireworks stand into which someone throws a lit match. In such cases, the preacher may need to help the congregation consciously choose either to do the things necessary to live and work together, or to become separate Christian communities. In the event of the latter, the pastor should help the congregation separate as amicably as possible. Hostility, after all, is not a Christian virtue.

Both folk and formal theologians share a characteristic that is decisive for the sermon: they want to know what the preacher thinks and why. Pastors need not pussyfoot around their deepest theological convictions. Quite the contrary. According to a study of listeners, parishioners respect pastoral honesty. Even when the listener holds an opinion opposite that of the preacher, the listener respects the preacher who articulates his or her opinion and is willing to dialogue about the disagreement. Indeed, listeners mistrust preachers who appear to hide key notions.[11] Of course, the preacher does not want to point a flaming homiletical blowtorch into a congregation that is more volatile than a fifty-gallon drum of gasoline. But in a context of respect and sensitivity toward all in the listening community, a preacher's straightforwardness is a sign of credibility and trustworthiness.

Sources of the Perception of God in the Sermon

All Christians, conservative or liberal, share qualities that differentiate them from many in the larger culture as Christians. Both groups believe in the existence of God. Conservatives and liberals believe that God has purposes for the world. Both groups believe that human beings can perceive something of God and God's purposes in the cosmos. But how do Christians come to understand God? Conservative and liberal Christians differ (though not in ways that are mutually exclusive) in their understanding and use of the sources of the perception of God.

Over the centuries, the church has drawn on four sources for understanding God: the Bible, Christian tradition, experience, and reason. When faced with an issue of belief or ethics, Christians may ask:

- What do we learn from the Bible about this matter?
- from Christian tradition?
- from our experience?
- from reason?

Christian communities in different times and places vary in the emphases they give to each source. Today, conservatives and liberals differ on the nature, authority, and interaction of these sources. However, such differences are not direct oppositions. George Rupp, president of Rice University, once said, "All liberals build on the past. All conservatives change."[15]

We need to say a word about the notion of revelation, that is, the idea that God reveals aspects of the divine character and purpose to us. For conservatives, revelation primarily took place in the past, especially through the Bible. Tradition clarifies revelation and applies it to new circumstances. Of course, most conservatives believe that God continues to speak in ways that are consistent with the revelation present in the Bible and explained in Christian tradition. The category of revelation faces rougher sledding among liberals.

Some liberals also acknowledge revelation. Many liberals see revelation taking place through the interaction of Bible, tradition, experience, and reason. Some liberals think that cultural conditioning and historical circumstance, along the interpretive quality of all perception, combine to give all awareness attributed to revelation a relative quality. That is, a community may be relatively more open to the fullness of revelation in one moment, while less open at other times. A community may actually misperceive what God intends to reveal. At a later time, the people may be more receptive to revelation, and hence, correct their earlier understanding of God's will. God does not change the divine mind, but the human perception of the divine will changes. A few liberals think that the cultural conditioning, historical circumstance, and consciousness are so shot through with interpretation that we can no longer meaningfully speak of revelation as a source of the perception of God. Instead, the community speaks of the best interpretation that it can reach at a given time on the basis of conversation among the Bible, tradition, experience, and reason.

Most folk theologians (and even some formal lay theologians) appear to be unaware of sources of understanding God other than the Bible. Relatively few people have a clear notion of the different ways in which conservatives and liberals understand these sources and make use of them. Preaching about this subject performs the pastoral function of helping the congregation grasp why it is sometimes so difficult for Christians to come to a common witness, and, indeed, why it is sometimes so difficult for Christians even to understand and talk with one another. Through preaching and teaching, the preacher can help the congregation understand the sources of perceiving God, how Christian communities use them, and the differences in Christian angles of vision.[16]

When making use of the sources of interpreting God, the preacher should ordinarily explain the content and importance of the sources that appear in the sermon. In today's congregation, the preacher simply cannot take for granted that the congregation will be familiar with the content or context of a biblical passage. The community is even less likely to recognize the importance of figures, events, or documents from Christian tradition. Listeners may not know that the preacher's appeal to experience is rooted in an honorable Christian practice and is not aped from the model of current media tell-all-in-public talk shows.

When conservatives and liberals have basic theological agreement on the issues at the heart of the sermon, the preacher can self-consciously use material in the sermon that will appeal to both. When conservatives and liberals have basic theological disagreement on the issues at the heart of the sermon, the preacher needs to help them understand the nature and depths of their differences. The preacher must assess the strengths and weaknesses of the differing perspectives.

The Bible

All Christians known to us honor the Bible as paradigm (or paradigms) of the divine presence and activity. The Bible contains a master story that points to God's character and to God's designs for the realms of humankind and nature. The Bible helps the church understand God and life. However, the church cannot glibly speak of the Bible as a source of the knowledge of God. For Christians have different understandings of the Bible.

The western Christian world has slightly different views of the contents of the Bible. Most Protestants regard the thirty-nine books in the First Testament and the twenty-seven books in the Second Testament as sacred scripture providing suitable bases for preaching and teaching. Roman Catholics add several other books to the sacred collection (e.g., Wisdom of Solomon, Sirach, Baruch, Tobit, Judith, Prayer of Manasseh, 1 and 2 Maccabees). Most Protestants refer to these additional books as apocryphal and regard them as valuable supplements to help the church understand the Bible and its world, but not as authoritative bases for preaching and teaching. However, diversity among Protestants is indicated by the Episcopal church's appointment of readings from the Wisdom of Solomon, Sirach, and Baruch to its lectionary.

Conservatives and liberals agree on a crucial perspective. They both believe that all interpreters are responsible to hear the biblical text speak its own word. They regard the text as a genuine other with its own integrity. They seek an exegesis of the text in its historical and literary contexts. However, both conservatives and liberals acknowledge that careful exegetes can come to different conclusions about the meanings of a text in its historical and literary contexts.

On the conservative end of the spectrum, Christians stress the divine authorship of the Bible, its unity, and its validity in every time and place. Conservatives disagree among themselves on the means and extent of divine authorship. Some conservatives believe that God moved the hands of the biblical writers. Most conservatives allow for a human element and cultural conditioning in the wording of the Bible. For instance, thoughtful conservatives regard the description of the mustard seed as "the smallest of all the seeds on earth" (Mk. 4:31) not as scientifically accurate but as reflective of the era in which the parable was spoken. But in matters of faith and ethics, the Bible is true because God wrote it. Liberals need to respect the differences among conservatives on inerrancy, infallibility, plenary verbal inspiration, and the vast network of related matters.

Conservatives also regard the Bible as making a consistent theological witness from era to era, from author to author, from text to text. As Ron once heard an eloquent conservative say, "The Bible speaks in one voice." The contents of the Bible are in essential agreement with one another.

Conservatives regard the Bible as valid in every time and place. If the Bible seems to contradict what the community otherwise believes to be true, the community needs to consider one of two possibilities: (1) the community may need to align its urges or understandings with that of the Bible in order to be in tune with God's will, or (2) the community may need to reexamine its understanding of the Bible. While the Bible itself is a reliable guide to faith and ethics, its human interpreters can misunderstand it. Fresh exegetical insights can reformulate how the church appropriates the Bible.

The preacher who wishes for a conservative to engage the sermon in a friendly spirit needs to bring the Bible and the tradition strongly into the sermon. Conservatives are often willing to entertain fresh interpretations of texts or aspects of the tradition.

The preacher who wishes to challenge a conservative viewpoint can sometimes use the Bible for that very purpose, particularly if the preacher thinks that the Bible offers different viewpoints on the issue in question. Some conservatives, hearing the preacher enumerate and describe multiple points of view in the Bible, ask, "Can these different perspectives be reconciled? If not, which seems the most authoritative, and why? Is it conceivable that a perspective from outside the Bible may make more sense?"[17]

As their designation implies, conservatives are not usually ready to reject a long history of interpretation on the basis of a few remarks (even passionate ones) from their pastor. The preacher needs to demonstrate that a revisionary understanding of a text or traditional affirmation rests on solid exegetical ground. The preacher who appears to be playing fast and loose with a biblical text or traditional concept for the sake of justifying a new fad will lose the respect of thoughtful conservatives and liberals alike.

Liberals, too, respect the Bible as an important witness to the divine life. However, liberals view aspects of the Bible quite differently from conservatives. Liberals tend to view the Bible as a human interpretation of the divine character and will. Some passages rise to marvelous heights of insight. But some texts are subject to human limitations in perception and do not measure up to the best of what we might believe about God or the world.

According to some liberal Christians, the Bible came about in the following way. The biblical authors became aware of the divine activity. They spoke and/or recorded their interpretations of God's character and work. Many of these interpretations were passed from one community to another and from one generation to another. People determined that some of the materials were able to help the people of God determine the divine presence and leading in situations other than the ones for which the passages and books were written. The value of these materials was confirmed by their usefulness to communities. Eventually, Israel and the church made formal decisions to create a canon of materials that had proven their ability to alert the community of faith in many different times and circumstances to God's presence and purposes in the world.[18] By creating the canon, the church determined that by engaging these texts under the prompting of the Holy Spirit, the canonical books could help the church interpret what God offers and asks in each generation. Later generations do what the biblical writers did in ancient times and places: come to as clear an understanding of God's will as is possible in the new circumstances.

Liberal Christians view the Bible as speaking not in a single theological voice, but in a plurality of voices. Liberals often say, "The Bible is not a book, but a library." Each author, book, or passage makes its own witness. To be sure, all the books of the Bible have a significant number of key tenets in common. For example, all biblical books agree the God of Israel is the sovereign of the universe. However, different authors and traditions often have their own nuances of interpretation of such matters. Some biblical writers disagree with one another. The Deuteronomist, for instance, assumes that obedience begets prosperity while disobedience calls forth a curse, but the book of Job says, "Not necessarily." Readers are advised in 1 Peter to be obedient to the emperor since the emperor is God's agent, but the book of Revelation regards the Roman Empire as an instrument of Satan.

The Bible is not a rigid anvil over which the church must bend its thinking, feeling, and actions. The many forms of pluralism of the Bible (e.g., cultural, theological, ethical) lead liberals to expect that some witnesses in the Bible will prove more useful to the later church than other parts.

For liberal Christians, the Bible is a collection of conversation partners. The church listens to the different voices in the Bible for ways in which the different voices may prove helpful in its later time and place, especially as the church brings the Bible into dialogue with tradition, experience, and reason.

According to some liberal interpreters, the Bible may contain material that is mistaken not only in its science, but also in its theology and ethical instruction. The liberal church is free to say, "While we understand the historical circumstances that gave rise to a particular text, we no longer consider that text authoritative."

A lot of liberal Christians understand that the past (especially as found in the Bible and Christian tradition) provides essential ingredients for understanding the present, and for having hope for the future. Liberals, however, do not feel imprisoned by ideas and practices from the past. A part of the liberal agenda is to keep a conversation ongoing to determine how the past can best inform the present.

The preacher needs to help liberals hear what the Bible says. Liberals rejoice when the Bible speaks in a single voice on a matter. In addition, liberal Christians then want to explore how that witness relates to contemporary experience. When the Bible (and the tradition) speaks in multiple voices, liberals want to become aware of this pluralism. Indeed, a pluralistic interpretation of a text or tradition is occasion for a different kind of rejoicing, for such diversity calls for a conversation with its concomitant excitement and adventure (as well as frustration and pain).

Tradition

Tradition, in this context, refers to texts, practices, and experiences of the Christian community after the biblical period and into the present day. The contributors to the tradition intend to apply, deepen, supplement, adapt–and occasionally understand themselves to correct– the insights of the Bible and the preceding generations of tradition.[19] When faced with an issue or situation, the contemporary church often turns to tradition and asks, how has the church perceived or acted in response to this issue in previous eras? If the church has not previously dealt directly with an issue or situation faced by the contemporary community, the current church is often able to locate analogous issues or situations in the tradition. If the preacher can find no analogy, the church is sometimes able to plot trajectories of thought that point to principles or analogies that are helpful to today's community.

Tradition, like the Bible, often provides a precedent for those who seek to preserve current beliefs, attitudes, or behaviors. Tradition can also provide a warrant for those who seek change, especially as the church comes to read the tradition in new ways or to hear voices in the tradition that have been overlooked or forgotten.

Nearly every sermon that moves from the Bible to the present passes through lenses that have been ground in the tradition. A Lutheran, for instance, usually reads the Bible (at least in part) through the eyes of Luther. However, preachers seldom clue the congregation in on the nature and effect of these lenses. Sermons often give the impression of jumping from the Bible to the present, as if bypassing interpretive traditions. In order to help the congregation increase its critical capacity, most preachers should help the congregation become more aware of how tradition influences the content of the sermon.

We cannot blithely speak of *the* tradition as if Christian tradition is a monolith. The elements of Christian tradition (even more than the books of the Bible) come from many different times and places.[20] Of course, the various components of Christian tradition share basic characteristics. But many communities express Christian tradition through the lens of their own cultures, practices, theologies, and other particularities. Conservatives and liberals both acknowledge that Christian tradition is pluralistic and diverse.[21]

While tradition is embodied in official statements and practices of the church, and in the formal writings of theologians that span time and space, congregations often have powerful traditions that are peculiar to them. In some instances "tradition" functionally consists of what laity remember (or have been told) about the assumptions and practices of their immediate community. The line in so many ecclesial parodies, "We've always done it that way," can refer to a convention that is only a few years old and is found in only one congregation. Nonetheless, while local precedent may not have centuries of force behind it, it is still very powerful.[22] Preachers need to account for conservative and liberal attitudes toward tradition at both official and popular levels.

Conservatives and liberals both ought to agree with Jaroslav Pelikan's distinction between tradition and traditionalism. "Tradition is the living faith of the dead, traditionalism is the dead faith of the living."[23] Conservatives and liberals both can drift into traditionalism. However, at their best, conservatives and liberals bring the faith of the dead to life, though they understand the nature of tradition itself and their relationship to it somewhat differently. In many respects conservative and liberal attitudes toward tradition parallel their attitudes toward the Bible.

Conservatives tend to think of tradition as a fixed and identifiable deposit of beliefs and practices to be preserved from generation to generation. In order to be Christian fully, a community must adhere to traditional affirmations and practices. These doctrines and beliefs are valid in all times and places. The purpose of the conservative church is to explain the deposit of doctrine and ethical prescriptions, to defend it against heresy, and to show how to put it into practice in the church's present time and place.

While conservatives disagree on many fine points of doctrine and ethics, most conservatives share a core of Christian beliefs and practices that they maintain are essential to Christian identity. These convictions derive, in part, from their reading of the "ecumenical consensus" represented by the Apostles' Creed, the Nicene Creed, the Chalcedonian formulation, and subsequent affirmations and interpretations. From these materials, conservatives identify a body of orthodox Christian doctrine and practices. Many conservative Christian thinkers regard orthodox tradition as filling out the details of the faith they find in the Bible.

Few Protestant conservatives regard the tradition as authored by God in the same way as the Bible. But many believe that the Holy Spirit has worked (and continues to work) to preserve the essential tenets of the faith through tradition.

Of course, conservatism itself is pluralistic and diverse. Conservatives debate how to understand specific points of the tradition. They ponder which points (and interpretations) of tradition are essential to the core of Christian identity, and which are nonessential. Some conservatives are quick to identify heresy. Others are more patient, waiting for time, reflection, and clear manifestations of the Holy Spirit to help them draw the line between the acceptable and the unacceptable. A sermon will prove persuasive to conservatives when it is clearly consistent with orthodox Christian tradition.

The preacher who hopes that conservatives might change a part of their interpretation of tradition might find resources in the tradition itself. A preacher can often locate voices within the tradition who offer alternative views of the matter under discussion. The presence of multiple voices in the Christian house can sometimes spark conservatives to ask which has the greatest claim to be authoritative.

The best liberals respect tradition and want to understand themselves in continuity with it. Liberals agree that Christian faith has an essence, a core, without which Christian faith is not Christian faith. However, for liberals, Christian tradition is a record of the process of interpretation as much as it is a fixed deposit. Clark Williamson, dean of Christian Theological Seminary, notes that the Latin *traditio* is a verb, not a noun.[24] Liberals understand the tradition to be the process by which Christian communities interpret Christian essence and its implications for the sake of (and in the light of) every new time and place. Liberals even speak of "traditioning" to describe the contemporary community's interaction with the tradition and its appearance in new circumstances. Throughout history, the community is in the position of

> receiving a tradition and encountering new situations, a receiving and an encountering that generate conflict between tradition and situation and that *can* also generate creativity. At every point in our historical life the community of faith, as well as the individual Christian, is faced with a hermeneutical task: we have to interpret this new situation in the light of the tradition in order to understand it and to incorporate it into this *living* tradition.[25]

The church receives the tradition and interprets it and reinterprets it from the perspective of the contemporary situation and worldview. The church understands its new moment in the light of the tradition. In the process, Christian understanding is sometimes reformulated, even transformed.

Williamson clarifies this process with a family analogy:

> When we pass on a tradition, which families do when they tell stories from the family history, we also incorporate people into a tradition. Not to be incorporated into a tradition is not to know

who you are, to whom you are related, where you come from, or where you are going...At the same time, one who has attended the same family reunion across a span of years recognizes that the stories and storytellers change, that this very traditional and traditioning activity is never the same twice.[26]

The preacher can help liberals regard the tradition as an assembly of conversation partners. When faced with an issue or situation, the preacher can ask questions such as, How have our predecessors in Christian history understood these matters? What are the strengths and weaknesses of our predecessors' perceptions? How do they help us? hinder us? Based on the best of what we think about God, the human situation, and nature, what should be our relationship to our predecessors' judgments?

Just as the tradition can help the community understand its present situation, so insights from the present situation can encourage the community to reconsider Christian tradition. In the process, the church can reaffirm long-established perspectives, enlarge understanding, add new elements, let other pieces drop away, put old components under new management, and challenge some assertions. The Christian community may conclude that a traditional affirmation is precisely what is needed in the present scene. The community may conclude that a traditional affirmation misrepresents the divine will.

Thoughtful liberals reinterpret Christian tradition carefully. While many new thoughts, feelings, and actions should be incorporated into the contemporary Christian house, many should not be. Contemporaneity is not sufficient criteria for a new element to affect Christian tradition. For example, "German Christians who supported Hitler offered new, but not therefore suitable, interpretations of the Christian faith."[27] Liberals need clear and cogent criteria by which to interpret and reinterpret the tradition in ways that are appropriate to the gospel as well as credible in the contemporary world.[28] The preacher needs to help the congregation identify such criteria and learn to employ them. Otherwise, liberal Christians are often in danger of using nothing more than the zeitgeist as the norm by which to gauge the Bible and tradition.

Occasionally liberals are cavalier and dismissive in their attitude toward tradition. The preacher often needs to work hard to help liberals seriously consider the possibility that tradition may offer significant guidance for the present. For this purpose, the preacher might point out that a particular body of tradition has proven immensely helpful in the experience of the church for several generations, for, as noted below, liberals honor experience as a norm.

Experience

The church's understandings and uses of experience have been a significant distinguishing point between conservatives and liberals in the modern era in coming to the knowledge of God. Many conservatives are more reserved in their use of experience, while liberals are more open.[29] Pentecostals are a variation on these themes. For while it tends to be conservative in theology, Pentecostal religion is highly experiential. In the Pentecostal view, valid experience is consistent with conservative interpretation of the Bible and Christian tradition. In any event, as the modern worldview gives way to the pluralism of postmodernity, the notion of experience is undergoing a transformation that complicates our discussion.[30]

The modern period began with the Enlightenment and continues into the present. Modernists held that pure, objective, unbiased, universally valid knowledge comes through scientific observation or through logical deduction from necessary first principles.[31] In this view, experience is what people receive through the five senses. That which is true can be confirmed through the senses or can be logically verified.

But the postmodern movement has become widely identified only in the last two decades. Postmodern thinkers claim that the modern notions of knowledge and experience are mistaken. Human beings cannot achieve objective, unbiased knowledge, because all perception is, inherently, interpretive.

Conservatives with a modern mind-set draw on experience in a limited way. They believe that Christians can experience the divine presence and divine will through their senses, as in worship, in the natural world, in interpersonal relationships, in prayer, in miniature and massive social events. However, conservatives insist that all *valid* Christian experience must be consistent with the Bible and the tradition. If Christians have experiences that lead them to think they can think or act in ways that contradict the Bible and the tradition, those perceptions are incorrect. Indeed, experience can be deceptive, even the tool of evil.

Conservatives welcome aspects of postmodernism's attitude toward experience, but find themselves in a quandary in other respects. They welcome the dethroning of experience as a universal standard for truth;

Christian faith need no longer be judged in the court of universal reason or scientific observation, as if Christian claims must pass muster before an authority higher than themselves. Further, the ambiguities of experience as a source for knowledge are now fully exposed.

In the emerging period, the conservative call is to articulate the Christian interpretation in its own language and on the basis of its own texts and practices.[32] Conservatives intend to draw primarily on the Bible and on Christian tradition. Conservatives then apply the implications of their discoveries to the church and the world.

In the sermon, then, the preacher can appeal to conservative understanding by showing how the Bible and tradition are confirmed in experience. If the preacher offers a revisionary understanding of some aspect of the orthodox Christian past, the reconstruction will seem more persuasive to conservatives if it is demonstrated through experience. Conservatives are not likely to depart from traditional understandings of the Bible, and from Christian belief and practice, on the basis of arguments or evidence from experience alone. However, the preacher may be able to help conservatives open the window to other viewpoints by referring to experiences that raise questions about the adequacy of traditional affirmations.[33]

In the modern era, liberals sought to understand Christian faith in ways that were compatible with modern experience. According to the liberal view, people who lived in the prescientific era sometimes misperceived dimensions of the natural world, human life, and the divine being and purposes. Modern liberals thought that the Enlightenment had removed much of the fog that obscured premodern vision of the world and the character of the divine. Modern Christians could understand the world and Christian faith objectively, without the accoutrements of myth and superstition that bedeviled premoderns. As the word *liberal* implies, liberals sought liberation from unenlightened ways of thinking and acting.

A theological correlate is crucial to the liberal theological position. Daniel Day Williams expressed this position with remarkable directness: "We know God in the same fundamental manner that we know anything else: to interpret our immediate experience to know what realities are impinging upon us."[34] The theological foundation of the liberal affirmation is simple. God is omnipresent, that is, present at all times and all places. Therefore, it is possible to come to know something of God at any time and place. On the basis of their more enlightened awareness of both the culture and the divine presence and will, liberals in modernity could accord experience an authority in the church equal to, or even superseding, aspects of the Bible and tradition. Liberal Christians identified claims that could be empirically demonstrated or that resulted from necessary first principles. A claim that could not be verified in experience was either rejected or interpreted in such a way that it seemed plausible inside the modern worldview.

Liberals found many elements in the Bible and in Christian tradition that fit hand in glove with modernity. They created hermeneutical methods to cross the gap between ancient and contemporary perspectives.[35] For instance, few liberals believed that miracles of the kind reported in the Bible happened in the way that they are described. However, they could understand the category of miracle as valid when they found surprising qualities in life (e.g., liberal sermons on "everyday miracles," such as love, hope, sharing). Liberals concluded that a few claims in the Bible and tradition were simply mistaken. Some liberals, for instance, deduced that the biblical pictures of God's gunning down the enemies of Israel, while understandable within the cultural assumptions of antiquity, were immoral.

Many liberals recognize that limitations in human perception make it impossible for human beings to know God fully.[36] Such liberals recognize that their awareness of experience is incomplete. But they believe they have enough knowledge to know God adequately.

Liberals modify their understanding of experience, and their use of it in the Christian house, in the light of postmodern emphases. Some postmodern Christians conclude that experience cannot be reduced to that which is received through the five senses. Experience also includes the element of feeling—awareness of depths that are difficult to conceptualize or discuss in terms of the five senses. As Bernard Meland puts it, "In a word …we live more deeply than we can think."[37]

Further, postmodern liberals agree that human beings always take in the world through lenses that shape (and bias) perception. We do have experience for what we see, hear, touch, taste, and smell. Our experience is particular to us and to the communities that shape our perceptual lenses. Experience is always interpretive.

The experience of a particular person or community may not be universal, but it is still experience, and as such, it is a norm by which to measure claims and experiences of others. Is the claim or event of another person or community similar to my experience? or different from it? The postmodern liberal does not immediately dismiss the experience of others (even those from premodern worlds) as deviant.

Thoughtful postmodern liberals regard differences as invitations to dialogue with others regarding their interpretations of experience.

Persons in the liberal spirit plumb the degree to which aspects of different life visions seem to correspond with the depth understanding of experience. Liberal Christians test Christian witness in the experience of others. Liberals test the viewpoints of others in Christian experience. In regard to a particular issue or situation, postmodern liberals ask of others, What is your experience of transcendent perspective on this matter? How does it compare and contrast with ours? Can we learn from you? Can you learn from us? Is our framework of understanding changed by this conversation? Liberals recognize that an encounter with another person or community may cause liberals to revise (even radically) their reading of their own experience, or the experience of others.

The preacher needs particularly to bring "evidential experiences" into the sermon.[38] These evidences are stories of real people and situations that verify the claims of the sermon. The congregation is particularly persuaded by stories from the preacher's own life.

At the same time, liberals and conservatives need to recognize that Christians can misuse the category of experience in coming to theological judgments. For instance, years ago Joey wrote a paper for a class he was taking with the noted Disciples historian Ronald Osborn in which Joey spoke innocuously of "the worship experience." This is what Osborn wrote on Joey's paper at that point:

> You have jangled one of my most sensitive nerves. Why can't Americans just say "worship" to denote an action of the church which needs no justification except sincerity and truth, which is justified in and of itself because it is a sincere offering to God? Why must we always say "worship experience" as though the really important thing about it were our own subjective feeling about this particular service? Why? Because ever since the Great Awakening and the emphasis on the subjective sense of conversion, Americans have emphasized and valued religion in direct proportion to the "kick" it provides, either spiritual (as they once tended to esteem it) or psychological in these secular times. Neither Chrysostom nor Luther would have known what the phrase "worship experience" was intended to signify. On this issue, American liberals and conservatives are in the same misguided camp. Only classical [Protestants] and

Catholics with a sense of the meaning of the liturgy can say "worship" with the understanding of its importance because of what it does in expressing our response to God rather than seeking to justify it because of the way it makes us feel.[39]

The gospel itself functions as a norm by which to measure our use of experience, just as our experience sometimes causes us to reconsider the ways in which we understand the gospel and its implication.

Reason

Both conservatives and liberals seek a faith that is reasonable, that is, a faith that is logically coherent and that makes sense in the light of the worldview of the community that holds it.[40] As a process of logical analysis, reason is—or should be—operative in all thinking about God and the Christian life, whether conservative or liberal. Reason is less a singular source, in the sense of being an identifiable datum, and more a process. Both conservatives and liberals use reason to help bring data from the other sources of the knowledge of God into a coherent picture.

The primary value of reason for conservatives is to establish logical consistency among all Christian affirmations. Conservatives wish to avoid statements or practices that logically contradict one another. Conservatives employ reason to demonstrate coherence among the claims of the Bible, orthodox Christian tradition, and the beliefs and practices of today's church. Conservatives can expend considerable energy showing how reason can lead them to harmonize parts of the Bible or Christian tradition that appear to offer variant views of Christian faith or practice.

Some conservatives use reason to explain why their version of Christian faith is credible in the face of competing, even challenging, understandings of Christian vision, as well as in comparison with other forms of belief (and nonbelief). Conservative Christians sometimes use reason to show why their worldview is believable amidst the challenges posed by modern and postmodern worldviews.

Some conservatives use scientific methods and principles to prove the truth of Christian claims. For instance, many conservatives use archaeological discoveries to confirm that events recorded in the Bible took place in the way that these events are described in the Bible.

Conservatives also use reason to deduce the outcome of biblical and traditional statements for contemporary communities. The careful use of reason may lead the Christian community to hitherto unrecognized, or undeveloped, implications of Christian faith. Reason alone cannot lead a person or community to certain knowledge of God. Any affirmation that results from reason must be tested for its logical coherence with the Bible and Christian tradition.

The preacher needs to help the conservative Christian understand how the claims of the sermon logically cohere with the heart of the Christian faith. If the preacher invites the congregation to accept an interpretation of Christian faith that falls outside usual conservative parameters, the preacher may win some conservative assent if the preacher can show that the fresh assertion is logically consistent (and even derives from) other statements or stories that conservatives regard as authoritative.

Liberals, too, seek faith and practice that are internally consistent. Liberals, too, wish to avoid logical contradiction. Liberals, too, use reason to explain why their version of Christian faith is credible today, even in the midst of the challenges of modern and postmodern worldviews. Liberals, too, use reason to draw out the hitherto undeveloped or unrecognized implications of Christian faith.

Some liberals believe that logical thought can lead to the knowledge of God. The divine omnipresence means that any act of thinking can respond to divine leading. Such reason can lead Christians past mistaken conclusions, or conundrums of the past and present, to fresh ways of understanding the divine character and purposes. Of course, new conclusions must be coherent with the essence of Christian faith.

Some liberals connect reason very closely with contemporary interpretations of experience. A statement or practice is reasonable to such liberals when it is consistent with a modern or postmodern worldview (depending on whether the liberal is a modern or postmodern). A claim or action that is incompatible with a modern or postmodern perception of the world may be unreasonable. Liberals aim for their views of God and the world to be consistent with what they generally believe to be true in everyday experience. As we noted in our discussion of experience, liberals regard differing claims as points of entry for conversation. Such a conversation may cause liberals to revise their conceptions of the reasonable and the unreasonable. They may conclude that they have previously had limited or otherwise erroneous concepts of God and the world.

In particular, the preacher needs to help the liberal understand how a text, doctrine, issue, situation, or practice correlates reasonably with contemporary experience. Liberals will not take with full seriousness a sermon whose authority is derived only from past sources. This point is one over which liberal preachers (and preachers who wish to speak to liberals) may need to reflect in their own preaching. A recent empirical study of more than 200 sermons preached in the Christian Church (Disciples of Christ) finds that most sermons are primarily composed of information about the biblical text that is the basis of the sermon, with some illustrations (many of them hackneyed) along the way. The purpose of the illustrations is presumably "to provide breaks in the continuous flow of information."[41] Indeed, in these sermons the four gospels are almost the only authorities cited. This observation suggests that many contemporary preachers need to be more persistent and careful in bringing past texts and traditions into dialogue with experience and reason if their sermons are to speak with maximal authority to liberals.

In summary, conservatives and liberals have somewhat different views of the nature of the Bible, tradition, experience, and reason as sources of the knowledge of God. Furthermore, conservatives give much greater weight to the Bible and tradition than to experience. Liberals have great respect for the Bible and tradition, but they recognize circumstances under which experience, and reason, can take precedence over scripture and tradition.

Concluding Pastoral Considerations

While the way in which the preacher handles theological considerations when preaching among conservatives and liberals is important, other qualities in the congregational setting are also vital. When these qualities are present, conservatives and liberals both tend to enter the world of the sermon. When these qualities are absent, the congregation is much less willing to give the sermon serious consideration, regardless of its theological clarity or homiletical artistry.

The most important of these qualities is a strong and trusted pastoral relationship between congregation and community.[42] Members tend to respect, and to be willing to listen to, a pastor whom they know cares for them, who proficiently and faithfully performs pastoral responsibilities, who acts with integrity, whose sermons give signs of thoughtful preparation. A congregation is more likely to give serious consideration to the sermon when the pastor calls regularly in nursing homes, provides pastoral care in times of personal crisis, deals competently and promptly with administrative responsibilities, owns up to mistakes, and signals the congregation that study time is important for the preparation of the sermon.

The ministry of Ernest Fremont Tittle at First Methodist Church in Evanston, Illinois, during the first part of the twentieth century, is an example of such a pastorate. Tittle preached on racial justice in a relatively conservative congregation two generations before the civil rights movement. This theme made some people in the congregation unhappy, but the congregation as a whole continued to support Tittle because of their profound appreciation for Tittle's pastoral ministry. He had been with them from house to house and hospital room to hospital room through multiple personal and communal crises over many years. They trusted him as pastor and as preacher. By the time of World War II, Tittle had become a pacifist. Because of his strong pastoral work, the congregation continued to support him and his preaching. Indeed, the local congregation even guaranteed a "free pulpit."[43]

When approaching a sensitive issue, the preacher needs to respect all who are related to the issue, even those with whom the preacher fundamentally disagrees. The gospel, after all, asserts that God loves each and all. This affirmation bestows on all Christians the responsibility to love one another. Of course the preacher will disagree with other interpreters in the Christian house. But in order to preach in ways that are consistent with the gospel, pastors need to take a cue from Ephesians and speak their understanding of the truth in love (Eph. 4:15), even when they must expose what they take to be misunderstandings and fallacies in the positions of other Christians. Furthermore, listeners quickly turn off when the preacher ridicules other people and viewpoints, or deals with them in caricature, or makes use of inflammatory or deriding language.[44]

The preacher needs to alert the congregation to conservative and liberal ways of thinking. The preacher also needs to help the congregation identify multiple interpretations of issues.[45] The pastor needs to describe the different interpretations with precision, respect, and sensitivity, and to evaluate them critically. When the congregation has a map of the interpretive landscape, they can locate themselves on it. Members can begin to think critically about their locations and about other locations.[46]

The preacher who propagandizes during the sermon is likely to lose the congregation. Propaganda, which can be practiced with equal malevolence by both conservative and liberal preachers, is the attempt to cause the congregation to think that their interpretative and behavioral options are more limited than they are. The propagandist tries to manipulate the hearers' perceptions into a single frame of reference and to shut down critical thinking. Most listeners in the long-established denominations want to think for themselves.[17] In the presence of propaganda, they feel treated as children, manipulated, violated.

A study of sermons has discovered that some people tend to hear what they want to hear, particularly if they like the preacher. Regardless of what the preacher actually says, these listeners interpret the sermon as confirming what they already believe. They may even unconsciously reconstruct the content of the message so that it will go along with their beliefs.[18] Some conservatives are going to hear the pastor as a conservative even when the pastor preaches a liberal sermon. The reverse is also true: some liberals will hear liberality in a conservative sermon. When such distortions come to the preacher's attention, it would be wise to make pastoral calls (or to take other means) to correct the impression. The trustworthiness of the preacher's relationship to the congregation is at stake.

Further, when some people are faced with evidence that contradicts their beliefs, they become even more convinced of the truth of their beliefs. Rather than change their ways of thinking, they will find a way to explain the contradiction between belief and affirmation. The classic illustration is groups who predict that the end of the world will occur at a specific time. They prepare for the moment. It does not occur. Do they abandon faith? No. They discover a flaw in their perception (or some other mistake) that caused a miscalculation. Indeed, in some cases, their fervor increases as they expect a new end-date.[19] When faced with such a mentality, the preacher is ethically obligated to attempt to call the listeners' attention to disagreements between belief and apparent fact.

In the end, of course, preachers must make a witness that they take to be truthful. While pastors ought to make a conscientious effort to shape sermons so that both conservatives and liberals can be persuaded, pastors ought not violate their own understandings of the gospel. To do so is to lose integrity. At times, the preacher must simply make the witness that seems most adequately to represent the divine purpose and leading. Pastors who are grounded in a vital relationship with the living God will be able to weather such storms as may result, and will receive appreciation with humility.

Reprise

We can imagine that a pastor reading this book could easily feel overwhelmed by the number of categories of listeners in a congregation and the call to develop sermons that connect with each one. After all, the Appendix that follows summarizes more than thirty-five different categories of listeners according to generation, patterns of mental operation, gender, cultural setting, social location, and theological orientation. Our list of varieties is not exhaustive.

When we discuss with ministers this wide range of different kinds of listeners in the congregation, we are frequently asked, "How can I, as a pastor, take account of every category in every sermon that I preach?" Our answer is, "You probably can't." As noted earlier, our suggestion is that a pastor identify the various listening tendencies present in a congregation. Each person or congregation is unique. While a book of this type can identify qualities that may be present, the local pastor is in position to determine their combination and proportion in the congregation. Over a season of preaching, the pastor can conscientiously integrate material that pertains to particular groups into particular sermons.

What we have suggested in this book affects more than sermon preparation alone. It affects pastors' entire ministries, the way pastors relate to their people. For example, take the fact that some pastors perceive the world visually, others through hearing, and still others through feeling (chapter 3). Ministers have their own tendencies along these lines. But some pastors forget that their preferences are not true for all their people. The wise pastor will spend some time every week stepping out of his or her world and into the worlds of the people, learning more about their generations, the ways they perceive the world, the ways they use language, the movies and TV shows they watch, the music they listen to, the books they read. Only by doing that can the pastor get a sense of the nuances of the listening community and of how to relate with people in settings beyond the sermon. Such insight can benefit pastors as they engage in teaching, pastoral counseling, administration, and other arenas of ecclesial life.

At the end of chapter 1, we sketch four approaches that a pastor might take to include the wide variety of patterns of listening in the speaking and listening center of the congregation. Ministers would likely select an approach from among the following based on their priestly listening to the congregation. Such pastoral attentiveness will help determine which strategy is appropriate for a particular time and context in the congregation's life.

1. A pastor might prepare a particular message (or a series of messages) to speak to a single cohort of listeners. For example, the preacher might develop a message that takes Boomer generational inclinations into account.

2. Pastors might also conscientiously integrate several distinct qualities in the sermon that enhance receptivity for a range of listener groups. For example, a sermon (or sermons) on an ethical problem might wrestle with the issue from the perspectives of persons whose mental operations are similar to Fowler's stages 2, 3, 4, and 5.

3. Through a season of sermons, a pastor might put together the approaches just discussed by making sure that multiple variables in the congregation's listening profile are discussed in sermons. The preacher could use the checklist in the Appendix to see that the sermon speaks to the spectrum of modes of perception over several Sundays.

4. The preacher might work in reverse on the relationship between the shaping of the sermon and the kinds of persons to be addressed. The preacher might concentrate on the biblical passage (or topic) as well as the purpose of the occasion, and then ask, *How will the listening groups at the assembly hear (or not hear) this sermon? Are some groups excluded? Will some groups feel that they received too much attention? How can I adapt the sermon to give an optimum opportunity for the configuration of listeners present to hear the sermon on their wavelengths?*

By taking one of the above approaches, the preacher breaks the task of speaking to multiple kinds of listeners in the congregation into bite-sized chunks. A pastor can work on one listening group, or one configuration of listening groups, at a time. That makes sermon preparation more manageable and less overwhelming.

As we have noted previously, interaction between preacher and congregation does not always follow predictable principles. People are not imprisoned in their particular configurations of listening preference. Communication in the sermon frequently transcends the tendencies that we have described. Furthermore, a wide range of factors, from the congregation's receptivity, to the ever present movement of the Spirit, through events in the wider world that affect the congregation's mind and heart, through what particular people had for breakfast, can affect the listening climate dramatically. A well-planned sermon designed to speak with a particular group in the community can die before the preacher has finished the introduction. A sermon that by most homiletical standards should not have been allowed in a pulpit can bring the gospel to life for a congregation. Nevertheless, many sermons will benefit when the preacher factors patterns of listening in the congregation into the development of the sermon.

Appendix

A Chart to Help Preachers Include Material for a Wide Range of Listeners

For a preacher who wants to consciously attempt to speak with the various listening communities in the congregation, a chart of the various groups and their characteristics could be helpful. After each sermon, the preacher can check those qualities that were incorporated into the sermon.[1] Over time, the chart will reveal those groups to whom the preacher speaks regularly and those whom the preacher may neglect. The following chart anticipates the subject matters of the book.

This chart is set up with age cohorts providing one axis and other listener traits the other. A preacher could easily put another kind of trait in the top axis. We include only the traits that are discussed in this book. We leave rows at the end so that a preacher can add other traits that are not discussed in this book.

	Gen13	Boomer	Silent	Builder
Persons with intuitive projective faith				
Persons with literal faith				
Persons with synthetic-conventional faith				
Persons with individuating-reflective faith				
Persons with conjunctive faith				
Persons with universalizing faith				

	Gen13	Boomer	Silent	Builder
Myers Briggs Type Indicator (MBTI) Extroverts				
MBTI Introverts				
MBTI Sensates				
MBTI iNtuitives				
MBTI Thinkers				
MBTI Feelers				
MBTI Judgers				
MBTI Perceivers				
Neuro-Linguistic Programming (NLP) Visual				
NLP Kinesthetic				
NLP Auditory				
Silent women				
Women who receive knowledge				
Women who are subjective knowers				
Women who are procedural knowers				
Women who are constructed knowers				
Heterosexual men				
Heterosexual women				
Gay men				
Lesbians				
Bisexual persons				
Transgendered persons				
Persons questioning their sexuality				
Asexual persons				
Anglo Americans				
African Americans				

	Gen13	Boomer	Silent	Builder
Latino Americans				
Asian Americans				
Native Americans				
Other cultures				
Strangers				
Silent minorities: older adults and children				
Poor people				
People with physical and mental disabilities				
Theological conservatives				
Theological liberals				

Notes

Introduction

[1]G. Edwin Osborn, *The Glory of Christian Worship* (Indianapolis: Christian Theological Seminary Press, 1960), 71–72. We have adapted these materials.

[2]This book partakes of the recent movement in preaching (and in wider pastoral ministry) that stresses the importance of understanding the congregation and its multiple contexts. For representative literature in this movement, see James Hopewell, *Congregation* (Philadelphia: Fortress Press, 1987); the bibliography in Allison Stokes and David A. Roozen, "The Unfolding Story of Congregational Studies," in *Carriers of Faith: Lessons from Congregational Studies*, ed. Carl S. Dudley, Jackson W. Carroll, and James P. Wind (Louisville: Westminster/John Knox Press, 1991), 183–192; Nancy T. Ammerman, Jackson W. Carroll, Carl S. Dudley, William McKinney, *Studying Congregations: A New Handbook* (Nashville: Abingdon Press, 1998); Thomas Edward Frank, *The Soul of the Congregation: An Invitation to Congregational Reflection* (Nashville: Abingdon Press, 2000). For this movement in preaching, see Don M. Wardlaw, "Preaching as the Interface of Two Social Worlds: The Congregation as Corporate Agent in the Act of Preaching," in *Preaching as a Social Act*, ed. Arthur Van Seters (Nashville: Abingdon Press, 1989), 55–94; Leonora Tubbs Tisdale, *Preaching as Local Theology and Folk Art*, Fortress Resources for Preaching (Minneapolis: Fortress Press, 1997). Unfortunately, we had finished most of our writing of this book before we were able to read the book by James R. Neiman and Thomas G. Rogers, *Preaching to Every Pew: Cross Cultural Strategies* (Minneapolis: Fortress Press, 2001).

[3]Recent theology emphasizes that by nature a congregation is more than a collection of individuals. A congregation is a *community*, that is, a body of persons who are integrally related with one another in much the same way that the various elements of the human body are interconnected. Individual Christians represent the Christian community in their words and actions. The congregation is embodied in individual Christians. Preaching intends, in part, to help form the congregation as community. This emphasis on interrelatedness is accompanied by a growing awareness of the importance of diversity in the human family. The congregation as community is not intended to be a homogenous group. To the contrary, an integral part of the vocation of the church is to bring together people who manifest different qualities (e.g., race, ethnicity, gender, age, social class) to witness to the great reunion that God intends for all peoples. In this reunion, individuals and groups do not lose their particularity in a great mush, but contribute their particularity to the life and witness of the larger group. On the emerging emphasis on congregation as community, see Ronald J. Allen, Barbara Shires Blaisdell, and Scott Black Johnston, *Theology for Preaching: Authority, Truth, and Knowledge of God in a Postmodern Ethos* (Nashville: Abingdon Press, 1997), 137–60.

[4]Nancy Eiesland, *The Disabled God: Toward a Liberatory Theology of Disability* (Nashville: Abingdon Press, 1994), 81.

Chapter 1: Varieties of Listeners in the Congregation

[1]Clement of Alexandria, "On Spiritual Perfection," trans. J. E. L. Oulton and Henry Chadwick, in *Alexandrian Christianity*, ed. Henry Chadwick, Library of Christian Classics (Philadelphia: The Westminster Press, 1954), 165. From *Stramata*, 7.18.

[2]Some readers may object to the comparison between fishing and preaching. Fishing is a violent act. Fishing assumes a domination paradigm in which the human being seeks to

dominate the fish. We agree. The purpose of preaching is not to "catch" listeners nor to dominate them, but to invite them into a conversation regarding how the gospel helps them interpret life (and how life helps them interpret the gospel). As with all images, the comparison between fishing and preaching has limitations, but when used critically it can still portray an aspect of the preacher's task.

[3]A congregation is not simply a collection of individual listeners or groups of listeners who share common traits, but is a system in which all parts work together. We do not have space to reflect on the implications of this insight for the kinds of differences among listeners discussed in this book. For a bibliography on the congregation as system, see Ronald J. Allen, *Preaching and Practical Ministry,* Preaching and Its Partners (St. Louis: Chalice Press, 2001), 7, n. 6.

[4]Clark M. Williamson, *A Guest in the House of Israel: Post-Holocaust Church Theology* (Louisville: Westminster/John Knox Press, 1993), 22. See further idem, *Way of Blessing Way of Life: A Christian Theology* (St. Louis: Chalice Press, 1999), 22–27.

[5]On the notion of mutual critical correlation, see the expositions in Clark M. Williamson and Ronald J. Allen, *A Credible and Timely Word* (St. Louis: Chalice Press, 1991), especially 71–120, and idem, *The Teaching Minister* (Louisville: Westminster/John Knox Press, 1991), 65–82. For an approach to preaching based on a hermeneutic of mutual critical correlation, see Ronald J. Allen, *Interpreting the Gospel: An Introduction to Preaching* (St. Louis: Chalice Press, 1998).

[6]Thomas G. Long, *The Witness of Preaching* (Louisville: Westminster/John Knox Press, 1989), 130.

[7]James A. Michener, *Iberia: Spanish Travels and Reflections* (New York: Random House, 1968), 450.

[8]Ibid., 349.

[9]Fred B. Craddock, *Overhearing the Gospel* (Nashville: Abingdon Press, 1978; 2d ed., St. Louis: Chalice Press, 2002).

[10]We owe the observation that careful preparation is a part of the preacher's code of ethics to David Kinsey, formerly a student at Christian Theological Seminary and now a pastor in the Society of Friends.

[11]Long, *The Witness of Preaching,* 132.

[12]Ibid., 131–32.

Chapter 2: Preaching and Different Generations

[1]An earlier form of this chapter appeared as Ronald J. Allen, "Preaching to Different Generations," *Encounter* 58 (1997): 369–400. It is used here by permission.

[2]In the following, we largely follow the descriptions of these generations in William Strauss and Neil Howe, *Generations: The History of America's Future from 1584 to 2069* (New York: William Morrow and Co., 1991). We draw only from the useful descriptions of the four cohorts that are the focus of our chapter. We do not discuss the larger, controversial, and probably too neat theory of the repetition of generational cycles through the history of the United States.

[3]Tom Brokaw, *The Greatest Generation* (New York: Random House, 1998).

[4]Strauss and Howe, *Generations,* 263.

[5]Ibid.

[6]Douglas Alan Walrath, *Frameworks: Patterns for Living and Believing Today* (New York: Pilgrim Press, 1987), 84.

[7]For a contemporary discussion of the sermon as an event of teaching and learning, see Ronald J. Allen, *The Teaching Sermon* (Nashville: Abingdon Press, 1995).

[8]Strauss and Howe, *Generations,* 286.

[9]Ibid., 285.

[10]Ibid., 287.

[11]Ibid., 281.

[12]Ibid., 279.

[13]Ibid., 282.

[14]Ibid.

[15]Ibid.

[16]Ibid., 285.

[17]Ibid., 293–94.

[18]Ibid., 307.

[19]Ibid., 301.

[20]Walrath, *Frameworks,* 74–87.

[21]Wade Clark Roof, *A Generation of Seekers* (San Francisco: HarperSanFrancisco, 1993).

[22]D. Newell Williams, "Future Prospects of the Christian Church (Disciples of Christ)," in *A Case Study of Mainstream Protestantism: The Disciples' Relation to American Culture, 1880–1989,* ed. D. Newell Williams (St. Louis: Chalice Press; Grand Rapids: Wm. B. Eerdmans, 1991), 561–63. See further Dean R. Hoge, Benton Johnson, and Donald A. Luidens, *Vanishing Boundaries: The Religion of Protestant Mainline Baby Boomers* (Louisville: Westminster/John Knox Press, 1994), 175–202.

[23]Roof, *A Generation of Seekers.* This expression, from the title of Roof's book, seems an especially apt description of Boomers.

[24]Ibid., 4–5.

[25]Ibid., 8.

[26]Ibid., 156–61.

[27]Ibid., 158.

[28]Ibid., 205–11.

[29]Ibid., 207.

[30]Ronald J. Allen, *Preaching the Topical Sermon* (Louisville: Westminster/John Knox Press, 1992).

[31]Joseph E. Faulkener, "What Are They Saying? A Content Analysis of 206 Sermons Preached in the Christian Church (Disciples of Christ) during 1988," in Williams, ed., *A Case Study of Mainstream Protestantism,* 422–26.

[32]Roof, *A Generation of Seekers,* 210.

[33]Ibid., 211.

[34]Strauss and Howe, *Generations,* 302.

[35]Roof, *A Generation of Seekers,* 190.

[36]Douglas Coupland, *Generation X: Tables for an Accelerated Culture* (New York: St. Martin's Press, 1991).

[37]Many members of this generation resent being called Baby Busters for several reasons: (1) they actually outnumber the Boomers; (2) the term Baby Busters inherently compares them to the Boomers, thus leaving them always in the shadow of the Boomers; (3) their major achievements are yet to come.

[38]George Barna, *Baby Busters: The Disillusioned Generation* (Chicago: Northfield, 1994). Cf. George Barna, *The Invisible Generation; Baby Busters* (Glendale, Calif.: Barna Research Group, 1992); George T. Holtz, *Welcome to the Jungle* (New York: St. Martin's Press, 1995), Susan Mitchell, *Generation X: The Young Adult Market* (Ithaca, N.Y.: New Strategist Publications, 1997); Rob Nelson and Jon Cowan, *Revolution X: A Survival Guide for Our Generation* (New York: Penguin Books, 1994); Tex Sample, *The Spectacle of Worship in a Wired World* (Nashville: Abingdon Press, 1998).

[39]Neil Howe and Bill Strauss, *13th Gen: Abort, Retry, Ignore, Fail?* (New York: Vintage Books, 1993), 3.

[40]Strauss and Howe, *Generations,* 321.

[41]Postmodernity also is eroding the confidence of many in other generations in the trustworthiness of Christian claims. Consequently, the preacher needs to build a base of authority for the sake of the congregation as a whole in order to help the community make its way through the confusion (and liberation) of diversity and relativism. See Ronald J. Allen, Scott Black Johnston, and Barbara Shires Blaisdell, *Preaching in a Postmodern Ethos: Truth, Authority, and Knowledge of God* (Nashville: Abingdon Press, 1997).

[42]Howe and Strauss, *13th Gen: Abort, Retry, Ignore, Fail?,* 55.

[43]Andres Tapia, "Reaching the First Post-Christian Generation," *Christianity Today* (September 12, 1994): 19.

[44]Howe and Strauss, *13th Gen: Abort, Retry, Ignore, Fail?,* 11.

[45]Tom Beaudoin, *Virtual Faith: The Irreverent Spiritual Quest of Generation X* (San Francisco: Jossey-Bass, 1998), xiv-xx.

[46]Andres Tapia, "X-ing the Church," *Christianity Today* (September 12, 1994): 21. For a

theological discussion of testimony, see Rebecca L. Chopp, "Bearing Witness: Traditional Faith in Contemporary Expression," *Quarterly Review* 17 (1997): 197–98; idem, "Theology and the Poetics of Testimony," *Criterion* 37 (1998): 2–12.

⁴⁷For an approach to Socratic style preaching, see Allen, *The Teaching Sermon,* 103–11.

⁴⁸Cited in Tapia, "Reaching the First Post-Christian Generation," 19.

⁴⁹Ibid., 20.

⁵⁰William Mahedy and Janet Bernardi even use this motif as the title of their book, *A Generation Alone: Xers Making a Place in the World* (Downers Grove, Ill.: InterVarsity Press, 1994), 17–34.

⁵¹Barna, *Baby Busters,* 109.

⁵²Cited in Tapia, "Reaching the First Post-Christian Generation," 22.

Chapter 3: Preaching and Different Modes of Mental Process

¹While these three particular ways of understanding human knowing and communicating are helpful, no one of the three patterns takes account of the full range of variables that are a part of every situation of human knowledge or communication. Nor do the three together comprise a complete grid of understanding. Other diversities include factors such as race, cultural assumptions and practices, social location, and theological point of view. We selected these three approaches because they illustrate a wide variety of angles by which to understand cognitive function. For a comprehensive survey of different ways in which theorists understand communication, see Stephen W. Littlejohn, *Theories of Human Communication,* 4th ed. (Belmont, Calif.: Wadsworth Publishing Co., 1992), as well as Em Griffin, *A First Look at Communication Theory,* 4th ed. (New York: McGraw Hill, 2000).

²All these studies designate categories to describe different patterns of thought, feeling, or behaving. Most of the researchers regard their categories as fluid. A person is seldom a pure expression of a single category to the exclusion of the characteristics of other categories. A person usually has a center of gravity typical of a particular trait, while incorporating traces of other traits into their mental functioning.

³Thomas G. Long, "Myers-Briggs and Other Modern Astrologies," *Theology Today* 49 (1992): 295.

⁴See James W. Fowler, *Stages of Faith: The Psychology of Human Development and the Quest for Meaning* (San Francisco: Harper & Row, 1981). Some Christian educators and others have criticized the developmental approach. Among the most incisive is Craig Dykstra, *Vision and Character: A Christian Educator's Alternative to Kohlberg* (New York: Paulist Press, 1981). A broad-ranging discussion is found in *Faith Development and Fowler,* ed. Craig Dykstra and Sharon Parks (Birmingham, Ala.: Religious Education Press, 1986).

⁵The term *stage* is potentially problematic, since it easily can be taken to imply a hierarchy of value. Fowler is clear that one stage is not better than another. "The faith stages…are not to be understood as an achievement scale by which to evaluate the worth of persons. Nor do they represent educational or therapeutic goals toward which to hurry people. Seeing their optimal correlations with psychosocial eras gives a sense of how time, experience, challenge, and nurture are required for growth in faith" (Fowler, *Stages of Faith,* 114).

⁶Robert Stephen Reid offers an alternative approach to using the insights of faith development theory in preaching. Reid draws on a taxonomy for understanding contemporary preaching developed by Lucy Rose that sees the preaching community divided into four different camps with respect to the nature of what happens in the event of preaching and that correlates a stage of adult faith development with each approach: traditional preaching speaks most naturally to persons at Fowler's stage 3; kerygmatic preaching correlates with Fowler's stage 4; practical postmodern preaching fits with stage 5; and thoroughly postmodern preaching corresponds to stage 6 development. See Reid's "Faithful Preaching: Preaching Epistemes, Faith Stages, and Rhetorical Practice," *The Journal of Communication and Religion* 21 (1998): 164–99. While we appreciate this groundbreaking effort, the taxonomy of preaching is not fully satisfactory (especially in the way in which it handles postmodern themes in contemporary preaching). Furthermore, we observe that each kind of preaching can manifest elements of each of the adult stages of faith development.

⁷Our discussion focuses primarily on listeners as individuals. However, Fowler has a definite concern for witness in the public arena. See Fowler, *Weaving the New Creation: Stages of the Faith and the Public Church* (San Francisco: HarperSanFrancisco, 1991).

⁸Fowler, *Stages of Faith Development*, 119-21.

⁹Ibid., 122-34. See further *Faith Development in Early Childhood*, ed. Doris A. Black (Kansas City: Sheed and Ward, 1989).

¹⁰On children in worship, see Janet Eibner and Susan Walker, *God, Kids and Us: The Growing Edge of Ministry with Children and the People who Care for Them* (Ontario: United Church Publishing House, 1996); Edith Bajema, *A Family Affair: Worshiping God with Children* (Grand Rapids: CRC Publications, 1994); Robbie Castleman, *Parenting in the Pew: Guiding Your Children into the Joy of Worship* (Downers Grove, Ill.: InterVarsity Press, 2002); Elizabeth Sandall, *Including Children in Worship: A Planning Guide for Congregations* (Minneapolis: Augsburg Fortress Press, 1991).

¹¹On this notion of practice, an accessible introduction is *Practicing Our Faith: A Way of Life for a Searching People*, ed. Dorothy C. Bass (San Francisco: Jossey-Bass, 1997), and Ronald J. Allen, *Preaching and Practical Ministry*, Preaching and Its Partners (St. Louis: Chalice Press, 2001).

¹²Fowler, *Stages of Faith*, 132.

¹³Carolyn C. Brown, *You Can Preach to the Kids Too! Designing Sermons for Adults and Children* (Nashville: Abingdon Press, 1994) calls for a broader notion of preaching and children and is among the best discussions of this subject. More narrowly focused on the children's sermon is Sara Covin Juengst, *Sharing Faith with Children: Rethinking the Children's Sermon* (Louisville: Westminster John Knox Press, 1994). Still significant is W. Alan Smith, *Children Belong in Worship* (St. Louis: CBP Press, 1984), esp. 49-85.

¹⁴Fowler, *Stages of Faith*, 135-50.

¹⁵Fowler points to a characteristic of Stage 2 perception (and one carrying into Stage 3) that can be theologically problematic. "The limitations of literalness and an excessive reliance upon reciprocity as a principle for constructing an ultimate environment can result either in an over controlling, stilted perfectionism, or 'works righteousness' or in their opposite, an abasing sense of badness embraced because of mistreatment, neglect, or the apparent disfavor of significant others" (Fowler, *Stages of Faith*, 150). These liabilities can also be manifest in the Stage 3 thinker, who can easily fall victim to what Sharon Parks calls "the tyranny of the they" (quoted in Fowler, *Stages of Faith*, 154). The preacher can counteract the negative qualities of such tendencies by overtly naming them as inappropriate to the gospel. The preacher can help Stages 2 and 3 thinkers to develop a sense of their own autonomy as deciding selves. The preacher can also tell stories that depict grace as the normative Christian reality and that help people imagine modes of relationship other than wooden reciprocity.

¹⁶Fowler, *Stages of Faith*, 151-74.

¹⁷Ibid., 174-83.

¹⁸Cf. James W. Fowler, *Becoming Adult, Becoming Christian: Adult Development and the Christian Faith* (San Francisco: Jossey-Bass, 2000).

¹⁹Ibid., 184-98.

²⁰Ibid., 187.

²¹For a fully developed sermon in this model, see Pablo Jiménez, "Paul's Subversive Partnership," in Ronald J. Allen, ed., *Patterns of Preaching: A Sermon Sampler* (St. Louis: Chalice Press, 1998), 98-103.

²²Ibid., 199-213.

²³An influential work for understanding this approach is Katherine Briggs and Peter Briggs, *Gifts Differing* (Palo Alto, Calif.: Consulting Psychologists Press, 1980). A popular adaptation of the theory is David Kiersy and Marilyn Bates, *Please Understand Me* (Del Mar, Calif.: Prometheus Nemesis Books, 1978). A book written for educators (whose ideas can be easily adapted for preaching) is Gordon Lawrence, *People Types and Tiger Stripes: A Practical Guide to Learning Styles*, 2d ed. (Gainesville, Fla.: Center for Application of Psychological Type, 1982). Otto Kroeger and Janet M. Thuesen, *Type Talk* (New York: Delacorte Press, 1992) is very practical. Cf. idem, *Type Talk At Work* (New York: Delacorte Press, 1994). Cf. Roy M. Oswald, *Personality Type and Religious Leadership* (Washington, D.C.: Alban Institute, 1988).

²⁴Virtually all people combine elements of all types. In each index, however, most people show at least a slight preference for one habit. But it is normal for people to discover that they mix characteristics from different habits.

²⁵Etta Jane Murphy, *Communication in Preaching and Personality: An Investigation of the Relationship of the Effectiveness of Communication in the Preaching Event and Personality Type as Measured by the Myers-Briggs Type Indicator* (D. Min. Project, Christian Theological Seminary, Indianapolis, Ind., 1985).

²⁶Some pastors have introduced the MBTI to the larger Christian community in order to help members understand themselves and others. Such knowledge can often help members transcend the limitations of their particular types in thinking bout God and the world, in making decisions, and in relating to others. Some church fights, for instance, result not from significant differences in theology or vision, but from personality types that operate very differently. See Lloyd Edwards, *How We Belong, Fight, and Pray: The MBTI as a Key to Congregational Dynamics* (Washington, D.C.: Alban Institute, 1993).

²⁷Lawrence, *People Types and Tiger Stripes,* 70–71; Kroeger and Thuesen, *Type Talk,* 17–18.

²⁸On embodiment as a reconception of "delivery," see *Learning Preaching: Understanding and Participating in the Process,* ed. Don M. Wardlaw (Lincoln, Ill.: Lincoln College and Seminary Press for the Academy of Homiletics, 1989), 160–66.

²⁹An excellent guide in sermon feedforward is John S. McClure, *The Roundtable Pulpit: Where Leadership and Preaching Meet* (Nashville: Abingdon Press, 1995). McClure does not work with MBTI categories in this volume.

³⁰The questions must probe the serious content of the sermon. Questions that are for rhetorical effect will likely bypass the Introvert as window dressing.

³¹Lawrence, *People Types and Tiger Stripes,* 72–73; Kroeger and Thuesen, *Type Talk,* 19–20.

³²Lawrence, *People Types and Tiger Stripes,* 74–75; Kroeger and Thuesen, *Type Talk,* 21–22.

³³Lawrence, *People Types and Tiger Stripes,* 76–77; Kroeger and Thuesen, *Type Talk,* 24–25.

³⁴The types are distributed unevenly in the population. Their approximate rates of occurrence in the adult population are:

Extrovert 70%, Introvert 30%,

Sensate 70%, iNtuitive 30%,

Thinkers (women) 40%, Feelers (women) 60%,

Thinkers (men) 60%, Feelers (men) 40%,

Judgers 55%, Perceivers 45%

(Lawrence, *People Types and Tiger Stripes,* 39).

³⁵Kroeger and Thuesen, *Type Talk,* 211.

³⁶Ibid.

³⁷The basic work is still John Grinder and Richard Bandler, *The Structure of Magic : A Book about Language and Therapy* (Palo Alto, Calif.: Science and Behavior Books, 1976), 2:6–26. Only a handful of people represent the world with olfactory and gustatory systems (4–5). Cf. idem, *The Structure of Magic : A Book about Language and Therapy,* vol. 1 (Palo Alto, Calif.: Science and Behavior Books, 1975); idem, *Frogs into Princes* (Moab, Utah: Real People Press, 1979).

³⁸Two guides are especially practical: Byron A. Lewis and Frank Pucelik, *Magic Demystified: A Pragmatic Guide to Communication and Change* (Lake Oswego, Oreg.: Metamorphous Press, 1982) and Stephen R. Lankton, *Practical Magic* (Cupertino, Calif.: Meta Publications, 1980). For the following descriptions, see Bandler and Grinder, *The Structure of Magic,* 2:15, and Lewis and Pucelik, *Magic Demystified,* 31–67.

³⁹Lewis and Pucelik, *Magic Demystified,* 60–62.

⁴⁰Mary Field Belenky, Blythe McVicker Clinchy, Nancy Rule Goldberger, Jill Mattuck Tarule, *Women's Ways of Knowing: The Development of Self, Voice, and Mind* (New York: Basic Books, 1986) says that people speak about knowledge in two different metaphor systems. Most men prefer visual terms, while most women prefer vocal terms. Neurolinguistic programming finds that some people represent the world in visual terms, others in auditory terms, and still others in kinesthetic terms. These interpretive grids do not consider parallel phenomena. Belenky and her colleagues specifically focus on how people speak about knowledge. Neurolinguistic programming deals with general human perception.

⁴¹Howard Gardner, *Frames of Mind: The Theory of Multiple Intelligences* (New York: Basic Books, 1983); idem, *Multiple Intelligences: The Theory in Practice* (New York: Basic Books, 1993). For an especially clear explanation of multiple intelligences and their use in the classroom (from which a preacher can easily extrapolate to the sermon), see David Lazear, *Eight Ways of Knowing: Teaching for Multiple Intelligences* (Palatine, Ill.: Skylight Publishing, 1998).

Chapter 4: Preaching and Gender

¹Adapted from a story by Deborah Tannen, *You Just Don't Understand: Women and Men in Conversation* (New York: Ballantine, 1990), 15.

²Ibid., 18.

³See Robert R. Howard, "Gender and Point of View in the Imagery of Preaching," *Homiletic* 24/1 (1999), for one such plea. Howard's essay is also an excellent bibliographical resource for feminist works in homiletics.

⁴Barbara Bate, "Gender, the World, and the Preacher," in *Papers of the Annual Meeting of the Academy of Homiletics* (1990), 14, cited in Howard, "Gender and Point of View," 1.

⁵Mary Field Belenky, Blythe McVicker Clinchy, Nancy Rule Goldberger, Jill Mattuck Tarule, *Women's Ways of Knowing: The Development of Self, Voice, and Mind* (New York: Basic Books, 1986).

⁶See further reflection on these themes in Nancy Goldberger, Blythe Clinchy, Mary Belenky, Jill Mattuck Tarule, *Knowledge, Difference, and Power: Essays Inspired by Women's Ways of Knowing* (New York: Basic Books, 1996). For a homiletical appropriation, see Leonora Tubbs Tisdale, *Preaching as Local Theology and Folk Art*, Fortress Resources for Preaching (Minneapolis: Fortress Press, 1997), 134–35.

⁷The conclusions of the research extend and nuance work in the relatively recent movement to trace the psychological development of women. Most studies of cognitive operation have studied more men than women, for example, William G. Perry, Jr., *Forms of Intellectual and Ethical Development in the College Years: A Scheme* (New York: Holt, Rinehart and Winston, 1970). From the perspective of women, Belenky et al. in *Women's Ways of Knowing*, reframe aspects of the typology of moral development articulated by Lawrence Kohlberg, *The Philosophy of Moral Development* (New York: Harper & Row, 1981); idem, *The Psychology of Moral Development* (New York: Harper & Row, 1984).

⁸The pioneering works are Christine M. Smith, *Weaving the Sermon: Preaching in a Feminist Perspective* (Louisville: Westminster/John Knox Press, 1989); Carol M. Norén, *The Woman in the Pulpit* (Nashville: Abingdon Press, 1991); Lee McGee, *Wrestling with the Patriarchs: Retrieving Women's Voices in Preaching*, Abingdon Preacher's Library (Nashville: Abingdon Press, 1996); Mary Donovan Turner and Mary Lin Hudson, *Saved from Silence: Finding Women's Voice in Preaching* (St. Louis: Chalice Press, 1999).

⁹Belenky et al., *Women's Ways of Knowing*, 18.

¹⁰Ibid.

¹¹Ibid., 23–34.

¹²Ibid., 31.

¹³Ibid., 35–51.

¹⁴Ibid., 48.

¹⁵Ibid., 60–65.

¹⁶Ibid., 60–61.

¹⁷The role of empathetic companion is not limited to the preacher. The church can become a community of empathetic companions.

¹⁸Belenky et al., *Women's Ways of Knowing*, 76–130.

¹⁹See John McClure, *The Roundtable Pulpit* (Nashville: Abingdon Press, 1995).

²⁰The preacher might also want to experiment with having the congregation speak out loud during the sermon itself (e.g., in dyads, buzz groups, or in response to questions the pastor asks). However, the authors of this book have never heard of such an experiment that succeeded.

²¹Belenky et al., *Women's Ways of Knowing*, 131–52.

²²For Tannen's key works, in addition to *You Just Don't Understand*, see *That's Not What I Meant: How Conversational Style Makes or Breaks Your Relations with Others* (New York: Morrow, 1986); *Gender and Conversational Interaction*, Oxford Studies in Sociolinguistics (New York: Oxford University Press, 1993); *Talking from 9 to 5: Women and Men in the Workplace: Language, Sex, and Power* (New York: Avon Books, 1995); *Gender and Discourse* (New York: Oxford University Press, 1994). These books introduce the wide-ranging bibliography of works regarding the relationship of gender and communication.

²³Tannen, *You Just Don't Understand*, 24–25.

²⁴Ibid., 25.

²⁵Fred Craddock, Lecture 3 at the Methodist Pastors Spring Conference, Arrowhead Springs, Calif., May, 1981.

²⁶Tannen, *You Just Don't Understand,* 75–76.

²⁷Ibid., 77.

²⁸Craddock, Lecture 3.

²⁹For a review of basic literature and issues, see Ronald J. Allen, "The Social Function of Language in Preaching" in *Preaching as a Social Act: Theory and Practice,* ed. Arthur Van Seters (Nashville: Abingdon Press, 1988), 167–204.

³⁰William G. Rowland, Jr., "Wordsworth and the Difficulty of 'Speaking to Men,'" in *Literature and the Marketplace* (Lincoln: University of Nebraska Press, 1996), 39–62.

³¹Robert Bly, *Iron John* (Reading, Mass.: Addison-Wesley, 1990), 2.

³²Ibid.

³³James E. Dittes, *The Male Predicament* (San Francisco: Harper & Row, 1985). See also James E. Dittes, *Driven by Hope: Men and Meaning* (Louisville: Westminster John Knox Press, 1996).

³⁴Bly, *Iron John,* 242. It should be noted that Bly has a thing about hair.

³⁵Dittes, *The Male Predicament,* 1. The remainder of this paragraph is based on Dittes' observations.

³⁶Ibid., 12.

³⁷See Tony Evans, "Spiritual Purity," in *Seven Promises of a Promise Keeper,* ed. Al Janssen and Larry K. Weedens (Colorado Springs: Focus on the Family Publishing, 1994), 79–80, cited by Tracy Dunn-Noland, "Promise Keepers or Patriarchal Kings," *Brite Student Journal* 2 (Spring 1996): 21.

³⁸Dittes, *The Male Predicament,* 12.

³⁹We recognize that the term *gender orientation* is imprecise, and perhaps even offensive to some readers. We use it to speak not only of sexual identity but of broader patterns of orientation to life that are variously associated with gender.

⁴⁰The way we label or describe one another is a task always fraught with peril, given the frequent shifts in generally accepted terminology and the possibility of being, even unintentionally, offensive. For example, the generally accepted non-offensive way of speaking about American persons of African descent has shifted over the past half-century from colored people to Negroes to Black people to African Americans. Americans from Europe have been variously called white, Caucasian, and European American. The growing Hispanic population has generally been labeled by language rather than race, thus Latino/a, Chicana/o, and Hispanic American. And these descriptions of Hispanic Americans have, unlike those of African Americans, tended to be cumulative rather than sequential. Perhaps the most difficult problem of all comes when speaking of persons in the sexual minority. *Homosexual* is a noninclusive word that is out of favor. Interestingly, *queer* has reappeared as a self-description of choice for many but not for all in the sexual minority. We confess our discomfort with it. So we are left with the very awkward acronym GLBTQA to save us from writing the perhaps more awkward and wordy "gay, lesbian, bisexual, transgendered, questioning, and asexual" phrase in every other sentence. We considered shifting the letters (e.g., BQLAGT) each time we used them to avoid a semblance of rank ordering, but felt that might be too confusing for readers. The bottom line is that we are writing at a difficult time for the way we understand one another, which, of course, is why we are writing about it in the first place.

⁴¹Categorization by Letha Scanzoni, cited in Christine Smith, *Preaching as Weeping, Confession, and Resistance* (Louisville: Westminster/John Knox Press, 1992), 89.

⁴²For a sermon along these lines, considering same-gender relationships (but not directly addressing bisexuality, transgendered, questioning, or asexual identity), see Ronald J. Allen, "Now that Homosexuality Is Out of the Closet, What Shall Christians Make of It?" in *Creative Styles of Preaching,* ed. Mark Barger Elliott (Louisville: Westminster John Knox Press, 2000), 69–76.

⁴³We believe that monogamous, covenantal relationships usually have the greatest possibility for fulfilling the divine purposes for sexuality. However, many in the Christian community (and beyond) think otherwise. For an alternative perspective, see Kathy Rudy,

Sex and the Church: Gender, Homosexuality, and the Transformation of Christian Ethics (Boston: Beacon Press, 1997).

⁴⁴Persons of all sexual orientations–heterosexual, lesbian, gay, bisexual, transgendered, and questioning–can violate the divine purposes of sexuality by sexual behaviors that violate the covenantal intention of sexuality, by exploiting other people, and by idolizing sex. Asexual persons can, likewise, make an idol of asexuality. Just as some heterosexual behaviors corrupt God's designs for sexuality, so can lesbian, gay, bisexual, transgendered, questioning, and asexual actions.

⁴⁵Walter Wink, "Homosexuality and the Bible," found in summer 2002 at http://www.melwhite.org/biblesays.html, 5–6.

⁴⁶Ibid.

⁴⁷Christine M. Smith, "Grace Transforms Condemnation–Heterosexism," in *Preaching as Weeping, Confession and Resistance*, 87–109; and "A Lesbian Perspective–Moving toward a Promised Place," in *Preaching Justice*, ed. Christine Smith (Cleveland: United Church Press, 1998), 134–53.

⁴⁸We owe these observations, and several others, to Andrew Shelton, a student at Brite Divinity School.

⁴⁹Andrew Shelton, personal correspondence.

⁵⁰Michael Piazza, "The Gay Advantage" (preached at the Cathedral of Hope, Dallas, Texas, 1996).

⁵¹Categories drawn from Smith, "A Lesbian Perspective," 141–44.

⁵²Ibid., 153.

Chapter 5: Preaching in Multicultural Settings

¹Fred Plog and Daniel Bates, *Cultural Anthropology* (New York: Alfred A. Knopf, 1980), 7.

²Eric H. F. Law, *The Wolf Shall Dwell with the Lamb: A Spirituality for Leadership in a Multicultural Community* (St. Louis: Chalice Press, 1993), 4–5, 9. Cf. idem, *Inclusion: Making Room for Grace* (St. Louis: Chalice Press, 2000).

³Stephen A. Rhodes, *Where the Nations Meet: The Church in a Multicultural World* (Downers Grove, Ill.: InterVarsity Press, 1998), 30–33. Cf. Stephen Kliewer, *How to Live with Diversity in the Local Church* (Washington, D.C.: Alban Institute, 1987).

⁴James Michener, *The Source* (New York: Random House, 1965), 823.

⁵J. S. Bowshill, in *1924 Congo Missionary Conference* (Bolobo, Haut-Congo, Congo: Baptist Mission Press, 1924), 6.

⁶From a conversation between Joseph Jeter and Justo González.

⁷Joel L. Swerdlow, "Global Culture," *National Geographic* 190.2 (August 1999): 3.

⁸Trevanian, *Incident at Twenty Mile* (New York: St. Martin's Press, 1998), 4.

⁹Rhodes, *Where the Nations Meet*, 53.

¹⁰Ibid., 33.

¹¹Joseph R. Jeter, Jr., "Together," (sermon for graduation exercises at Brite Divinity School, Fort Worth, Texas, December 18, 1999).

¹²For detailed consideration of the multiple cultures in congregations, see James R. Neiman and Thomas G. Rogers, *Preaching to Every Pew: Cross Cultural Strategies* (Minneapolis: Fortress Press, 2001).

¹³From a prayer by The Rev. Joe Wright, pastor of the Central Christian Church in Wichita, Kansas, offered before the Kansas Legislature in 1995 and now available in a variety of forms.

¹⁴S. T. Karnick, "The Everything Culture," *American Outlook Magazine* (Summer 1999): 2.

¹⁵See http://multiculturalism.aynrand.org/.

¹⁶See Aart M. van Beek, *Cross-cultural Counseling* (Minneapolis: Fortress Press, 1996), 40.

¹⁷For broader discussion of the minister as leader in multicultural communities, see Charles R. Foster, *Embracing Diversity: Leadership in Multicultural Congregations* (Bethesda, Md.: Alban Institute, 1997) and idem with Theodore Brelsford, *We Are the Church Together: Cultural Diversity in the Congregation* (Valley Forge, Pa.: Trinity Press, International, 1996).

¹⁸Christine M. Smith, ed., *Preaching Justice: Ethnic and Cultural Perspectives* (Cleveland: United Church Press, 1998) brings together essays that, while focusing specifically on preaching justice

in eight different ethnic and cultural settings, illustrate how a preacher can take cultural factors into account in the formulation of the sermon.

[19]Ronald E. Osborn, in a discussion of his book *Creative Disarray* (St. Louis: Chalice Press, 1991).

[20]Osborn, *Creative Disarray*, 176–77. Phrases in quotes are from Dietrich Bonhoeffer and Fred B. Craddock.

[21]Lucy Atkinson Rose, *Sharing the Word* (Louisville: Westminster John Knox Press, 1997), 5.

[22]Ibid., 98.

[23]Ibid., 107.

[24]Lloyd Stone, "This is my Song," *Chalice Hymnal* (St. Louis: Chalice Press, 1995), no. 722.

[25]The authors have heard this saying frequently in Craddock's lectures.

[26]Lawrence A. Hoffman, "Jewish-Christian Services—Babel or Mixed Multitude," *Cross Currents* (1990): 13.

[27]Ibid., 14.

[28]Conversation with Joey Jeter, December 1, 1999.

[29]George Hamilton Combs, *I'd Take This Way Again* (St. Louis: Bethany Press, 1944), 172.

[30]John McClure, ed., *Best Advice for Preaching* (Fortress Press, 1998). Many theological seminaries also have lists of suggestions for ministers' libraries. For a more extensive list of works, see the online Vanderbilt Research Bibliography in Homiletics, edited by Robert Howard (http://divinity.library.vanderbilt.edu/bibs/homiletics.htm#Textbooks). And for a useful guide to online resources, see the Wabash Guide to Internet Resources in Religion, edited by Charles Bellinge (www.wabashcenter.wabash.edu/Internet/front.htm.).

[31]Brian Wren, *What Language Shall I Borrow? God-Talk in Worship: A Male Response to Feminist Theology* (New York: Crossroad, 1989).

[32]Hoffman, "Jewish-Christian Services," 17.

[33]Barbara Kingsolver, *The Poisonwood Bible* (New York: HarperCollins, 1998), 213–14, 276.

[34]James Fowler, cited in Foster and Brelsford, *We Are the Church Together,* 167.

[35]Ibid., 116.

[36]Fred Craddock, in a lecture on preaching given at Arrowhead Springs, Calif., in May, 1981.

[37]George Cladis, *Leading the Team-based Church* (San Francisco: Jossey-Bass, 1999), 4.

[38]See John S. McClure, *The Roundtable Pulpit: Where Leadership and Preaching Meet* (Nashville: Abingdon Press, 1995), and Rose, *Sharing the Word.*

[39]Robert Bellah, *Beyond Belief: Essays on Religion in a Post-Traditional World* (New York: Harper & Row, 1970), xix–xxi.

[40]Leslie Weatherhead, *Thinking Aloud in War-Time* (New York: Abingdon Press, 1940), 61.

[41]For example, see Brian K. Blount and Leonora Tubbs Tisdale, eds., *Making Room at the Table: An Invitation to Multicultural Worship* (Louisville: Westminster John Knox Press, 2001); Kathy Black, *Worship Across Cultures: A Handbook* (Nashville: Abingdon Press, 1998); idem, *Culturally-Conscious Worship* (St. Louis: Chalice Press, 2000); Eric H. F. Law, *The Bush Was Blazing but Not Consumed: Developing a Multicultural Dialogue and Liturgy* (St. Louis: Chalice Press, 1996).

[42]Law, *The Wolf Shall Dwell with the Lamb,* 48ff.

[43]Ibid., 49.

[44]Adapted from Clovis Chappell, *Values That Last* (Nashville: Abingdon Press, 1939), 124–25.

[45]Jung Young Lee, *Marginality: The Key to Multicultural Theology* (Minneapolis: Fortress Press, 1995), 164–68.

[46]Ibid., 173.

[47]Michael Mata, cited in Manuel Ortiz, *One New People* (Downers Grove, Ill.: InterVarsity Press, 1996), 149.

[48]From a lecture by William Sloan Coffin at Brite Divinity School, Forth Worth, Texas, February 10, 1987.

Chapter 6: Preaching and the Least of These

[1]We strongly recommend Christine M. Smith, *Preaching as Weeping, Confession, and Resistance: Radical Responses to Radical Evil* (Louisville: Westminster/John Knox Press, 1992)

as a penetrating theological and homiletical analysis of how to preach in relationship with a wide range of persons who are on the margins of church and society and (or) who suffer injustice.

[2]Albert Schweitzer, *The Quest of the Historical Jesus*, trans. W. Montgomery (New York: Macmillan, 1961), 403.

[3]Francis W. Nichols, *Christianity and the Stranger* (Atlanta: Scholars Press, 1995), 1. See further Patrick W. Keifert, *Welcoming the Stranger: A Public Theology of Worship and Evangelism* (Minneapolis: Fortress Press, 1992); Presbyterian Church (U.S.A.) Advisory Committee on Social Policy, "Building Community Among Strangers: Church Wide Study Developed by the Task Force on Building Community Among Strangers," (Louisville: Presbyterian Church [U.S.A.], 1997).

[4]William H. Shea, "Fundamentalism: How Catholics Approach It," in Nichols, *Christianity and the Stranger*, 286.

[5]For efforts in this regard, see Ronald J. Allen, "The One Shot Preaching Assignment," *Preaching* 7/2 (1991): 41–46

[6]W. E. Sangster, cited in Gerald Kennedy, *While I'm On My Feet* (Nashville: Abingdon Press, 1963), 140.

[7]We are grateful to Wade Killough, student at Brite Divinity School, for this observation.

[8]See Cheryl J. Sanders, *Ministry at the Margins: The Prophetic Mission of Women, Young and the Poor* (Downers Grove, Ill.: InterVarsity Press, 1997).

[9]Henri J. M. Nouwen and Walter J. Gaffney, *Aging* (Garden City, N.Y.: Doubleday, 1976), 101–2.

[10]Walter J. Burghardt, "Aging: A Long Loving Look at the Real," in *Graying Gracefully: Preaching to Older Adults*, ed. William J. Carl, Jr. (Louisville: Westminster John Knox Press, 1997), 27.

[11]Martin Luther, *TR 3: 3421*, cited in Fred W. Meuser, *Luther the Preacher* (Minneapolis: Augsburg, 1983), 53.

[12]Carolyn C. Brown, *Forbid Them Not* (Nashville: Abingdon Press, 1994), 7.

[13]See Richard Batey, *Jesus and the Poor* (New York: Harper & Row, 1972), 5ff.

[14]Pope Paul VI, cited in George V. Pixley and Clodovis Boff, *The Bible, The Church, and the Poor*, trans. Paul Burns (Maryknoll, N.Y.: Orbis Press, 1989), xi.

[15]David Buttrick, remark made at the Scott Lectures, Phillips Theological Seminary, 1993.

[16]Pixley and Boff, *The Bible, The Church, and the Poor*, xii.

[17]For Ron's reflections on being a member of a congregation in an urban area, see his "What I Need from Urban Preaching," *Christian Ministry* 30/6 (1999): 20–22.

[18]Eddy Hall, "Do the Poor Feel Welcome in Your Church?" in *Caring for the Least of These*," ed. David Caes (Scottsdale, Pa.: Herald Press, 1992), 73–80.

[19]Tex Sample, *Hard Living People and Mainstream Christians* (Nashville: Abingdon Press, 1993), 50f.

[20]Charles Spurgeon, "Preaching for the Poor," sermon no. 114 in *The New Park Street Pulpit*, available online in summer, 2002 at http://www.spurgeon.org/sermons/0114.htm .

[21]David Buttrick, "Preaching, Hermeneutics and Liberation," in *Standing with the Poor*, ed. Paul Plenge Parker (Cleveland: Pilgrim Press, 1992), 103.

[22]Enda McDonough, "…The Image of God," in *The Dignity of the Despised of the Earth*, ed. Jacques Pohier & Dietmar Mieth (New York: Seabury Press, 1979), 118.

[23]See Batey, *Jesus and the Poor*, 18–22.

[24]Harry Lee, "My Master Was So Very Poor," no. 216 in *Christian Worship: A Hymnal* (St. Louis: The Bethany Press, 1953).

[25]Eric Bazilian, "One of Us," performed by Joan Osborne on the album *Relish* (Blue Gorilla, 1995).

[26]Kathy Black, *A Healing Homiletic: Preaching and Disability* (Nashville: Abingdon Press, 1996), 50–51. Cf. Nancy Eiesland, *The Disabled God: Toward a Liberatory Theology of Disability* (Nashville: Abingdon Press, 1994).

[27]It has been suggested that the reason for this was simple. Bishops could control what was preached and taught. But they could not control healing. Out of control healers could—and did—disrupt church order. Of course, the ministry of healing never fully disappeared; it found a home on the margins of church life.

[28]Laurie Devine, *Nile* (New York: Dell Books, 1983), 61.

[29]Black, *A Healing Homiletic*, 22.

[30]Jean Vanier, *Community and Growth* (New York: Paulist Press, 1979), xi.

[31]Ibid., 154–64.

³²Ibid., 163.

³³For more information, see Lisa Gwyther, *You Are One of Us* (Durham, N.C.: Duke University Medical School, 1995.)

³⁴Perry LeFevre, quoted in Denise Dombkowski Hopkins, "Failing Brain, Faithful Community," *Memphis Theological Seminary Journal* 32 (1994): 37. A revised form of this lecture was published in Donald K. McKim, ed., *God Never Forgets: Faith, Hope, and Alzheimer's Disease* (Louisville: Westminster John Knox Press, 1997).

³⁵Samuel Balentine, in Hopkins, "Failing Brain, Faithful Community," 35.

³⁶Robert Davis, *My Journey into Alzheimer's Disease* (Wheaton, Ill.: Tyndale House, 1989).

³⁷Davis, in Hopkins, "Failing Brain, Faithful Community," 34.

³⁸Ibid., 36.

³⁹Ibid., 20.

Chapter 7: Preaching in a Congregation of Conservatives and Liberals

¹James Davison Hunter, *Culture Wars: The Struggle to Define America* (New York: Basic Books, 1991), 43–45.

²Some ministers have had remarkable success building congregations around a particular theological viewpoint. People join such a congregation, in part, because it is self-consciously liberal or conservative. Our impression is that such congregations often spend less time on internal theological dispute, and they often mobilize for Christian witness more efficiently and forcefully than congregations that must mediate between conservative and liberal perspectives. In Oklahoma City, for instance, pastor Robin Meyers has led the Mayflower Congregational Church (United Church of Christ) to become a distinctly liberal alternative in a predominately conservative religious climate. That congregation is growing at the rate of 100 new members a year. However, most pastors in the long-established denominations inherit congregations that are theologically mixed. Even if a pastor decides to lead the congregation toward singularity in theological viewpoint, the minister is ethically obligated to understand the views of those who differ and to treat those persons with care and respect, even when critiquing their views and explaining why the congregation is adopting a single theological slant.

³Hunter points out that the orthodox and progressive tendencies in the culture wars embrace much more than we usually associate with the terms *conservative* and *liberal*, especially as these terms are used in the political and religious arenas (*Culture Wars*, 42). Orthodoxy and progressivism, in Hunter's usage, sum up vast and complicated interpretive webs. Obviously, however, religious conservatism is usually associated with cultural orthodoxy, and religious liberalism with cultural progressivism.

⁴Hunter's terms, *orthodox* and *progressive*, seem to us to be even more polarizing (and, therefore, potentially disruptive of communication) than the designations *liberal* and *conservative*. The term *progressive* could be taken to imply that orthodoxy is regressive. The use of the term *orthodox* as a synonym for conservative would be particularly problematic in the religious community. In Christian circles, the term *orthodox* is often associated with Eastern Christianity (e.g., the Greek Orthodox Church). Furthermore, both conservative and liberal Christians can seek to be exponents of the orthodox (in contrast to heretical) Christian tradition.

⁵William C. Placher, "The Nature of Biblical Authority: Issues and Models from Recent Theology," in *Conservative, Moderate, Liberal: The Biblical Authority Debate,* ed. Charles R. Blaisdell (St. Louis: CBP Press, 1990), 1.

⁶For a useful survey of different theological options and their outcomes in preaching, see Donald K. McKim, *The Bible in Theology and Preaching* (Nashville: Abingdon Press, 1994). For a more technical survey of contemporary theological options, see *The Modern Theologians,* ed. David Ford, 2d ed. (Oxford: Basil Blackwell, 1997). The five-family typology that follows is neither Ford's nor McKim's, but is Ron's. For a different approach, see W. Paul Jones, *Theological Worlds: Understanding the Alternative Rhythms of Christian Belief* (Nashville: Abingdon Press, 1989); idem, *Worlds Within a Congregation: Dealing with Theological Diversity* (Nashville: Abingdon Press, 2000).

[7]For characterization of these families with an eye toward the implications of each for preaching, see Ronald J. Allen, *Interpreting the Gospel: An Introduction to Preaching* (St. Louis: Chalice Press, 1998), 73–80.

[8]Professor Allen (no relationship to Ron Allen) made these remarks in a class session on liberal and conservative approaches to the Bible.

[9]Hunter notes that this tendency is true in the larger culture war as well (*Culture Wars,* 43).

[10]Remarks made at a conference at Christian Theological Seminary in 1989 on liberal, moderate, and conservative approaches to the Bible.

[11]Delwin Brown, *Boundaries of Our Habitations: Tradition and Theological Construction* (Albany: State University of New York Press, 1994), 49–54.

[12]Similarity of theological worldview does not, of course, guarantee communion of spirit. Differences in personality, the possession and use of power in the congregation, local church politics, and a host of other factors can disrupt the relationship between theologically compatible people.

[13]Ron first heard the expression "agree to disagree and to do so agreeably" from Sharon E. Watkins, pastor of Disciples Christian Church (Disciples of Christ) in Bartlesville, Oklahoma.

[14]Hans Van Der Geest, *Presence in the Pulpit: The Impact of Personality on Preaching,* trans. Douglas W. Stott (Atlanta: John Knox Press, 1981), 113–14.

[15]George Rupp, address during Ministers Week at Texas Christian University, February 11, 1987.

[16]Teaching sermons provide an ideal vehicle for accomplishing this task. See Ronald J. Allen, *The Teaching Sermon* (Nashville: Abingdon Press, 1995). However, the goal is probably larger than can be accomplished by preaching alone; it needs to be addressed in multiple settings throughout the congregational system. For this larger perspective, see Ronald J. Allen, *Preaching and Practical Ministry,* Preaching and Its Partners (St. Louis: Chalice Press, 2001).

[17]This technique is sometimes called creating cognitive dissonance. Listeners experience cognitive dissonance when they become aware that valued ways of thinking and acting are dissonant with other possibilities. The awareness of cognitive dissonance often initiates a search to resolve the dissonance. See Allen, *The Teaching Sermon,* 45–48.

[18]For convenient and insightful overviews of the formation of the canon, with bibliography, see James A. Sanders and Harry Y. Gamble, "Canon," *The Anchor Bible Dictionary,* ed. David Noel Freedman et al. (New York: Doubleday, 1992), 1:837–61

[19]One of the classic distinctions between Roman Catholics and Protestants is the relative authority of the Bible and tradition in coming to the knowledge of God. Both Roman Catholics and Protestants acknowledge the priority of the Bible, but Roman Catholics accord tradition a higher authority than do Protestants. However, this distinction is one of degree and is not an absolute demarcation between the two churches.

[20]For two classic descriptions of tradition and its development, see Yves M.-J. Congar, *Tradition and Traditions,* trans. Michael Naseby and Thomas Rainborough (New York: The Macmillan Co., 1966), and Jaroslav Pelikan, *The Christian Tradition: A History of the Development of Doctrine* (Chicago: University of Chicago Press, 1971–1989).

[21]The categories and subcategories along which tradition may be subdivided are numerous. Denominational similarity is a major one. For instance, the three main subtraditions within Christianity are Orthodoxy, Roman Catholicism, and Protestantism. Within each of these major families are further subtraditions. Greek Orthodox and Russian Orthodox are quite similar, but each has its own individualities. The Evangelical Lutheran Church in America, the Southern Baptist Convention, the Presbyterian Church (USA), the community Bible churches, and the Pentecostal Holiness Church are all recognizably Protestant, but they lift up different emphases. Other categories along which tradition may be divided include theological family (e.g. fundamentalism, evangelical, neoorthodox, liberation, postliberal, revisionary theology), race, ethnicity, nationality, orientation as to liberal or conservative, and particularities of practice. Within each of these movements, we could locate still further subdivisions. A congregation can usually locate itself as within identifiable streams of the Christian influence. Some of the divisions may appear obvious only to those within very closely

related traditions. For instance, a congregation might describe itself as being in the one cup Southern tradition of the Church of Christ.

[22]One of the preacher's tasks is to understand local tradition—its content, why it is important to the community, its relationship to larger Christian tradition, points at which local loyalties can be used to enhance the community's relationship to the wider Christian community, or points at which local tradition needs to be critiqued and changed for it to manifest the best of Christian witness. The relatively new discipline of congregational studies helps pastors with this task. See James Hopewell, *Congregation* (Philadelphia: Fortress Press, 1987); Nancy T. Ammerman, Jackson W. Carroll, Carl S. Dudley, and William McKinney, *Studying Congregations: A New Handbook* (Nashville: Abingdon Press, 1998); and the bibliography in Allison Stokes and David A. Roozen, "The Unfolding Story of Congregational Studies," in *Carriers of Faith: Lessons from Congregational Studies,* ed. Carl S. Dudley, Jackson W. Carroll, and James P. Wind (Louisville: Westminster/John Knox Press, 1991), 183–92; Thomas Edward Frank, *The Soul of the Congregation: An Invitation to Congregational Reflection* (Nashville: Abingdon Press, 2000). For preaching, see Don M. Wardlaw, "Preaching as the Interface of Two Social Worlds: The Congregation as Corporate Agent in the Act of Preaching," in *Preaching as a Social Act,* ed. Arthur Van Seters (Nashville: Abingdon Press, 1989), 55–94, and Leonora Tubbs Tisdale, *Preaching as Local Theology and Folk Art,* Fortress Resources for Preaching (Minneapolis: Fortress Press, 1997); James R. Nieman and Thomas G. Rogers, *Preaching to Every Pew: Cross Cultural Strategies for Preaching* (Minneapolis: Fortress Press, 2001).

[23]Jaroslav Pelikan, *The Vindication of Tradition* (New Haven, Conn.: Yale University Press, 1984), 65.

[24]Clark M. Williamson and Ronald J. Allen, *The Teaching Minister* (Louisville: Westminster/John Knox Press, 1991), 73.

[25]Ibid., 74.

[26]Ibid.

[27]Ibid.

[28]Three criteria that many liberals find helpful are (1) appropriateness to the gospel, (2) intelligibility, and (3) moral plausibility. See ibid., 75–82, as well as Clark M. Williamson and Ronald J. Allen, *A Credible and Timely Word: Process Theology and Preaching* (St. Louis: Chalice Press, 1991), 71–90; Williamson, *A Guest in the House of Israel: Post-Holocaust Church Theology* (Louisville: Westminster/John Knox Press, 1993), 22; and idem, *Way of Blessing, Way of Life: A Christian Theology* (St. Louis: Chalice Press, 1999), 22–27.

[29]While not dealing with experience from the standpoint of the liberal-conservative divide, Nicholas Lash, *Easter in Ordinary: Reflections on Human Experience and the Knowledge of God* (Charlottesville: University Press of Virginia, 1988) is an insightful guide into the history of the Christian understanding of experience.

[30]For a discussion of the relationship of the modern and postmodern worlds and their implications for the preacher, see Ronald J. Allen, Scott Black Johnston, and Barbara S. Blaisdell, *Theology for Preaching: Authority, Truth, and Knowledge of God in a Postmodern Ethos* (Nashville: Abingdon Press, 1997).

[31]An exceptionally clear discussion of this matter can be found in William C. Placher, *Unapologetic Theology: A Christian Voice in a Pluralistic Conversation* (Louisville: Westminster/John Knox Press, 1989), 24–38.

[32]At this point, the complexity of the current theological scene and difficulties in using the terms *conservative* and *liberal* become very clear. Many postliberal preachers have views of the Bible that are more similar to the views of liberals (as described above) than of conservatives. However, many postliberal theologians espouse views of the church and its purposes that are similar to the views that I have just described as conservative. In some respects postliberalism is liberal, but in other respects it is conservative. See Timothy R. Phillips and Dennis L. Okholm, eds., *The Nature of Confession: Evangelicals and Postliberals in Conversation* (Downers Grove, Ill.: InterVarsity Press, 1996).

[33]This possibility is another example of cognitive dissonance.

[34]Daniel Day Williams, *God's Grace and Man's Hope* (New York: Harper and Brothers, 1949), 45–56.

[35]Rudolf Bultmann's program of demythologizing was one of the most famous examples of modern hermeneutics.

[36]D. Newell Williams, ed., *A Case Study of Mainstream Protestantism: The Disciples' Relation to American Culture, 1880–1989* (St. Louis: Chalice Press; Grand Rapids: Wm. B. Eerdmans, 1991), 47–48.

[37]Bernard Meland, *Fallible Forms and Symbols: Discourses of Method in a Theology of Culture* (Philadelphia: Fortress Press, 1976), 28.

[38]Van Der Geest, *Presence in the Pulpit*, 114–21.

[39]Ronald E. Osborn, comments on a paper by Joseph R. Jeter, Jr., School of Theology at Claremont (1979).

[40]Philosophers debate the precise understanding and function of reason. For a survey of opinions, see G. J. Warnock, "Reason," in *The Encyclopedia of Philosophy*, ed. Paul Edwards (New York: Macmillan, 1967), 7:83–85.

[41]Joseph Faulkener, "What Are They Saying? A Content Analysis of 206 Sermons Preached in the Christian Church (Disciples of Christ) During 1988," in Williams, ed., *A Case Study of Mainstream Protestantism*, 439.

[42]See Van Der Geest, *Presence in the Pulpit*, 31–68; Bonita L. Benda, *The Silence is Broken: Preaching on Social Justice Issues* (Th.D. diss., Iliff School of Theology, Denver, Colo., 1983), 251–52.

[43]For these remarkable aspects of Tittle's ministry, see Robert M. Miller, *How Shall They Hear Without a Preacher? The Life of Ernest Fremont Tittle* (Chapel Hill: University of North Carolina Press, 1971), 332–60, 392–476.

[44]Kelly Miller Smith, *Social Crisis Preaching* (Macon, Ga.: Mercer University Press, 1984), 83.

[45]William E. Dorman and Ronald J. Allen, "Preaching on Emotionally Charged Issues," *Ministry* 1 (1992): 51–52; cf. Ronald J. Allen, *Preaching the Topical Sermon* (Louisville: Westminster/John Knox Press, 1992), 104–5.

[46]For strategies to help the congregation to learn to think critically, see Allen, *The Teaching Sermon*, 39–62, 149–51.

[47]Van Der Geest, *Presence in the Pulpit*, 113–26.

[48]Kenneth I. Pergament and Donald V. DeRosa, "What Was That Sermon About? Predicting Memory for Religious Messages from Cognitive Psychology Theory," *Journal for the Scientific Study of Religion* 24 (1985): 192.

[49]Leon Festinger, Henry W. Riecken, and Stanley Schachter, *When Prophecy Fails* (Minneapolis: University of Minnesota Press, 1956).

Appendix

[1]A limited version of this chart appears in Ronald J. Allen, *Interpreting the Gospel: An Introduction to Preaching* (St. Louis: Chalice Press, 1998), 42–43.